2. Acceptanc... D0125208

XXIII

Energy and Natural Resources Law—see also Oil and Gas

Environmental Law—see also Energy and Natural Resources Law; Sea, Law of

FINDLEY AND FARBER'S ENVIRONMENTAL LAW IN A NUTSHELL, Second Edition, 367 pages, 1988. Softcover. (Text)

RODGERS' HORNBOOK ON ENVIRONMENTAL LAW, 956 pages, 1977, with 1984 pocket part. (Text)

Equity—see Remedies

Estate Planning—see also Trusts and Estates; Taxation—Estate and Gift

LYNN'S AN INTRODUCTION TO ESTATE PLANNING IN A NUTSHELL, Third Edition, 370 pages, 1983. Softcover. (Text)

Evidence

BROUN AND BLAKEY'S BLACK LETTER ON EVIDENCE, 269 pages, 1984. Softcover. (Review)

GRAHAM'S FEDERAL RULES OF EVIDENCE IN A NUTSHELL, Second Edition, 473 pages, 1987. Softcover. (Text)

LILLY'S AN INTRODUCTION TO THE LAW OF EVIDENCE, Second Edition, 585 pages, 1987. (Text)

McCORMICK'S HORNBOOK ON EVIDENCE, Third Edition, Student Edition, 1156 pages, 1984, with 1987 pocket part. (Text)

ROTHSTEIN'S EVIDENCE IN A NUTSHELL: STATE AND FEDERAL RULES, Second Edition, 514 pages, 1981. Softcover. (Text)

Federal Jurisdiction and Procedure

CURRIE'S FEDERAL JURISDICTION IN A NUTSHELL, Second Edition, 258 pages, 1981. Softcover. (Text)

REDISH'S BLACK LETTER ON FEDERAL JURISDICTION, 219 pages, 1985. Softcover. (Review)

WRIGHT'S HORNBOOK ON FEDERAL COURTS, Fourth Edition, Student Edition, 870 pages, 1983. (Text)

Future Interests—see Trusts and Estates

Health Law—see Medicine, Law and

Human Rights—see International Law

VI

Immigration Law

WEISSBRODT'S IMMIGRATION LAW AND PROCEDURE IN A NUTSHELL, (Second Edition, 438 pages, 1989, Softcover. (Text)

Indian Law—see American Indian Law

Insurance Law

DOBBYN'S INSURANCE LAW IN A NUTSHELL, Second Edition, 316 pages, 1989. Softcover. (Text)

KEETON AND WIDISS' INSURANCE LAW, Student Edition, 1359 pages, 1988. (Text)

International Law—see also Sea, Law of

BUERGENTHAL'S INTERNATIONAL HUMAN RIGHTS IN A NUTSHELL, 283 pages, 1988. Softcover. (Text)

BUERGENTHAL AND MAIER'S PUBLIC INTERNATIONAL LAW IN A NUTSHELL, Second Edition, approximately 255 pages, 1990. Softcover. (Text)

FOLSOM, GORDON AND SPANOGLE'S INTERNATIONAL BUSINESS TRANSACTIONS IN A NUTSHELL, Third Edition, 509 pages, 1988. Softcover. (Text)

Interviewing and Counseling

SHAFFER AND ELKINS' LEGAL INTERVIEWING AND COUNSELING IN A NUTSHELL, Second Edition, 487 pages, 1987. Softcover. (Text)

Introduction to Law—see Legal Method and Legal System

Introduction to Law Study

HEGLAND'S INTRODUCTION TO THE STUDY AND PRACTICE OF LAW IN A NUTSHELL, 418 pages, 1983. Softcover (Text)

KINYON'S INTRODUCTION TO LAW STUDY AND LAW EXAMINATIONS IN A NUTSHELL, 389 pages, 1971. Softcover. (Text)

Juvenile Justice

FOX'S JUVENILE COURTS IN A NUTSHELL, Third Edition, 291 pages, 1984. Softcover. (Text)

Labor and Employment Law—see also Employment Discrimination, Social Legislation

LESLIE'S LABOR LAW IN A NUTSHELL, Second Edition, 397 pages, 1986. Softcover. (Text)

NOLAN'S LABOR ARBITRATION LAW AND PRACTICE IN A NUT-

Labor and Employment Law— Continued

SHELL, 358 pages, 1979. Softcover. (Text)

Land Finance—Property Security—see Real Estate Transactions

Land Use

HAGMAN AND JUERGENSMEYER'S HORNBOOK ON URBAN PLANNING AND LAND DEVELOPMENT CONTROL LAW, Second Edition, Student Edition, 680 pages, 1986. (Text)

WRIGHT AND WRIGHT'S LAND USE IN A NUTSHELL, Second Edition, 356 pages, 1985. Softcover. (Text)

Legal Method and Legal System—see also Legal Research, Legal Writing

KEMPIN'S HISTORICAL INTRODUCTION TO ANGLO-AMERICAN LAW IN A NUTSHELL, Second Edition, 280 pages, 1973. Softcover. (Text)

REYNOLDS' JUDICIAL PROCESS IN A NUTSHELL, 292 pages, 1980. Softcover. (Text)

Legal Research

COHEN'S LEGAL RESEARCH IN A NUTSHELL, Fourth Edition, 452 pages, 1985. Softcover. (Text)

COHEN, BERRING AND OLSON'S HOW TO FIND THE LAW, Ninth Edition, approximately 700 pages, 1989. (Coursebook)

Legal Writing

SQUIRES AND ROMBAUER'S LEGAL WRITING IN A NUTSHELL, 294 pages, 1982. Softcover. (Text)

TEPLY'S LEGAL WRITING, ANALYSIS AND ORAL ARGUMENT, 576 pages, 1990. Softcover. (Coursebook)

Legislation

DAVIES' LEGISLATIVE LAW AND PROCESS IN A NUTSHELL, Second Edition, 346 pages, 1986. Softcover. (Text)

Local Government

MCCARTHY'S LOCAL GOVERNMENT LAW IN A NUTSHELL, Second Edition, 404 pages, 1983. Softcover. (Text)

REYNOLDS' HORNBOOK ON LOCAL GOVERNMENT LAW, 860 pages, 1982, with 1987 pocket part. (Text)

Mass Communication Law

ZUCKMAN, GAYNES, CARTER AND DEE'S MASS COMMUNICATIONS LAW IN A NUTSHELL, Third Edition, 538 pages, 1988. Softcover. (Text)

Medicine, Law and

HALL AND ELLMAN'S HEALTH CARE LAW AND ETHICS IN A NUTSHELL, Approximately 389 pages, 1990. Softcover (Text)

KING'S THE LAW OF MEDICAL MALPRACTICE IN A NUTSHELL, Second Edition, 342 pages, 1986. Softcover. (Text)

Military Law

SHANOR AND TERRELL'S MILITARY LAW IN A NUTSHELL, 378 pages, 1980. Softcover. (Text)

Mortgages—see Real Estate Transactions

Natural Resources Law—see Energy and Natural Resources Law, Environmental Law

Office Practice—see also Interviewing and Counseling

HEGLAND'S TRIAL AND PRACTICE SKILLS IN A NUTSHELL, 346 pages, 1978. Softcover (Text)

Oil and Gas

HEMINGWAY'S HORNBOOK ON OIL AND GAS, Second Edition, Student Edition, 543 pages, 1983, with 1989 pocket part. (Text)

LOWE'S OIL AND GAS LAW IN A NUTSHELL, Second Edition, 465 pages, 1988. Softcover. (Text)

Partnership—see Agency—Partnership

Patent and Copyright Law

MILLER AND DAVIS' INTELLECTUAL PROPERTY—PATENTS, TRADEMARKS AND COPYRIGHT IN A NUTSHELL, 428 pages, 1983. Softcover. (Text)

Products Liability

PHILLIPS' PRODUCTS LIABILITY IN A NUTSHELL, Third Edition, 307 pages, 1988. Softcover. (Text)

Professional Responsibility

ARONSON AND WECKSTEIN'S PROFESSIONAL RESPONSIBILITY IN A NUTSHELL, 399 pages, 1980. Softcover. (Text)

ROTUNDA'S BLACK LETTER ON PROFESSIONAL RESPONSIBILITY, Second Edition, 414 pages, 1988. Softcover. (Review)

WOLFRAM'S HORNBOOK ON MODERN LEGAL ETHICS, Student Edition, 1120 pages, 1986. (Text)

Property—see also Real Estate Transactions, Land Use, Trusts and Estates

BERNHARDT'S BLACK LETTER ON

Property—Continued

PROPERTY, 318 pages, 1983. Softcover. (Review)

BERNHARDT'S REAL PROPERTY IN A NUTSHELL, Second Edition, 448 pages, 1981. Softcover. (Text)

BURKE'S PERSONAL PROPERTY IN A NUTSHELL, 322 pages, 1983. Softcover. (Text)

CUNNINGHAM, STOEBUCK AND WHITMAN'S HORNBOOK ON THE LAW OF PROPERTY, Student Edition, 916 pages, 1984, with 1987 pocket part. (Text)

HILL'S LANDLORD AND TENANT LAW IN A NUTSHELL, Second Edition, 311 pages, 1986. Softcover. (Text)

Real Estate Transactions

BRUCE'S REAL ESTATE FINANCE IN A NUTSHELL, Second Edition, 262 pages, 1985. Softcover. (Text)

NELSON AND WHITMAN'S BLACK LETTER ON LAND TRANSACTIONS AND FINANCE, Second Edition, 466 pages, 1988. Softcover. (Review)

NELSON AND WHITMAN'S HORNBOOK ON REAL ESTATE FINANCE LAW, Second Edition, 941 pages, 1985 with 1989 pocket part. (Text)

Regulated Industries—see also Mass Communication Law, Banking Law

GELLHORN AND PIERCE'S REGULATED INDUSTRIES IN A NUTSHELL, Second Edition, 389 pages, 1987. Softcover. (Text)

Remedies

DOBBS' HORNBOOK ON REMEDIES, 1067 pages, 1973. (Text)

DOBBYN'S INJUNCTIONS IN A NUTSHELL, 264 pages, 1974. Softcover. (Text)

FRIEDMAN'S CONTRACT REMEDIES IN A NUTSHELL, 323 pages, 1981. Softcover. (Text)

MCCORMICK'S HORNBOOK ON DAMAGES, 811 pages, 1935. (Text)

O'CONNELL'S REMEDIES IN A NUTSHELL, Second Edition, 320 pages, 1985. Softcover. (Text)

Sea, Law of

SOHN AND GUSTAFSON'S THE LAW OF THE SEA IN A NUTSHELL, 264 pages, 1984. Softcover. (Text)

Securities Regulation

HAZEN'S HORNBOOK ON THE LAW OF SECURITIES REGULATION, Student Edition, 739 pages, 1985, with 1988 pocket

Securities Regulation—Continued

part. (Text)

RATNER'S SECURITIES REGULATION IN A NUTSHELL, Third Edition, 316 pages, 1988. Softcover. (Text)

Social Legislation

HOOD AND HARDY'S WORKERS' COMPENSATION AND EMPLOYEE PROTECTION IN A NUTSHELL, 274 pages, 1984. Softcover. (Text)

LAFRANCE'S WELFARE LAW: STRUCTURE AND ENTITLEMENT IN A NUTSHELL, 455 pages, 1979. Softcover. (Text)

Sports Law

SCHUBERT, SMITH AND TRENTADUE'S SPORTS LAW, 395 pages, 1986. (Text)

Taxation—Corporate

WEIDENBRUCH AND BURKE'S FEDERAL INCOME TAXATION OF CORPORATIONS AND STOCKHOLDERS IN A NUTSHELL, Third Edition, 309 pages, 1989. Softcover. (Text)

Taxation—Estate & Gift—see also Estate Planning, Trusts and Estates

MCNULTY'S FEDERAL ESTATE AND GIFT TAXATION IN A NUT-SHELL, Fourth Edition, 496 pages, 1989. Softcover. (Text)

Taxation—Individual

HUDSON AND LIND'S BLACK LETTER ON FEDERAL INCOME TAXATION, Second Edition, 396 pages, 1987. Softcover. (Review)

MCNULTY'S FEDERAL INCOME TAXATION OF INDIVIDUALS IN A NUTSHELL, Fourth Edition, 503 pages, 1988. Softcover. (Text)

POSIN'S HORNBOOK ON FEDERAL INCOME TAXATION, Student Edition, 491 pages, 1983, with 1989 pocket part. (Text)

ROSE AND CHOMMIE'S HORNBOOK ON FEDERAL INCOME TAXATION, Third Edition, 923 pages, 1988, with 1989 pocket part. (Text)

Taxation—International

DOERNBERG'S INTERNATIONAL TAXATION IN A NUTSHELL, 325 pages, 1989. Softcover. (Text)

Taxation—State & Local

GELFAND AND SALSICH'S STATE AND LOCAL TAXATION AND FINANCE IN A NUTSHELL, 309 pages, 1986. Softcover. (Text)

Torts—see also Products Liability

KIONKA'S BLACK LETTER ON TORTS, 339 pages, 1988. Softcover. (Review)

KIONKA'S TORTS IN A NUTSHELL: INJURIES TO PERSONS AND PROPERTY, 434 pages, 1977. Softcover. (Text)

MALONE'S TORTS IN A NUTSHELL: INJURIES TO FAMILY, SOCIAL AND TRADE RELATIONS, 358 pages, 1979. Softcover. (Text)

PROSSER AND KEETON'S HORNBOOK ON TORTS, Fifth Edition, Student Edition, 1286 pages, 1984 with 1988 pocket part. (Text)

Trade Regulation—see also Antitrust, Regulated Industries

MCMANIS' UNFAIR TRADE PRACTICES IN A NUTSHELL, Second Edition, 464 pages, 1988. Softcover. (Text)

SCHECHTER'S BLACK LETTER ON UNFAIR TRADE PRACTICES, 272 pages, 1986. Softcover. (Review)

Trial and Appellate Advocacy—see also Civil Procedure

BERGMAN'S TRIAL ADVOCACY IN A NUTSHELL, Second Edition, 354 pages, 1989. Softcover. (Text)

GOLDBERG'S THE FIRST TRIAL (WHERE DO I SIT? WHAT DO I SAY?) IN A NUTSHELL, 396 pages, 1982. Softcover. (Text)

HEGLAND'S TRIAL AND PRACTICE SKILLS IN A NUTSHELL, 346 pages, 1978. Softcover. (Text)

HORNSTEIN'S APPELLATE ADVOCACY IN A NUTSHELL, 325 pages, 1984. Softcover. (Text)

JEANS' HANDBOOK ON TRIAL ADVOCACY, Student Edition, 473 pages, 1975. Softcover. (Text)

Trusts and Estates

ATKINSON'S HORNBOOK ON WILLS, Second Edition, 975 pages, 1953. (Text)

AVERILL'S UNIFORM PROBATE CODE IN A NUTSHELL, Second Edition, 454 pages, 1987. Softcover. (Text)

BOGERT'S HORNBOOK ON TRUSTS, Sixth Edition, Student Edition, 794 pages, 1987. (Text)

MCGOVERN, KURTZ AND REIN'S HORNBOOK ON WILLS, TRUSTS

Advisory Board

XIV

CONTRACTS
IN A NUTSHELL

THIRD EDITION

By

GORDON D. SCHABER

Dean and Professor of Law,
McGeorge School of Law
University of the Pacific

and

CLAUDE D. ROHWER

Professor of Law,
McGeorge School of Law
University of the Pacific

ST. PAUL, MINN.
WEST PUBLISHING CO.
1990

COPYRIGHT © 1975, 1984 By WEST PUBLISHING CO.
COPYRIGHT © 1990 By WEST PUBLISHING CO.

50 West Kellogg Boulevard
P.O. Box 64526
St. Paul, MN 55164–0526

Library of Congress Cataloging-in-Publication Data

Schaber, Gordon D.
   Contracts in a nutshell / Gordon D. Schaber and Claude D. Rohwer.
  —3rd ed.
    p.   cm.
   ISBN 0–314–73434–1
   1. Contracts—United States. I. Rohwer, Claude D. II. Title.
  KF801.Z9S3 1990
  346.73'02—dc20
  [347.3062]

                        90–35216
                        CIP

ISBN 0–314–73434–1

DEDICATION

To our friends and colleagues in Eastern Europe
and The Peoples' Republic of China who are
striving to create or reestablish a system of
commercial law that will provide a basis for a free
market economy with the attendant individual
freedoms that such laws can foster.

*

PREFACE

Professors teaching Contracts can choose from among various alternatives for sequencing materials. Available casebooks on the subject use a variety of approaches. The authors have selected a sequence that we think contributes to ease in understanding. For example, the chapter on Remedies precedes the chapter on Performance because we believe that performance problems are more manageable if one has a general knowledge of the remedies that will be available for a given breach. However, the odds are that our organization will not track precisely with that used by any particular Contracts professor.

Students using this book can consult the outline or the index to locate the materials that relate to what is currently being covered in their classes. Each chapter is designed to be comprehensible regardless of the order in which the materials are studied.

The authors acknowledge the very capable and dedicated editorial assistance of Anna Orlowski, class of 1991. We also received helpful comments and suggestions from Professors Charles D. Kelso,

Anthony M. Skrocki and Michaela M. White for which we are most grateful.

GDS
CDR

Sacramento, California
April, 1990

IV. Statute of Frauds

VIII. Remedies

IX. Performance

XI. Assignment of Rights and Delegation of Duties

*

TABLE OF CASES

References are to Pages

TABLE OF CASES

CONTRACTS

IN A NUTSHELL

THIRD EDITION

*

CONTRACTS

I. INTRODUCTION

§ 1. Basis for Enforcement of Promises

Contract law is initially concerned with determining what promises the law will enforce or otherwise recognize as creating legal rights. The following is a brief description of the bases which our courts use to determine what promises are enforceable.

(a) A promise made as a bargained exchange for some legally sufficient consideration is enforced in the common law system. This requires some agreement between the contracting parties which may take the form of an offer by one party and an acceptance of it by the other. The agreement may be manifested in either written or oral words and thus be an express contract. It may be manifested by conduct or some combination of words and conduct, in which case it will be characterized as an implied contract. Promises can be enforced whether they are the product of an express or an implied agreement.

(b) A duty to perform may also arise when a promise reasonably induced another person to change position in reliance on the promise. This basis for recognition of a duty to perform a promise, usually termed "promissory estoppel" or "detrimental reliance," has arisen in the last one hundred years and is now generally accepted by American courts. Older cases treated promissory estoppel as a substitute for consideration but it is now generally recognized as an alternative basis for promise enforcement. It is a substitute for the bargained exchange and thus may be used to enforce a promise in the absence of offer, acceptance and consideration.

(c) Courts have traditionally found legal justification to enforce promises to pay preexisting obligations that have become unenforceable because the time permitted by law for bringing suit has expired (the statute of limitations has run) or because the debt has been discharged in bankruptcy. These are properly categorized as new promises to perform previously existing obligations. Where the original oral promise was unenforceable because the law required a writing, the courts will enforce a new written promise or written acknowledgment. A promise to perform an obligation that was unenforceable when made because the promisor lacked legal capacity will also be enforced. These latter two categories are technically not promises to pay preexisting legal obligations because the prior "obligation" was never legally owing. The lack of a writing or the promisor's lack of capacity made the promise unenforceable from the beginning, yet the new promise to pay this "obligation" will be enforced.

(d) Courts enforce promises because statutory enactments by legislative bodies decree that such promises be enforced. Sections 2–205 and 2–209(1) of the Uniform Commercial Code provide convenient examples of this.

(e) A very few cases exist in which courts have enforced a subsequent promise to pay for material benefits previously conferred but for which no legal obligation to pay existed. Enforcement was permitted because of the "moral obligation." Careful examination of these few cases usually discloses that the court also identified an alternative basis for enforcing the promise in question (cf. § 67, *infra*).

(f) The final category is fundamentally different from those listed above. Courts have found good reason to impose an obligation of a quasi-contractual nature upon certain persons. For instance, parties who are deemed to have been unjustly enriched by receiving a benefit from another for which they rightfully should pay may be liable for the reasonable value of the benefit conferred. The obligation which is imposed has been deemed to be more analogous to a contract obligation as distinguished from tort, and thus is sometimes referred to as quasi-contract or implied-in-law contract. In many jurisdictions this type of obligation is referred to as restitution or unjust enrichment.

These are non-consensual obligations in which the party to be charged did not in fact make any promise or did not make a legally effective promise. The court is imposing a "promise" upon that party as a first step in the process of finding liability of the kind which would exist had a legally enforceable promise in fact been made. This law is a part of the subject of restitution and is discussed generally in Chapter III.

§ 2. Sale of Goods and the Uniform Commercial Code

The Uniform Commercial Code (referred to herein as the U.C.C.) consists of numerous articles which deal with different areas of commercial law. Students of contract law should know that Article One (in which all section numbers begin with "1") contains general principles of law and definitions that apply to the entire U.C.C., and that Article Two (in which all section numbers begin with "2") applies to all "transactions in goods" other than security transactions. Transactions in goods are "security transactions" where the purpose of the transaction is to secure a loan or other obligation. (See U.C.C. section 2–102.)

Articles Three through Nine deal with other commercial matters. For example, Article Three deals with the law relating to promissory notes and checks. These articles of the U.C.C. have no direct bearing upon the study of the law of contracts except for certain portions of Article Nine. Article

Nine produces significant changes in the common law relating to assignments. (See Chapter XI.)

There is a new article of the U.C.C. expressly dealing with leasing and rental of goods. This article has been officially designated as Article 2A (in which all section numbers begin with "2A"). It has been submitted to the various states for their consideration and has been adopted in some states. One state, California, has departed from the "Article 2A" designation and has adopted this new article as number "10" (which becomes "Division 10" under the California system of codification).

Because the U.C.C. makes important changes in the common law relating to the sale of goods (Article 2) and the leasing of goods (Article 2A), it is important to understand the definition of "goods." U.C.C. section 2–105(1) provides in part: " 'Goods' means all things (including specially manufactured goods) which are moveable at the time of identification to the contract. . . ." The "time of identification to the contract" can vary in different contexts but will most frequently refer to the time of performance. Therefore, the key question is whether the contract involves things that are moveable when performance is rendered. The goods need not be in existence when the contract is made.

A contract for a special machine to be designed and built by the seller and delivered to the buyer is a contract for goods. A contract for construction of a building is a service contract and not a contract for goods. While the builder will use goods to build the structure, those goods will not be moveable when the performance is rendered.

A contract may involve both goods and services in which case one must decide which is the dominant part of the transaction. A contract to change oil and lubricate a car is probably a service contract because the goods (oil and grease) are incidental. A contract for a piano in which the seller is to deliver it and tune it after it is moved is a transaction in goods because the services involved are incidental to the sale of the goods. A contract in which an artist is to paint a portrait is probably a service contract. The artist is to deliver the completed painting which could be viewed as specially produced goods, however the dominant nature of the contract is probably the service of the artist painting the picture.

Contracts for growing crops or trees are contracts for goods if the contract contemplates the severing of the crops or trees from the land. A contract for the sale of minerals or a structure to be removed from realty is a transaction in goods only if it is to be severed by the seller. (See U.C.C. sections 2–105 and 2–107 and the comments to these sections.)

To the extent that the U.C.C. has not changed the law relative to sales of goods and other transactions in goods, principles of common law and equity are applicable (U.C.C. section 1–103). In making reference to the U.C.C., the essence of certain sections will be summarized or paraphrased for the purpose of explaining their significance. Such summaries obviously should not be treated as substitutions for a careful reading of the original.

The U.C.C. applies to all persons and entities. A few limited sections and portions of sections are applicable only to merchants or to transactions between merchants. The term merchant is not defined in its ordinary sense, and the definition varies depending upon the context (U.C.C. section 2–104 and comment 2).

U.C.C. section 1–203 provides: "Every contract or duty within this Act imposes an obligation of good faith in its performance or enforcement." This simple sentence can have substantive impact in many contract situations, and should not be viewed as a simple mouthing of honorable intentions. U.C.C. section 1–201(19) provides: " 'good faith' means honesty in fact in the conduct or transactions concerned." U.C.C. section 2–103(1)(b) provides: " 'good faith' in the case of a merchant means honesty in fact and the observance of reasonable commercial standards of fair dealing in the trade." This latter definition is applicable only to merchants and is usually held to apply only in those cases in which a section of Article Two expressly requires good faith, e.g. 2–305.

§ 3. Contracts Which Constitute a Bargained Exchange

The primary basis for enforcing a promise in the common law system is that it was made as part of a bargained exchange. There must be an agreement between the contracting parties pursuant to which the bargain is made, and the elements of this bargained exchange are typically stated to be offer, acceptance and consideration.

§ 4. Necessity for Agreement on Terms

Bargained exchange contracts must involve an agreement. Both parties must manifest their intention to be bound to an agreement, the terms of which are sufficiently definite and certain to be legally enforceable. This may involve oral negotiations, an exchange of written proposals, the execution of a standard form or non-verbal conduct which manifests an agreement. It is not uncommon for parties to engage in a series of discussions in which the various terms of an agreement are delineated. Ultimately, the parties may shake hands, literally or figuratively, manifesting their assent to the total understanding. In such circumstances, an agreement has been reached without either party making a specific offer which the other accepted. Realizing that one may not be able to find a specific offer and acceptance in every contract agreement, it is nonetheless best to approach this topic by examining the basic elements involved in identifying offers and acceptances.

II. CONTRACT FORMATION

A. MUTUAL ASSENT TO A BARGAIN

1. OFFER

§ 5. Manifestation of Assent to Be Bound

An offer is a communication that creates in the offeree the power to form a contract by accepting in an authorized manner. In the words of the Restatement, Second, Contracts, (herein referred to as Restatement, Second) it must be a "manifestation of willingness to enter into a bargain, so made as to justify another person in understanding that his assent to that bargain is invited and will conclude it." Thus the first element of an offer is a manifestation of an intention to be presently bound subject only to an appropriate acceptance.

An offer may be found where words arouse an expectation in the mind of a reasonable person in the position of the offeree that if he makes a promise or performs an act as requested, nothing further need be done by either party in order to form a contract. Words which arouse such an expectation create a power of acceptance in the offeree. On the other hand, words which arouse a lesser expectation, merely inviting further discussion or an offer from the other party may be considered preliminary negotiations. Restatement, Second, section 26 provides:

9

Sec. 26. Preliminary Negotiations. A manifestation of willingness to enter into a bargain is not an offer if the person to whom it is addressed knows or has reason to know that the person making it does not intend to conclude a bargain until he has made a further manifestation of assent.

Whether a communication is an offer or is simply preliminary negotiations is a question of fact. If the recipient is aware that the proposal is addressed to other parties, it is less likely to be an offer as such conduct tends to negate an intention to be presently bound. Where intention to be bound is not clear, the more definite a proposal the more likely it is that a trier of fact will conclude that the party making it is willing to be presently bound.

§ 6. Subjective and Objective Intent

Contract liability is primarily predicated upon the intention a party objectively manifests rather than unexpressed subjective intent. While subjective intention will sometimes be a factor in interpreting the parties' communications (§§ 88–90, *infra*), the focus is ordinarily upon what the person to whom the communication was directed should reasonably have understood.

In determining what intention is manifested by a given communication, the message is construed as a whole in light of all correspondence and prior transactions. Common sense, as well as the law, dictates that later expressions are controlling over inconsistent earlier expressions; that language added by the parties controls over printed materials in a standard form; that language is to be interpreted in light of the custom and usage in the trade or community and in accordance with any prior course of dealing between the parties.

While finding and following the objective intent manifested by the parties is the norm in contract law, there are circumstances in which subjective intent is relevant. Followed to its literal conclusion, the application of objectively manifested intent instead of the actual or subjective intention of the parties could result in a contract based upon communications between two parties, neither of whom actually meant to be bound. If it is apparent that the subjective intent of each party was the same, that intent will control. Contract law is concerned with protection of the reasonable expectations of the parties and there is ordinarily no reason to enforce manifested bargains which neither party actually intended or wanted.

Where a mutual misunderstanding exists, the subjective intention of the parties is considered. There is no mutual assent where each party knew or had reason to know the different meaning attached by the other. Section 20 of the Restatement, Second, takes the further position that there is no mutual assent if the parties attach materially different meanings to their manifestations and neither knew or had reason to know of the meaning attached by the other. (See §§ 108–114, *infra*.)

Proposals that appear to be seriously made and accepted do not create enforceable obligations if the parties were jesting or for other reasons did not intend their words to have legal effect. Contracts professors and students make many hypothetical bargains in the classroom and no legally enforceable rights result. People reach agreements relating to matters such as social dates with no intent that there be legally enforceable rights and duties. If the person to whom a proposal is made knows or should have known that the proposal is not meant to result in a legally enforceable bargain, then no contract results.

§ 7. Certainty of Terms in the Offer

To have an enforceable contract, the parties must manifest their assent to a bargain that is sufficiently definite and certain to permit a court to fashion an appropriate remedy for breach. It should be noted that it is the contract and not the offer which must contain the required degree of certainty as to subject matter. An offer may propose the sale of either a certain two story house or a certain one story house. The choice can be left to the buyer. It does not matter that the offer is uncertain so long as the resulting contract will be specific when the offeree makes an effective acceptance, which in this case would require the election of one house or the other.

A second point to keep in mind is that in some cases, contract disputes do not develop until after the parties have been performing the contracts for a period of time. Courts can and do look to the course of performance of the contract to find the parties' intentions as to terms. Thus even if an agreement was too vague or indefinite to be enforced when it was first made, it might become an enforceable contract after the parties have rendered and accepted some performances and thereby manifested what they in fact both intended their agreement to be.

Older court opinions state that the agreement must contain all of the "essential" terms of the contract. Many of these opinions contain statements to the effect that the function of courts is to enforce contracts or provide remedies for their breach, not to write contracts for the parties.

Recent decisions are more likely to focus upon the question whether the contract is sufficiently definite to permit the court to grant the relief the plaintiff seeks. If the plaintiff seeks money damages, the court must be able to determine whether the contract was breached and what damages were caused. If the plaintiff seeks a court order to compel performance, more certainty may be required as the court is being asked to order the defendant to do something and the judge will want a clear picture of what it is the defendant agreed to do.

The degree of certainty or definiteness which is required for an enforceable contract varies with the subject matter. For example, in real property transactions, the parties ordinarily proceed with due care and deliberation, setting forth their agreement in considerable detail. Much significance is also attached to the transfer of real property, and aggrieved parties often seek the remedy of specific performance which requires particular certainty of contract terms. Possibly for these reasons, courts generally will not enforce an agreement for the sale of land unless it is certain and definite as to all material terms. It is sometimes stated that the material terms include the parties, price, subject matter, and time of performance. The identity of the parties to the contract is usually obvious. Time of performance is found to be within a reasonable time where no time is specified. Subject matter and price will be important in transactions such as land contracts, but there are situations, for example, dealership agreements, in which even price and subject matter are not crucial terms.

Rather than attempting to memorize a list of material terms, one should appreciate that the essential terms will vary from transaction to transaction. In a cash transaction, interest rates have no significance, but a provision that the price will be paid over a period of 10 years at an interest rate to be agreed upon may make the entire agreement unenforceable due to uncertainty. However, one can find recent cases that enforce such agreements where the parties' intention to be presently bound was clear.

An analysis of common law decisions in contract cases leads to the generalization that more certainty of terms is required in land contracts than is required in service contracts such as employment contracts or construction contracts. Common law decisions involving transactions in goods required even less certainty. The practice of the market place often involved making agreements with the intent to be presently bound despite the absence of terms on matters which could be rather important. This common law approach to transactions in goods has been carried forward by the U.C.C. as discussed in the next section.

The Restatement, Second, section 33, takes the following position on the subject of certainty:

(1) Even though a manifestation of intention is intended to be understood as an offer, it cannot be accepted so as to form a contract unless the terms of the contract are reasonably certain.

(2) The terms of a contract are reasonably certain if they provide a basis for determining the existence of a breach and for giving an appropriate remedy.

(3) The fact that one or more terms of a proposed bargain are left open or uncertain may show that a manifestation of intention is not intended to be understood as an offer or as an acceptance.

There is a definite relationship between certainty of terms and manifestation of intent to be bound. If parties have reached an agreement but there are significant terms to be settled, a court might properly find that the parties have not yet manifested their intent to be presently bound but have only expressed an intention to continue to negotiate and try to work out a deal. Where intent to be bound is not clear, missing terms may tip the scales to produce a finding that there was no such intent manifested yet. Conversely, the presence of complete terms is some indication that the parties had concluded an agreement.

§ 8. Certainty of Terms Under the U.C.C.

Section 2–204(3) of the U.C.C. provides:

(3) Even though one or more terms are left open a contract for sale does not fail for indefiniteness if the parties have intended to make a contract and there is a reasonably certain basis for giving an appropriate remedy.

There are other sections such as 2–207(3) which direct a court to enforce a contract where the parties have expressed by words or conduct their intention to be bound despite the fact that one or more terms are the subject of disagreement.

To facilitate enforcing contracts despite unsettled terms, sections 2–304 through 2–311 provide "gap filling" provisions to assist a court in fashioning an appropriate remedy. Unspecified terms can also be supplied by looking to the course of performance of the parties under the contract before the dispute arose, their course of dealing in prior transactions and usage of the trade or industry. (See sections 1–205 and 2–208.)

It becomes apparent that under the U.C.C., the crucial issue is ordinarily whether the parties manifested an intent to be presently bound. If they did, one can usually find a way to establish contract terms. This is also the modern trend in common law decisions involving subject matter other than goods.

§ 9. Terms Established by External Standards

A contract may leave terms of performance to be established by external standards. A contract for the sale of goods may provide for a price equal to the price of similar goods on a certain commodity market. Interest on an obligation may be fixed at one percent over the prime rate established by a designated bank.

While reference to an external source for a contract term does not prevent enforcement of an otherwise enforceable agreement, a serious issue is presented where the external standard fails, e.g., the commodity market closes or the designated bank ceases the practice of establishing or publicizing a prime rate. Many common law decisions demonstrate a reluctance to "rewrite" the contract for the parties. If an alternative standard is not inferred in the contract terms, the contract may fail for lack of certainty. If the subject matter is goods, U.C.C. section 2–305(1)(c) directs that where an external price standard fails, the court shall substitute a reasonable price at the time of delivery if the court finds that the parties intended this result (cf. U.C.C. section 2–305(4)).

The approach taken in transactions in goods has had an influence on the common law of contracts. Where there is a failure of the formula or device selected by the parties to fix the price or another contract term, modern decisions frequently focus upon the question whether the parties intended to be bound in the event the formula failed. If it is found that they did intend to be bound, the court can be expected to substitute reasonable terms and enforce the contract.

The parties may fix quantity in terms of the requirements of the buyer or the output of the seller. The principles applied to these contracts are discussed in § 57, *infra.*

Contracts may also provide that one or the other of the parties shall specify a term of performance. Where this is what the parties bargained for, the term specified will be enforced so long as the specification was made in good faith. This principle was recognized at common law and has been adopted by the U.C.C. (section 2–311) which specifies that the exercise of discretion must be in good faith and "within limits set by commercial reasonableness."

§ 10. Advertisements, Mass Mailings, and Price Quotations

An advertisement typically indicates a willingness, even an eagerness, to enter into a bargain. One is thus tempted to label such an advertisement as an offer. However, it must be recalled that in order to be an offer, the manifestation must be so made as to justify another person in understanding that assent to the bargain is invited and will conclude the bargain. This latter element is usually found to be lacking in the typical advertisement.

The terms which are generally found to be lacking in the typical advertisement are certainty as to quantity and the identity and number of intended offerees. If these terms can be satisfied without further promise by the advertiser, a valid offer may be found. Advertisements that promise a reward for a certain act are thus typically found to constitute an offer. An advertisement which manifests a willingness to sell a specific item on stated terms to the first person who accepts may also be found to be an offer. However, the typical ad which offers items such as lawn chairs for a stated price is usually treated as an invitation to make offers. While this conclusion may offend one's sense of justice, it is suggested that societal concerns with prevention of deceptive advertising and improper practices such as bait-and-switch are most effectively addressed by consumer protection legislation that can impose meaningful civil or criminal penalties.

Mass mailings are typically treated the same as advertisements in the media. A communication which expresses a willingness to sell a specific item of property and which is sent to a large number of persons ordinarily does not exhibit an intention to be presently bound subject only to an acceptance from one of the recipients. Assuming that the material sent is of such a nature that the fact of wide distribution is readily apparent, the recipients are not justified in assuming that their assent will conclude a bargain.

Distributions of catalogues, price lists, and the like, ordinarily communicate a desire to solicit orders or offers from the public. People in business frequently use the term "price quote" which ordinarily implies that there is no present intention to be bound. However, a communication which is sent in response to a buyer's specific request for goods or in response to a seller's specific solicitation of an order is more likely to be found to manifest an intention to be presently bound and thus constitute an offer. The communications combine to create certainty as to parties, quantity and availability, and thus may generate an expectation in the recipient that an acceptance will form a contract. A "price quote" may likewise reasonably create in the recipient an understanding that assent by him will conclude a bargain where the context of the entire communication and surrounding facts and circumstances justify such an inference.

§ 11. Receipt of the Offer

Restatement, Second, section 23, provides: "It is essential to a bargain that each party manifest assent with reference to the manifestation of the other." The primary concern of contract law is to protect reasonable expectations which are created by the promises of others. Such expectation ordinarily exists only if an offer has been communicated, and a contract will be formed only if an offeree has knowledge of an offer at the time of the purported acceptance.

Assume that X places a reward offer in the newspaper. Y performs the requested act without knowledge of this offer. No bargained exchange has occurred and no contract results. Y has no expectations to be protected or fulfilled unless Y knew of the existence of the offer. Most cases permit a person who learns of an offer after he has rendered part of the requested performance to accept by completing the performance with the intention of accepting the offer. Reward offers made by governmental entities have been recognized as creating rights in persons who perform the requested act without knowledge of the reward, but such rights are properly categorized as bounties or statutorily created rights rather than contract rights.

X sends an offer to Y by mail. Y mails an identical offer to X which crosses in the mail. No contract results from the sending and receipt of these offers. It should be noted, however, that either party may accept the offer which has been received and that conduct by either or both may accomplish this result.

§ 12. Communication in the Intended Manner

An offer does not manifest an intention to be bound until it has been intentionally communicated to the offeree. Thus, one does not have the power to accept an offer until it has been communicated in an intended manner. If X learns from Z that Y intends to make an offer to X, X does not have the power to accept.

However, the law is designed to protect the reasonable expectations of a party which are created by the words or actions of another. Thus if an offeror volitionally communicates an offer although not intending to do so, the offer is effective when received by the offeree so long as the offeree does not know or have reason to know of the mistake. Assume a party prepares and signs a letter that manifests an offer and then decides not to mail it. Thereafter, the party inadvertently mails the letter. The offer will be effective assuming the offeree has no reason to know of the mistake.

§ 13. Assignment of Offers

Since an offer is intended only for the person to whom it is communicated by the offeror, an offer is not assignable to another. An exception to this rule is the paid-for offer, otherwise known as an option contract. If an offeree has given consideration for a promise not to revoke an offer, he has a property right therein which is ordinarily assignable. (See §§ 23, 167 and 174, *infra*.)

§ 14. Duration of an Offer

An offer terminates at the end of the time stated in the offer, and an attempted acceptance after that time is merely a counter-offer. The usual inference is that time for acceptance of an offer begins to run when the offer is received. If S mails an offer on July 1 giving B 10 days in which to accept and the letter arrives in the ordinary course of mail on July 3, the inference is that the offer will lapse at the end of the day on July 13 if it is not otherwise terminated before that time.

If there is a delay in communication and the offeree knows or should know of this fact, then the reasonable inference is that the offeror intended the time for acceptance to begin to run from the date on which the offer would ordinarily have been received. If the above-described letter were postmarked on July 1 and would ordinarily be delivered in two days, the offer will lapse on July 13, even if it is delivered on July 12. If it is not delivered until July 14, then there was never an effective offer that the recipient could accept. However, if the offeree does not know or have reason to know that the letter was delayed, his reasonable expectations which are created from reading the letter will be protected, and he will have 10 days from receipt to accept.

If no time is stated in the offer, it will lapse after a reasonable time. The duration of a reasonable time is a question of fact, dependent upon the nature of the contract, business usages, and other circumstances of which the offeree either knows or should know. The nature of the subject matter, e.g. a fluctuating commodity, and the mode of communication, e.g. telegraph, are important in that they indicate the degree of urgency connected with the transaction. In some cases, even twenty-four hours may be beyond a reasonable time.

In face-to-face or telephone communications, most cases result in a factual determination that an offer made in the course of the conversation lapses when the conversation is terminated. The offer would remain open if there were some reasonably clear indication that such was intended by the offeror.

It is frequently stated that an acceptance must be seasonably made. The word "seasonable" is used to mean within the time permitted by law. This would be the time fixed by the offeror or a reasonable time if no time is fixed and before the occurrence of an event that would terminate the offer. (See §§ 15–19 and 21, *infra*.)

§ 15. Termination of the Offer by Death or Insanity

Death or insanity of the offeror terminates the offeree's power of acceptance, and despite the objective theory of contracts, no notice to the offeree of these operative facts is necessary. Death or insanity of an offeree also terminates contractual possibilities, not because the offer is terminated but because only the intended offeree can accept. The above rules do not apply if the offer was irrevocable and the contemplated performances were not personal to the parties involved. (See §§ 23 and 176, *infra.*)

§ 16. Termination of the Offer by Death or Destruction of a Person or Thing Essential to Performance

Death or destruction before acceptance of a person or thing essential for performance of the proposed contract terminates the offer. An offer for a personal services contract will be terminated by death or incapacity of the one who was to perform the services. If S offers to sell a specific cow to B, death of that cow prior to acceptance terminates the offer. If the cow had died before the offer was made and B accepted the offer, S could seek to be excused on the grounds of mistake (§ 109, *infra*). If the cow died after acceptance but before delivery and before risk of loss had passed to the buyer, the contract would have been formed but S could seek to be excused from performance on the basis of impossibility (§ 176, *infra*). If the cow died while being transported from S's farm to B's farm, the problem might be one of risk of loss (U.C.C. sections 2–509 and 2–510).

§ 17. Termination by Supervening Illegality

If, after an offer is made but prior to acceptance, the proposed contract becomes illegal, the offer is terminated. Hence, if R offers to lend E $1,000 for one year at 12% interest, and thereafter, but prior to acceptance, a usury law is enacted prohibiting interest at more than 10% on future loans, the offer is terminated. Note that if the proposed contract were illegal when the offer was made, the problem would involve the defense of illegality (§ 120, *infra*), whereas if it became illegal after acceptance but prior to timely performance, the problem would involve excuse from performance based upon impossibility (§ 176, *infra*).

§ 18. Termination by Rejection by the Offeree

An unqualified rejection terminates an offer, and it cannot thereafter be revived by the offeree's attempt to accept it. An offer is rejected when the offeror is justified in inferring from the words or conduct of the offeree that the offeree does not intend to accept the offer nor take it under advisement. Under the majority view, a rejection is not effective until it is received by the offeror. Thus, the offeree's power to create a contract by accepting is not terminated merely by sending a rejection. Sending a rejection may, however, change the time when an acceptance is effective (§ 42, *infra*).

§ 19. Termination by Counter-Offer

The making of a counter-offer impliedly manifests a rejection of the offer and therefore terminates the offer. To illustrate, consider the following:

(1) S offers to sell Blackacre for $50,000 to B. B replies: "I will pay you $20,000 cash and a one year note at 10% interest for the balance." Since the offer implicitly contains the term of cash, this is a counter-offer and rejection of the original offer. The rejection will be effective upon receipt by S.

(2) S makes the same offer as above. B replies: "I am keeping your offer under advisement. Will you take $20,000 cash and a one year note at 10% interest for the balance?" This communication, which expressly reserves decision on the offer may be an "inquiry into terms." Even if it is found to contain a counter-offer, it does not impliedly reject the offer.

The significant point is that the making of a counter-offer ordinarily communicates to the offeror that the offeree does not wish to accept the offer. Where the offeree manifests an intention not to reject the offer, a rejection should not be found despite the fact that the offeree proposes an alternative bargain.

§ 20. Termination by Revocation

The common law of contracts operates under the premise that all offers are revocable prior to the time of acceptance. Exceptions to this general rule exist where there is an option contract (§ 23, *infra*), where there is detrimental reliance by the offeree upon a promise not to revoke the offer (§ 24, *infra*), where the offer is made irrevocable by statute (§ 25, *infra*), or, in the case of an offer for a unilateral contract, where the offeree has begun to perform the requested act (§ 26, *infra*). In the absence of one of these exceptions, an offeror may revoke prior to acceptance even where a promise has been made to keep the offer open for a stated period of time.

Normally offers are revoked by words communicated to the offeree which indicate that the offeror no longer wishes to be bound by the terms of his offer. The offeror need not say, "I revoke." It is sufficient if he states, "You have missed a wonderful opportunity." Or, "I am reconsidering whether to sell Blackacre." If a reasonable person in the position of the offeree would understand that the offeror no longer intends to be presently bound by the terms of his offer, the offer is revoked.

§ 21. Revocation by Indirect Communications of Facts Inconsistent With Intent to Be Bound

If an offeree receives information from a reasonably reliable source which indicates that the offeror no longer intends to be bound by the terms of the offer, then this is effective as a revocation of the offer. Where the offer was to sell a parcel of land, learning from a reliable source that the offer-

or has sold the land to another is enough to terminate the offer because the offeree knows that the
offeror no longer intends to be bound by the terms
of the offer.

§ 22. Time When Revocation Effective

The law is concerned with protecting the reasonable expectations of the parties, and for that reason, the offeree is not charged with knowledge of
any attempted revocation that has not yet been
received. Therefore, a revocation must be received
before it is effective. Thus, an acceptance that
became operative prior to the receipt by the offeree
of a revocation will create a contract.

Under the very old common law principles, an
offer was revoked when an offeror changed his
mind even though that change was not communicated to the offeree. This was the product of
emphasizing a subjective "meeting of the minds"
theory which was rejected in the nineteenth century. This requirement of coincidence of subjective
intent is no longer the law, and the term "meeting
of the minds" is misleading and should be avoided.

A few states (including California, South Dakota,
North Dakota and Montana) have statutes which
provide that revocations are to be treated in like
manner as acceptances. The implication of these
sections is that a revocation might be effective
when sent (§ 42, *infra*). At least one of these
states (South Dakota) has so interpreted this statutory language.

§ 23. Irrevocability by Virtue of Option Contracts

If legally sufficient consideration is given in exchange for a promise to keep an offer open during a stated period of time, an option contract is created. The promise not to revoke is enforceable, thus the offer is irrevocable for the period stated. The option contract is not terminated by the subsequent death or insanity of the offeror or offeree. Most decisions hold that such irrevocable offers are not terminated even by an express rejection by the offeree.

Assume that S offers to sell Blackacre to B for $50,000 and that B pays S $100 in exchange for S's promise not to revoke this offer for 90 days. These facts would give rise to an option contract. One month later, B advises S that B has turned his attention away from real property and will not accept S's offer. The prevailing view is that there is no termination of the offer by virtue of this rejection because B has paid for a 90 day option. Had S changed position to his detriment in reliance upon B's stated intention not to accept the offer, then B should be estopped from denying the effectiveness of his rejection.

§ 24. Irrevocability by Reliance on Promise Not to Revoke

An express or implied promise not to revoke an offer will be enforced in many jurisdictions when the offeror could foresee that the offeree might rely to his substantial detriment upon the promise not to revoke and the offeree does in fact so rely. This concept is analogous to an option contract (§ 23, *supra*). Instead of a bargained for option contract, there is a promise not to revoke which was gratuitous but which is enforced because of the foreseeable reliance which in fact occurred (§ 69, *infra*).

The Restatement, Second, section 87(2) provides:

"An offer which the offeror should reasonably expect to induce action or forbearance of a substantial character on the part of the offeree before acceptance and which does induce such action or forbearance is binding as an option contract to the extent necessary to avoid injustice."

The Restatement does not expressly provide the offeror must promise not to revoke the offer. However, it would be an exceptional situation in which the offeror does not at least impliedly promise not to revoke and yet should reasonably foresee the offeree relying upon the offer. The implications of the final phrase ". . . to the extent necessary to avoid injustice" will be explored in § 69, *infra*.

§ 25. Offers Made Irrevocable by Statute

Various states have adopted statutes which make certain types of offers irrevocable. When a merchant makes an offer to buy or sell goods and gives assurance in a signed writing that the offer will be held open, the offer is irrevocable for the stated period of time or for a reasonable time if no time is stated, but in either event, not to exceed three months (U.C.C. section 2–205). Numerous jurisdictions provide that bids (offers) made to public agencies are irrevocable for stated periods. There are a few state statutes making other types of offers irrevocable where the offeror has promised not to revoke. For example, New York General Obligations Law section 5–1109 provides for the enforcement of signed written promises not to revoke despite the absence of consideration.

§ 26. Irrevocability of Offers for Unilateral Contracts

There are various theories justifying the result, but almost all jurisdictions conclude that in the case of an offer for a unilateral contract (§§ 29 and 32, *infra*), once the offeree has begun to perform, the offeror may not revoke but must give the offeree reasonable time and opportunity to complete the requested performance. Once the offeree has commenced to do acts which are clearly in performance of the contract, the offeror is bound to permit the offeree to finish the requested act even though the offeree is not obligated to finish.

At least three theories have been used to prevent revocation of an offer for a unilateral contract after performance has begun. (1) Beginning of performance constitutes an acceptance and the contract is formed at that time with the offeror's duty of performance being conditional upon the offeree completing the requested act or forebearance. (2) The offer for a unilateral contract carries with it an implied promise not to revoke if the offeree begins performance. Thus, the beginning of performance is an acceptance of this offer for an option contract. The option contract prevents the offeror from revoking the principal offer until the offeree has had reasonable time and opportunity to finish. (3) Offers for unilateral contracts become irrevocable once performance is begun. This approach is less a theory than simply a dogmatic assertion. It might be questioned, however, whether any independent "theory" is needed to support this rule. (See generally Restatement, Second, section 45.)

With few exceptions, cases draw a distinction between preparation which does not destroy the offeror's right to revoke, and commencing performance which protects the offeree from revocation. Preparation may be substantial and costly, but the rules noted above protect only the offeree who has made some start on performance. Careful analysis of the offer to determine precisely what acts the offeror requested is necessary to determine whether the offeree is preparing to perform or has commenced to perform the requested acts. A minority position protects the offeree where he has undertaken significant preparation for performance.

Assume that X offers to pay $100,000 to the first person who flies from Florida to Cuba in a human-powered aircraft before a fixed date. Several interested parties, including Y, spend substantial time and money on research, development and training for the task. X revokes his offer, and thereafter Y performs the act before the fixed date. Y probably has no rights under Restatement, Second, section 45 or related theories because Y had not begun to perform at the time X revoked. Y might maintain a successful action against X on the theory that Y detrimentally relied upon X's implied promise not to revoke. (See § 24, *supra* and § 69, *infra.*)

2. ACCEPTANCE

§ 27. Offeror's Control Over Manner and Medium of Acceptance

The offeror is the master of the offer and may dictate not just the terms of the proposal but also the manner and medium of acceptance. "Medium of acceptance" is used here to refer to such matters as whether the acceptance is to be in writing or can be oral, or whether the acceptance should be sent by mail or by facsimile or hand-delivered. It is sometimes referred to as "method of acceptance." "Manner of acceptance" which is discussed in the next section refers to whether acceptance is to be by making a promise or simply by performing the requested act.

Matters relating to medium of acceptance can raise two quite distinct questions. It is possible for an offeror to dictate a particular medium or method of acceptance which is the only way in which the offer can be accepted. This is a rare phenomenon. An offeror can state: "If you wish to accept this offer, you must attend the basketball game Friday in a red shirt and wave your hat in the air while singing Yankee Doodle." Where the offeror's unusual directive is clearly expressed, a court will no doubt respect this requirement and find that acceptance can be effected only by attending the basketball game, wearing a red shirt, etc. This point is developed in § 41, *infra.*

The term "authorized medium of acceptance" is also used when dealing with a different issue. As discussed in §§ 41 and 42, *infra,* an acceptance is ordinarily effective when sent if sent by an authorized medium. If it is sent by an unauthorized medium, it is not effective until received. For example, if mail is an authorized medium of acceptance, a contract may be formed when the acceptance is mailed. If mail is not authorized, the acceptance will not be effective until the letter is received. (But if received in timely fashion, it may be found to be operative as of the time of dispatch. See § 42, *infra.*) If the letter is lost in the mail, the difference is obviously quite significant. (See § 15, *supra.*)

When dealing with this latter problem the court does not assume that the offeror has manifested an intention that no contract can ever be formed unless the offeree uses a certain medium to communicate the acceptance. "Authorized medium" is not used to refer to the *only* medium by which a contract can be formed. It is used to refer to the medium of acceptance that the offeror invited the offeree to use which will ordinarily have the legal effect of making the acceptance effective when sent.

§ 28. Alternate Approaches to Manner of Acceptance

When the formal structuring of the law of contracts was in vogue, it was considered necessary to divide all offers into one of two categories. Those that sought formation of the contract by a return promise from the offeree were termed offers for bilateral contracts and those which sought only action or forbearance rather than a promise were termed offers for unilateral contracts. Having characterized the offers as seeking one or the other of the possible responses, the courts set about the task of determining whether the offeree chose the proper manner of acceptance.

The modern approach to this problem involves recognition of the fact that many offers do not clearly indicate whether acceptance is to be effected by making a promise or commencing performance. U.C.C. section 2–206 and Restatement, Second, section 30(2) provide that unless otherwise indicated by the language or circumstances, an offer invites acceptance in any manner and by any medium reasonable under the circumstances. Thus acceptance either by making a return promise or by commencing performance is appropriate unless the offeror has manifested a desire to have one or the other.

§ 29. The Traditional Approach; Bilateral and Unilateral Characterization

The Restatement, First, recognized a structure in which an offer is either an offer for the formation of a unilateral contract or a bilateral contract. This requires that one characterize the nature of the contract which the offeror proposes in order to determine whether the purported acceptance is appropriate to create a contract.

An offer in which the offeror promises to do or not to do something in exchange for a promise by the offeree to act or refrain from acting in a certain manner is an offer for a bilateral contract. The proposed contract is bilateral, or "two-sided", because if the offeree accepts by making the requested promise, both sides will be contractually bound. This is the more common type of contract in business transactions.

An offer in which the offeror makes a promise in exchange solely for an act or forbearance by the offeree is an offer for a unilateral contract. This type of contract is "one-sided" because only the offeror, who makes the promise, will be legally bound. The offeree may act or refrain from acting as requested, but he cannot be sued in contract for failing to perform or even abandoning performance once commenced because he has not made any promises. When the offeree's performance is completed, only one enforceable promise exists because the offeree has already performed.

Virtually all offers seek to induce the offeree to act or refrain from acting in a certain way. The critical question is whether the offeror wanted the offeree to promise to act or forbear (and subsequently to fulfill his promise), or whether he simply wanted an act or forbearance with no commitment or promise by the offeree. The position of the Restatement, First, is that offers which are uncertain as to manner of acceptance should be treated as offers for bilateral contracts.

By way of example: (1) The offer states: "If you will meet me at the airport and drive me home when I return next Thursday at 11:00 P.M., I will pay you $20." Certainly the offeror is requesting an act, but it would be reasonable to conclude that he wants a promise to act from the offeree. This may properly be construed as an offer for a bilateral contract. (2) The offer states: "I will sell you my book if you will promise to pay me $25 at the end of the semester. You may accept by waving your hat at me in class." The waving of the offeree's hat is an act, but it is being used as a method of communicating a promise to pay $25. The contract will be a bilateral contract; a promise to deliver a book in exchange for a promise to pay $25. (3) The offer states: "I will pay you $500 if you will swim across the Hudson River at Albany, N.Y., on July 4." This is most likely an offer for an act—an offer for a unilateral contract—but there is still room to analyze all the circumstances to determine whether the offeror manifested a desire for a promise to perform. If the matter is in doubt, the preferred interpretation is to treat it as one for a bilateral contract. There are some offers which clearly seek bilateral responses, but there are very few business offers which are so clearly for unilateral contracts that the matter is not open to discussion. Common examples of offers for unilateral contracts include reward offers and transactions such as those in which a party is invited to put money in a machine or in a box or through the hole in a window.

§ 30. Effect of Traditional Unilateral-Bilateral Determination Upon Attempted Acceptance

If the court determines that an offer is one for a bilateral contract, then the appropriate manner in which the offeree may accept is by making the requested return promise. This might effectively be done by a written or oral expression or by conduct which implies a promise to perform in the circumstances presented. However, if the offeree misconstrued the offer to be one for a unilateral contract and failed to make the required return promise, no contract would exist. If the offeree simply began to perform the requested act, he might be protected if the offeror was aware of his conduct and acquiesced in this manner of communicating an implied promise to perform. But if the offeror was unaware of the offeree's activities, the rendering of part performance would not create a contract.

If the determination of the court is that an offer was one for a unilateral contract, then the appropriate manner of acceptance was to perform or forbear as the case may be. If the offeree mistakenly assumed that the offer was one for a bilateral contract and attempted to accept by rendering a return promise, no contract would be formed thereby. The offeree might logically assume that a contract existed which could result in loss to him due to his reliance. This loss might not be compensable. (But see § 69, *infra*.)

The characterization by the court of the offer as having been one for a bilateral or unilateral contract occurs after the actions of the parties with respect to formation. The court is called upon to determine what a reasonable person in the position of the offeree should have understood to be the intention and desire of the offeror based upon the manifestations of the offeror and the surrounding circumstances. The court has the offeree standing before it and the court knows how this offeree interpreted the offer. Unless it is apparent that the offeree was reacting unreasonably, the court will be disposed to interpret the offer as the offeree interpreted it. This is not to say that offers are interpreted as offerees read them. It is simply stating that when an offeror did not think enough about the manner of acceptance to indicate with some degree of clarity what was sought, the court may be likely to follow along with whatever manner of acceptance the offeree reasonably concluded to be appropriate. To be sure, each court reached its determination for the stated reason that it so interpreted the objective manifestations of the offeror. The traditional common law decisions did not indicate that the offeree had an option as to the manner of acceptance.

A fundamental criticism which can be made of the traditional approach is that many offerors are rather unconcerned about whether the offeree is to accept by communicating a promise or by simply rendering the requested performance. While notice of what is transpiring may be significant, the offeror might be quite indifferent to the manner of acceptance. Thus while the law preserves the right of an offeror to specify a manner of acceptance, there is little purpose to be served by the court developing a greater concern for the matter than the offeror exhibited.

§ 31. Modern Approach to Manner of Acceptance

The U.C.C. and the Restatement, Second, divide offers in three categories rather than two. (1) Those offers which reasonably communicate a desire for a return promise will be treated as offers for bilateral contracts and a contract will result when the offeree accepts in that manner. (2) Those offers which communicate a desire for performance without any return promise being sought will be treated as offers for unilateral contracts and will require acceptance by performance and not by the making of a return promise. (3) Offers which do not clearly communicate what the offeror desires can be accepted in whichever manner the offeree chooses. Restatement, Second, section 32 provides: "In case of doubt an offer is interpreted as inviting the offeree to accept either by promising to perform what the offer requests or by rendering the performance, as the offeree chooses."

Both the U.C.C. and the Restatement, Second, avoid the use of the terms "bilateral" and "unilateral," however these remain useful labels to describe offers that invite or require acceptance by return promise (bilateral) and offers that invite or require acceptance by performance (unilateral).

§ 32. Acceptance by Promise or by Performance; When the Parties Are Bound

In the case of an offer for a bilateral contract, acceptance must be by return promise that unequivocally manifests an intent to be bound and is effective when communicated to the offeror as described in § 42, *infra*. If the offeree begins to perform and the offeror acquires knowledge of the fact, this may effectively communicate an implied promise to perform. In such a case, this acceptance would be effective and both parties would be bound when the offeror learns that the offeree has begun to perform and acquiesces in this informal manner of acceptance.

In the case of an offer for a unilateral contract, the offeror becomes bound when the offeree has begun to perform. The different theoretical bases for this result are discussed in § 26, *supra*. The result is the same under each of the different theories. The offeror is bound when the offeree has begun to perform and must give the offeree reasonable time and opportunity to finish the requested performance. Since the offer was one for a unilateral contract, the offeree does not become contractually bound to complete the requested performance even though performance is begun.

If the court treats an offer as one which invites acceptance either by promise or by performance, then the beginning of performance by the offeree creates a binding bilateral contract under the Restatement, Second view. Thus, the beginning of performance binds the offeror without regard to whether the offeror is aware of this event, and by beginning performance, the offeree impliedly promises to render complete performance.

§ 33. Notice of Acceptance

Common law courts have been reluctant to impose upon offerees a requirement of notifying the offeror that an acceptance has been rendered. In the case of offers for unilateral contracts, giving notice of the fact of performance was not necessary to form the contract unless expressly requested. A few cases indicate that where the offeree has reason to know that the offeror has no convenient way of learning of the performance, then the offeree must use reasonable efforts to notify the offeror of this fact or lose the right to enforce the contract.

This minimal requirement has been adopted in Restatement, Second, section 54 which provides:

Sec. 54. Acceptance by Performance; Necessity of Notification to Offeror

(1) Where an offer invites an offeree to accept by rendering a performance, no notification is necessary to make such an acceptance effective unless the offer requests such a notification.

(2) If an offeree who accepts by rendering a performance has reason to know that the offeror has no adequate means of learning of the performance with reasonable promptness and certainty, the contractual duty of the offeror is discharged unless

(a) the offeree exercises reasonable diligence to notify the offeror of acceptance, or

(b) the offeror learns of the performance within a reasonable time, or

(c) the offer indicates that notification of acceptance is not required.

A similar requirement is imposed by U.C.C. section 2–206(2) which provides:

(2) Where the beginning of a requested performance is a reasonable mode of acceptance an offeror who is not notified of acceptance within a reasonable time may treat the offer as having lapsed before acceptance.

An offer which requests a return promise will ordinarily produce effective notice for the offeror.

However, an offer can provide that acceptance shall be accomplished by such things as signature by the offeree in the space provided. Such offers raise the issue whether notice of acceptance is required. Some cases indicated that the offeror was certainly empowered to request notice if desired, and since it was not requested, it need not be given. The Restatement, Second, takes a strong position on this point, providing in section 56 that except for acceptance by silence and situations in which notice is waived, ". . . it is essential to an acceptance by promise either that the offeree exercise reasonable diligence to notify the offeror of acceptance or that the offeror receive the acceptance seasonably."

§ 34. Non–Promissory Offers

An offer may be made in which the offeror's performance is completed when the offeree accepts the offer. X's horse is being boarded at Y's stable. X states: "If you will promise to pay me $1,000 for that horse, he is yours." Y is already in possession of the horse. No delivery or tender of performance by X is needed.

R fills out a form for a one year term life insurance policy under his company's health plan and submits it to the company with his check. The form expressly provides that the company must approve the application. The company's approval forms the contract and R's performance is already completed.

The Restatement, Second, sections 1 and 55 take the position that a non-promissory offer which requests an act from the offeree is not a contract because a contract is a promise or set of promises for the breach of which the law gives a remedy. Thus, an exchange of performances is not a "contract." While this may be a valid point, it should be observed that an offer for a reverse unilateral contract in which a merchant offers to let a customer keep the goods in the customer's possession upon payment of $500 will be treated as a sale of goods for purposes of implying a warranty of merchantability (U.C.C. section 2–304). Of course, one could find a "sale" to have occurred despite the absence of a "contract", however, the basic standards which must be met to satisfy the warranty are defined in terms of the "contract description." One would also assume that the law of mistake, misrepresentation, duress, lack of capacity, and undue influence would also be applicable to such a transaction.

Bargained exchanges of performances may properly be categorized as not being contracts, but much of the law of contracts and of sales will be applied to such transactions.

§ 35. Requirement of an Acceptance Responsive as to Terms

At common law, an acceptance must be unequivocal and must comply with the terms of the offer as to the promise to be made or the performance to be rendered. The offer constitutes a manifestation of intent by the offeror that he is willing to be presently bound to the terms proposed subject only to the condition that the offeree accept. The offer creates in the offeree the power to form a contract by accepting the terms proposed. In order to have an acceptance, the offeree must exercise his power to form a contract by accepting the terms proposed and thus completing the formation process.

A proposed acceptance which requires the offeror's consent to terms which are additional to or different from those offered is not an acceptance but a counter-offer. Such a communication does not conclude the contract. It is a continuation of the formation process. It manifests the offeree's intent to be presently bound but subject to the offeror's consent to the additional or different terms. Thus it is a counter-offer and the original offeror is now the party who has the power to form a contract by accepting in the authorized manner.

§ 36. Acceptances Which Propose Additional or Different Terms

A communication in which the offeree agrees to be bound by the offeror's terms is effective as an acceptance even though the offeree requests a change in those terms. So long as the communication is not made dependent upon the offeror agreeing to some changes or additions, it is effective as an acceptance.

The parties who make a contract are free to modify that contract in the absence of some intervening third party's rights. There is no theoretical or practical problem with an offeree accepting an offer, thus concluding the contract, and proposing a modification of the contract in the same communication. So long as there is an unequivocal acceptance of the offeror's proposal, the contract is formed.

§ 37. Impact of the U.C.C. Upon Acceptances That Vary From Terms of the Offer

Section 2–207 of the U.C.C. was designed to change the common law rules relating to responses to offers that appear to be expressions of acceptance but contain different or additional terms. While common law cases were not uniformly consistent on the subject, most court decisions held that a response by an offeree which varied the terms of the offer did not operate as an acceptance but as a counter-offer. (See §§ 35 and 36, *supra.*) If a prospective buyer sent an order for goods requesting shipment on Monday, a response which purported to be an acceptance (e.g., "We are pleased to accept your order.") would likely be held not to operate as an acceptance if it indicated that shipment would not be made until Tuesday. In actual practices, the two parties might consider themselves to be bound, but if the seller failed to perform, seller's attorney could defend on the grounds that no contract had been formed.

The intent behind section 2–207 is to alter this result. Subsection (1) of 2–207 provides that a definite and seasonable (meaning timely) expression of acceptance operates as an acceptance even though it contains terms additional to or different from those offered. (Subsection (1) also deals with written confirmations that are sent following the making of an oral contract, but that is a separate problem which will be discussed in § 38, *infra.*)

The key phrase in section 2-207(1) is "expression of acceptance," a term which is not defined in the Code and which had no particular meaning at common law. To have an "expression of acceptance," one must find that the offeree has manifested an intent to be presently bound without further communication of approval by the offeror. It might be best understood when it is distinguished from an "expression of counter-offer" which would require further assent from the offeror. If the offeree expressly conditions his assent upon the offeror agreeing to the different or additional terms contained in the offeree's response, then a contract is not yet formed. This response would be a counter-offer because it requires assent by the offeror to complete the bargaining process.

Professor Karl Llewellyn, the principal author of Article Two of the U.C.C., was asked to address this issue while testifying before the New York Law Revision Commission in 1954. He is quoted as saying: "We were attempting to say, whether we got it said or not, that a document which said 'This is an acceptance only if the additional terms we state are taken up by you' is not a definite and seasonable expression of acceptance but is an expression of a counter-offer."

"Expression of acceptance" must be interpreted more broadly than the term "acceptance." If it were synonymous with "acceptance," then subsection (1) would end up providing that "an acceptance . . . operates as an acceptance." Such an interpretation would make subsection (1) meaningless. "Expression of acceptance" can be interpreted as referring to the apparent intention of the offeree whereas "operates as an acceptance" refers to the legal effect.

To further assist the courts in the interpretation of subsection (1), the authors added a final clause which provides: "unless acceptance is expressly made conditional on assent to the additional or different terms." This clause has been the focus of attention in many court opinions that interpret subsection (1). It should not be. In fact, it is almost redundant. From Professor Llewellyn's testimony and from the plain language of the subsection it is evident that any response by an offeree which adds or changes terms and expressly requires that the offeror assent thereto before the offeree is willing to be bound is not an "expression of acceptance." It would be an expression of counter-offer.

When attempting to resolve the issue whether a response by an offeree is or is not an acceptance under the Code, the inquiry must focus upon whether the response is an expression of acceptance. The inquiry should not focus upon whether that response adds terms or changes terms because that fact does not preclude the response from operating as an acceptance. Of course, if the response is expressly conditioned upon the offeror agreeing to those different or additional terms, it is not an expression of acceptance.

A response by an offeree may be found to be an expression of acceptance and thus form a contract even if it makes an addition or change which is material. One must be very careful not to read into subsection (1) any requirement that the additional or different term be non-material. There is no implication of such a requirement in subsection (1) and subsection (2)(b) would be rendered meaningless (see § 38, *infra*) if subsection (1) only permitted contracts to be formed where the additional or different terms proposed by the offeree were not material.

A second common interpretation error is to try to read into subsection (1) the requirement that it apply only to transactions between merchants. Subsection (1) applies to all transactions in goods that are governed by Article Two.

If a contract is found under subsection (1), the terms of the contract are the terms proposed by the offeror. (If a court applies the "knockout" rule discussed in § 38, *infra*, then there would be an exception to this conclusion.) Some students of contract law find that they can accept this statement as accurate in theory but have a hard time applying it to an actual fact situation.

Assume that X offers to sell a generator to Y for a stated price. Y responds stating: "We are pleased to accept your offer for the generator but it will be necessary for you to install it in our power plant as we have neither trained people nor equipment to perform this task." If it is concluded that this is a definite expression of acceptance and that it is not expressly conditioned upon X assenting to the additional terms relating to installation, a contract is formed. The terms of the contract are simply a generator for the stated price. The contract does not include any terms relating to installation. This is a hard result for some to accept. How can the offeree be bound to accept a generator without installation when it expressly stated that this was what it needed? The answer, plainly and simply, is that section 2–207(1) clearly provides that the offeree is accepting the offeror's offer and that offer was for a generator with no provision for installation. When the law provides, as section 2–207(1) does, that two non-responsive communications can form a contract, a choice must be made as to whose terms prevail. Section 2–207 makes a clear choice; the offeror's terms control, at least where the offeree sought to add an additional term.

To determine whether the offeree's additional term relating to the duty to install ever became part of the contract, one must look to subsection 2–207(2) which is analyzed in § 38.

§ 38. Contract Terms Following a Non-Responsive Acceptance

When an offer is accepted by an expression of acceptance which states a term additional to those contained in the offer, subsection 2–207(2) must be applied to determine whether this additional term becomes part of the contract. It should be noted that subsection (2) is never applicable in any fact situation whatsoever unless a contract has been found pursuant to subsection (1). Any attempt to incorporate subsection (2) factors such as materiality or merchant status into subsection (1) determinations is erroneous.

As a result of the application of the first sentence of subsection (2), the offeree's proposed additional terms will become part of the contract if the offeror assents to them. (Pursuant to section 2–209(1), no consideration is needed for such a modification.) In addition, if both parties are merchants, the offeree's proposed additional terms will be accepted by the offeror's silence if they do not materially alter the contract, provided that the offeror has not already indicated that he objects to this addition or to any addition to the contract. Unless the proposed additional terms are accepted in a manner described in this paragraph, they do not become part of the contract. Some people tend to get confused when they observe that the parties proceeded to perform the contract after the offeree "accepted" with an added term. One might be tempted to conclude that by performing, the offeror was manifesting assent to the additional term which the offeree proposed. However, since the expression of acceptance formed a contract on the offeror's terms, the fact that the offeror proceeds with the performance of the contract that he proposed does not in any way manifest assent to the additional terms which the offeree wished to add. Of course, if the offeror actually performs in accordance with the proposed additional term, this conduct would manifest assent to add that term to the contract.

The above discussion all relates to additional terms. If the offeree's expression of acceptance contained different terms as distinguished from additional terms, a serious problem of Code interpretation is presented. Subsection (2) expressly applies to "additional" terms and makes no mention of "different" terms. One might conclude that this is simply a drafting error or oversight particularly when one considers comment 3 to section 2–207 which begins: "Whether or not additional or different terms become part of the agreement depends upon the provisions of subsection (2) . . ." However, when the State of Wisconsin and later the State of North Carolina attempted to "cure" the apparent oversight by adding "or different" in subsection (2), these modifications of the Code were disapproved by the Permanent Editorial Board for the U.C.C. with the following comment:

Reason for Rejection. The stated purpose is to conform the language of subsection (2) with that of subsection (1). The change is harmless as it affects the first sentence of subsection (2), but "different terms," as distinguished from "additional terms," do not become part of the contract under the second sentence of subsection (2), since they have already been objected to. See subsections (2)(c) and (3) and Comment 6. Moreover, it is the express policy of the subsection that an offeror is not to be subjected to the hardship or surprise of terms which are "different" in that they materially alter the original bargain.

This issue was addressed in Steiner v. Mobil Oil Co. (1977). The court concluded that while writers were in disagreement as to what to do with different terms, the question whether they ever were to become part of the contract should properly be decided by applying subsection (2). Since the offeror had not expressly consented to the different terms, the first sentence of subsection (2) did not resolve the problem. Since the transaction in that case was between merchants, the court applied the second sentence of subsection (2) and concluded that the different terms were not accepted by silence for two reasons: a) the change was material, and b) since the offeror had himself proposed different terms in the offer and had expressly discussed his desires on the subject with an employee of Mobil Oil, he had already given notice of objection to the change. Using this logic, it becomes evident that if different terms are analyzed under subsection (2), they will never become part of the contract unless the offeror expressly consents to them. While the California Supreme Court did not cite and perhaps was unaware of the comment of the Permanent Editorial Board quoted above, it should be noted that the Board reached the same conclusion as to the result which would be reached if subsection (2) was applied to different terms. It stated that different terms "have already been objected to" and that "they materially alter the original bargain."

If one were to conclude that different terms should not properly be analyzed under subsection (2), the obvious problem is determining where else to turn to determine what to do with this change of terms which the offeree indicated it wanted. The answer given by some writers and courts is to turn to subsection (3). This seems to be the only alternative.

It is difficult to apply subsection (3) to this problem given its language. Subsection (3) provides: "Conduct of both parties which recognizes the existence of a contract is sufficient to establish a contract for sale although the writings of the parties do not otherwise establish a contract. In such case the terms of the particular contract consist of those terms on which the writings of the parties agree, together with any supplementary terms incorporated under any other provisions of this Act." On its face, this would appear to apply to two situations. The first situation would be one in which the parties exchanged correspondence that discussed terms but did not manifest an intention to be presently bound following which they both proceeded with performance. (Section 2–204 discusses contract formation and can also be applied to this problem.) The second situation to which subsection (3) applies is one in which an offer is made to which the offeree responds with an "expression of counter-offer" thus not forming a contract under subsection (1). (For an example of this second situation, see C. Itoh & Co. v. Jordan Int'l Co. (1977).)

If a court does decide to apply subsection (3) to determine the terms of a contract formed under subsection (1), the different terms in the offer and acceptance will "knock each other out" because subsection (3) directs that the contract terms "consist of those terms on which the writings of the parties agree, together with any supplementary terms incorporated under any other provisions of this act." Thus if the offeror orders goods for shipment on Monday and the offeree sends an expression of acceptance that states that the goods will be shipped on Tuesday, the resulting contract does not have an express shipment date because the writings of the parties do not agree on that point. The court must then turn to "other provisions of this act" and would apply section 2–309. The result is a contract for goods to be shipped within a reasonable time.

This "knockout" rule or approach was applied in Southern Idaho Pipe & Steel   v. Cal-Cut Pipe &

Supply, Inc. (1977). Some writers also find support for the knockout rule in comment 6 to section 2-207 although that comment appears to apply to confirming memoranda sent after an oral contract is formed.

Applying the alternative theories discussed above to a specific hypothetical produces the following results. Assume that a merchant seller offers to sell certain goods to a non-merchant buyer. In the offer, the seller gives certain express warranties (section 2–313) and effectively disclaims all other warranties, express or implied (section 2–316). The offeree responds stating that it is "pleased to accept the offer" but that it wants to have the implied warranty of merchantability (section 2–314). (This is presumably a "different" term as the offeror disclaimed all implied warranties.) No further communications are exchanged and the goods are delivered and accepted. Subsequently a dispute develops over the scope of the warranties given.

Assuming that the response by the offeree is an expression of acceptance, a contract was formed under subsection (1) when that acceptance was sent. If the "knockout" rule is not applied, this contract must be on the offeror's terms. Thus there was a contract with no implied warranty of merchantability since that warranty was disclaimed in the offer.

If the court turns to subsection (2) to analyze the different term which the offeree requested, it will find that the term was not expressly accepted by the offeror. Since the buyer is not a merchant, the second sentence of subsection (2) is not available to permit finding that the offeror accepted by silence. Even if both were merchants, there would be no acceptance of this term by silence because it is a material modification and because the offeror has already impliedly objected to it. The final contract will thus be found to have no implied warranty of merchantability. Buyer will lose.

If the court turns to subsection (3) to analyze the contract terms, it will find that a contract exists on the terms on which the writings of the parties agree. The writings of the parties agree on all matters except the inclusion or exclusion of an implied warranty of merchantability. As to this issue, the court will have to look elsewhere in the Code. It will apply section 2–314 and conclude that because the seller was a merchant with respect to goods of this kind, there is an implied warranty of merchantability. Buyer will win.

Note that this result would be the same even if the seller refused to ship the goods unless buyer agreed to seller's terms relating to warranties. The contract is already formed and seller is bound to warranty terms to which it did not consent and never had an opportunity to object. The knockout rule permits the offeree to change the terms of the offer and bind the offeror. The offeror does not appear to have any way to protect itself from this result which seems highly unfair. For example, assume Buyer makes an offer to buy goods on credit and Seller responds with an expression of acceptance that states the terms will be cash. If the knockout rule is applied, there is a contract with no express agreement as to time of payment. The court will look to the Code which will provide that the payment will be cash on delivery. Buyer becomes bound to this term with no opportunity to reject it.

There is one final 2–207 issue to be discussed. Assume that Buyer and Seller enter into an oral contract and thereafter Seller sends a confirming memorandum which adds a term not orally agreed upon or changes a term in the oral agreement. This confirming memorandum is a sufficient writing to satisfy the statute of frauds even though it misstates the terms of the oral contract. (See the last sentence of section 2–201(1).) The question is what effect this writing has upon the terms of the oral contract that the parties had already concluded. Section 2–207(1) refers to this problem in a very inartful and indirect manner ("or a written confirmation which is sent within a reasonable time," referring to a reasonable time after the making of the oral contract). It is difficult to find a precise meaning in subsection (1), but it is apparent that courts are directed to look to subsection (2) to determine whether additional terms in a written confirmation become part of the contract which the parties had already orally concluded. Whether a court should look to subsection (2) or subsection

(3) to determine what to do with different terms could be analyzed as discussed above. However, it is suggested that if the parties in fact have a valid (although perhaps unenforceable) oral contract, no party should be permitted to "knockout" any term of that contract by sending a written confirmation which contains a different term. That party has already agreed to be bound by the terms of the oral contract and cannot unilaterally change or "knockout" those terms.

§ 39. Acceptance by Conduct Under U.C.C. Section 2–206

U.C.C. section 2–206 allows an offeree to accept an offer in any manner and medium reasonable under the circumstances unless the offeror directs otherwise. Thus, where the manner of acceptance is not specified, the offeree can accept by return promise or by commencing performance if either manner of acceptance is reasonable under the circumstances. Unless the offeror has specifically indicated otherwise, any medium of acceptance such as mail, telegram or telefax is permitted if it is reasonable under the circumstances.

Subsection 2–206(1)(b) relates specifically to offers to buy goods for prompt or current shipment and permits acceptance either by a prompt promise to ship or prompt shipment of conforming or nonconforming goods. The rationale for finding an acceptance where the offeree has shipped non-conforming goods is best understood by considering a hypothetical problem and contrasting the results that might be reached at common law and under the Code.

Assume that Buyer orders a machine specifying that the internal components be made of a certain type of alloy. Thereafter, Seller ships a machine of the type requested that does not contain internal parts made of the requested alloy. The shipment is accompanied by an invoice that reflects the price Buyer offered to pay. Buyer accepts the machine and pays the price. Upon discovering that the machine is not what was ordered, Buyer seeks a remedy.

At common law, Seller is in a position to argue that if he did not ship what Buyer ordered, then he did not accept Buyer's offer. What he shipped was tendered for the price stated (a counter-offer by Seller), and Buyer's acceptance of the goods and payment manifests Buyer's assent to this counter-offer.

Subsection 2–206(1)(b) takes this argument away from Seller by providing that the shipment of non-conforming goods is an acceptance unless Seller seasonably notifies Buyer that the shipment is not what was ordered but is being offered only as an accommodation to Buyer. By shipping non-conforming goods without such notice, Seller has accepted Buyer's offer and breached the contract.

Subsection 2–206(2) provides that where acceptance is made by beginning performance, Seller will lose the right to enforce the contract if notice of acceptance is not given to the offeror within a reasonable time. This simply confirms the common law rule that one who accepts an offer for a unilateral contract by performing must notify the offeror if the offeror has no convenient way of learning whether the act is being performed.

§ 40. Agreements That Contemplate a Future Writing

An expressed intention or desire to reduce an agreement to writing or to a more formal written form does not necessarily justify the conclusion that a contract does not presently exist. The parties may manifest an intent to be presently bound to an oral agreement or to an agreement which is reflected in various informal writings. An expressed desire to reduce the contract to writing or to set forth the terms of the contract in a more formal writing is not inconsistent with an intention to be presently bound.

When one or both parties specify or insist that an agreement be reduced to writing or to a more formal writing, it may be for purposes of properly and conveniently memorializing the agreement while the details are still fresh in everyone's mind. On the other hand, it may be a manifestation of one party's intention that he not be legally bound until he has approved the requested writing. This is a factual question that is resolved by focusing upon the term "presently bound."

A related problem arises when a person executes an agreement with qualifying language such as "subject to the approval of my attorney." The ordinary interpretation of such language might be that the party has manifested intent to be presently bound with the stated condition relating only to the legal sufficiency of the documents. Circumstances might justify a factual determination that the condition is more fundamental and manifests an intent to obtain general advice and counsel concerning the wisdom of the transaction. In the latter case, the party in question has apparently not yet manifested an intent to be presently legally bound.

Based upon the foregoing analysis, common law opinions often reached the conclusion that "agreements to agree" did not result in any enforceable obligations. However, a preliminary understanding or agreement, though not yet enforceable as a binding contract, might be found to impose upon both parties an obligation to meet and make a good faith effort to complete the contract negotiations. In this case, an abrupt and unwarranted termination of negotiations by one party might entitle the other to recover at least such damages as are appropriate to compensate for reliance upon the tentative agreement. (See § 95, *infra.*)

§ 41. Offers That Require a Specific Method of Acceptance

An offer may prescribe the place, time, manner or medium of acceptance. If the offer is interpreted to mandate a specific method of acceptance as the only one permissible, then that is the only method by which the offeree is empowered to accept and form a contract. (See § 27, *supra*.)

X mails an offer to Y and states: "If you wish to accept, you will wire your acceptance to my agent in Hong Kong, Z. No other form of acceptance is permitted." Y wires an acceptance to X. It would be likely that no contract would result. If X acquiesces in Y's unauthorized method of acceptance, a contract could be found.

Where the offer states how acceptance is to occur but does not definitely assert that this is the only possible method of acceptance, the ordinary interpretation is that another method of acceptance which fulfills the same apparent needs as to place, time and form will be effective to form a contract.

X mails an offer to Y and states: "If you wish to accept, you must respond by return mail." Y receives the offer on Friday. An acceptance mailed on Friday would not reach X until Monday. Y hand delivers an acceptance to X on Sunday. A contract will most likely result.

Assume the same facts except that Y phones X on Sunday and says: "I accept." This is less likely to be found to result in a contract. X has asked for a written response which contemplates a signed writing. If X does not acquiesce in this form of acceptance, no contract should be found.

Assume again that there is a request for a response by return mail which would have arrived on Monday. Y responds in writing, but sends the communication by Federal Express, a private company which promises overnight delivery service. If this medium of acceptance were found not to be authorized, the acceptance will not be effective until it is received. (See § 42, *infra*.) In this situation, the use of the "unauthorized" medium of response does not mean that a contract cannot result. There is no basis for concluding that use of the mail was a condition without which the offeror refused to be bound. So long as the offer has not been terminated and the signed writing arrives within the time authorized for acceptance, a contract will result.

§ 42. Time When Communications Are Effective

Since an offer cannot be accepted by one who has no knowledge of its terms, an offer is not effective until it is actually communicated to and thus made known to the offeree.

The offer may specify the time when an acceptance will be effective. For example, an offeror could simply provide that "no acceptance will be effective unless actually delivered to me." In the absence of such a specification, a properly dispatched acceptance which is made by an authorized medium is effective when sent. A contract is formed at the time regardless of whether the acceptance is ever received by the offeror. Where an acceptance is sent by other than an authorized medium, it is ordinarily effective when received (cf. § 41, *supra*). It is generally held that acceptances of option contracts are not effective until received.

The apparent reason for this rule is that the offeree has "bought and paid for" a given period of time and must get the acceptance to the offeror within that period.

In the absence of special circumstances which are known to the offeree, an offer that does not expressly prescribe a medium of communicating acceptance may be interpreted as impliedly authorizing the same medium as was used to communicate the offer. Most courts interpret the rule as requiring the acceptance to be sent by the same medium or better, meaning faster. U.C.C. section 2–206 authorizes "any medium reasonable in the circumstances." It is anticipated that this logical approach will be applied by analogy to transactions not within the U.C.C.

Common law decisions have proceeded on the premise that acceptances are effective at one point in time for all purposes. If sent by an authorized medium, they are generally effective on dispatch. If sent by a different medium or if improperly dispatched, they are effective when received. The Restatement, Second, suggests a different approach in section 67 which provides:

> Where an acceptance is seasonably dispatched but the offeree uses means of transmission not invited by the offer or fails to exercise reasonable diligence to insure safe transmission, it is treated as operative upon dispatch if received within the time in which a properly dispatched acceptance would normally have arrived.

Application of this section can avoid some technical problems in the acceptance process. If the offeror expressly requests response by letter and the offeree sends a wire, the wire will not be effective until it is received but it will be operative as of the time of its dispatch. If the wire is lost in transmission or is delayed for an extended period, no contract will result. But if the acceptance arrives within the time in which a letter would have been received, it is operative as of the time of dispatch. Thus an intervening revocation would not defeat the formation of a contract.

Section 67 will also avoid the issue that can arise when a communication is not properly dispatched, for example a letter sent with the wrong zip code or inadequate postage. Such a communication will not be effective unless received in a timely fashion, but if it is received within the time contemplated, it will be operative as of the time of dispatch.

Revocations are not effective until received by the offeree. Thus an acceptance that becomes operative prior to receipt of a revocation forms the contract. Statutes in some jurisdictions may have the effect of making a revocation effective when sent (§ 22, *supra*).

A rejection is effective when received by the offeror. The dispatch of a rejection followed by the dispatch of an acceptance by an authorized medium creates the potential for problems. It has been held that the acceptance is still effective when sent and a contract is formed. If the offeror receives the rejection first and changes position in reliance thereon, the offeree will be estopped from enforcing the contract.

Another approach to this problem holds that the sending of a rejection takes from the offeree the power to have his subsequently dispatched acceptance become effective when sent. The result is that the rejection and the subsequently dispatched acceptance will be effective only when received. If the acceptance arrives first, there will be a contract. If the rejection arrives first, there will be no contract.

§ 43. Acceptance by Silence

The basic proposition applied in the law of contracts is that silence does not constitute an acceptance. Exceptions have been recognized only in specific limited situations.

One situation involves parties who have had prior dealings in which the offeree has led the offeror reasonably to understand that the offeree will accept all offers unless the offeree sends notice to the contrary. An offer of the same type as involved in the prior dealings which the offeror has reason to believe will be accepted is deemed to be accepted if the offeree had an opportunity to reject and failed to do so. The cases which have applied this rule have involved an offeree engaged in a business. The business has an established price or prices which have been communicated to the offeror and the offeror has been invited to make an offer.

The Restatement, Second, section 69 recognizes a different situation in which a contract may result from silence. This is "where the offeror has stated or given the offeree reason to understand that assent may be manifested by silence or inaction, and the offeree in remaining silent and inactive intends to accept the offer." The second sentence of U.C.C. section 2–207(2) also provides for acceptance by silence of an offer to modify a contract.

§ 44. Acceptance by Exercise of Dominion and Control Over Goods or by Receipt of Benefits or Services

One who receives goods with knowledge or reason to know that they are being offered for a price is bound by the terms of the offer if he exercises dominion and control over the goods or does any act inconsistent with the offeror's ownership. The abuse of this common law rule by the senders of unsolicited merchandise has led to statutes in many jurisdictions which avoid placing contractual liability upon the recipient. One form of statute simply provides that the receipt of unsolicited merchandise is conclusively presumed to be a gift. In the absence of such statutes, however, the common law rule is still applicable.

One who knows or has reason to know that services are being offered with the expectation of compensation is liable for the reasonable value or stated value of such services if he takes the benefit of them under circumstances in which there was a reasonable opportunity to reject.

§ 45. Auctions

An auction is with reserve unless otherwise stated. This means that the owner may refrain from holding the auction or may interrupt the auction and terminate it even after the bidding has begun. The owner may likewise bid in and buy his own property in an auction with reserve. However, unless the right to do so has been announced, he may not "run up" a legitimate bidder and thereby inflate the price. Where this is done, the successful bidder has the right to enforce a contract at the price of the last legitimate bid which was made before the owner improperly entered the bidding. The U.C.C. gives the successful bidder the alternative remedy of avoiding the sale (section 2–328(4)).

In an auction with reserve, the auctioneer solicits offers from the potential bidders. The bids are offers. The fall of the hammer or other customary words or action constitutes the acceptance. Prior to acceptance, the bid or offer may be revoked. The auctioneer may reject all offers or may reject a particular offer, usually because it is not a sufficiently large increase over the prior bid. When the auctioneer recognizes a higher bidder, e.g., by saying: "I now have $300," he communicates a rejection of the previous bid. Thus, the revocation of a bid by the bidder does not reinstate a prior bid which had been surpassed.

U.C.C. section 2–328(3) provides: "In an auction without reserve, after the auctioneer calls for bids on an article or lot, that article or lot cannot be withdrawn unless no bid is received within a reasonable time." This section does not deal with the situation in which the auctioneer does not call for bids.

The term "without reserve" or comparable language is used to manifest a promise by the owner that the property in question will in fact be sold to the highest bidder and that nothing will be held back or withdrawn from sale. This promise is customarily made in advertising to encourage attendance and bidding. At the time it is made, it is a bare promise and is unenforceable. However, it is quite reasonably interpreted by a potential bidder to be a promise for a unilateral contract which commits the offeror to hold an auction without reserve if the prospective bidder will attend the auction. Thus, the failure to hold or to proceed with an auction which has been advertised as without reserve could be a breach of this collateral contract.

The interruption of an auction without reserve by the owner and his refusal to complete the sale gives rise to an action by the party who made the highest bid before the auction was interrupted. By the terms of the collateral contract, the owner was legally obligated to accept the highest bid. Thus, the court can find a contract between the parties at that price. Where the owner refuses to start the auction, it is more difficult for a frustrated potential bidder to find a cause of action. No individual can prove that he would have been the successful bidder nor can one prove what the successful bid would have been. There is no reasonably certain basis for specifically enforcing a contract or for giving damages for the loss of the expectancy of the bargain. There is a good theoretical basis for awarding reliance damages in such situations to compensate the frustrated bidder for costs reasonably incurred in attending the auction or otherwise preparing to bid. (See §§ 69 and 134, *infra.*)

The collateral contract which is discussed above imposes upon the owner an obligation to proceed with the auction once the potential bidders have performed the requested act. Depending upon the interpretation used, the requested act may be attending the auction or making a bid. The structure of the sales contract in the auction without reserve can be analyzed in the same manner as in an auction with reserve. The bids are offers. They may be withdrawn before acceptance. The acknowledgment of a higher bid impliedly rejects a prior bid. The fall of the hammer is the acceptance which terminates the bidding and forms the contract.

There is another theory which is sometimes discussed in this area. This approach holds that in an auction without reserve, the owner makes an offer to sell and each bid is an acceptance which forms a contract subject to the condition that the contract will be terminated if a higher bid is made. The courts and writers who discuss this approach take the position that bidders can nonetheless revoke their bids before the auctioneer "accepts" by the fall of the hammer. This is, of course, inconsistent with the notion that the bid is an acceptance which creates a binding contract of sale subject to a higher bid.

The source of confusion which gives rise to this latter theory would appear to be the fact that some courts fail to define with care the offer which the seller makes by advertising an auction without reserve. It is mistakenly assumed that the seller's offer is an offer to sell as distinguished from an offer to be bound to accept the highest bid. Once this error is made, several problems arise. Each bid becomes an acceptance forming a contract which is conditional upon no higher bid being made. Yet despite the existence of a contract, the bidder can withdraw the bid before the fall of the hammer.

When you have completed your study of this chapter, you may wish to analyze questions 1–9 at the end of this book and compare your analysis with the one given there.

3. CONSIDERATION

§ 46. Introduction to Consideration

Every legal system distinguishes between promises that it chooses to enforce and promises that it will not enforce. One who seeks to enforce a promise in a common law jurisdiction must affirmatively establish a basis for finding the promise to be enforceable. There are three bases for finding a promise to be enforceable: 1) because the promise was made for valid consideration; 2) because the promisee has detrimentally relied upon the promise (§ 69, *infra*), or 3) because the promise comes within a statute which makes it enforceable despite the absence of consideration (some examples in § 68, *infra*).

Consideration is the primary basis for promise enforcement in the common law system. A distinction is made between gratuitous promises and those which are made as part of a bargained exchange. While there are special rules which will permit enforcement of certain gratuitous promises (§§ 62–69, *infra*), the first inquiry should be to determine whether a promise was given in return for something or whether it was gratuitous.

It will assist in understanding the law of consideration if one keeps in mind the fact that we are dealing with a formality. It is a formality which is being used to validate a promise or make it enforceable.

In drawing lines of distinction between promises that are made as a part of a bargain and promises which the law deems to be gratuitous, common law courts have generally followed a very formalistic approach. If there is any legal detriment incurred by the promisee which can be viewed as a bargained exchange for the promisor's promise, that is sufficient. Courts have not concerned themselves with the adequacy or fairness of the consideration but only with finding the presence of some legal detriment incurred as part of a bargain. Conversely, if there is no legal detriment or no bargain, courts will find no consideration despite what might be viewed as the equities of the situation.

The application of this approach produces some results that are difficult to justify when viewed from a broad perspective of justice. Unlike the French system which asks whether there is proper cause to enforce a promise and which invokes issues of morality and common business practices to determine the presence or absence of such cause, the common law decisions usually turn on the technical question of whether some legal detriment and bargain are present. Thus a promise by an employer to pay a pension to an employee when she retires in the future is supported by consideration, but the same promise made to the employee after she retires is not supported by consideration because the employee is incurring no detriment as a bargained exchange for the promise. (See § 47, *infra.*)

Because a formal requirement such as consideration may produce results that are viewed as unfair, a number of special rules have been developed and many court opinions bend the rules a bit to get to what the judges consider a proper result. Therefore, the proper role of an attorney or law student is first to understand the basic requirements of the law of consideration so that one will be fully aware of situations in which it presents a problem. When this has been accomplished, the second task is to identify the situations in which the law has recognized exceptions or in which a given court might be induced to interpret the facts in such a way as to find the requirement to be satisfied.

§ 47. Requirement of a Bargained Exchange

Restatement, Second, section 71(1) provides: "To constitute consideration, a performance or a return promise must be bargained for." "Bargained for" does not require a bargaining process of offers and counter-offers such as might take place in a flea market. To be "bargained for," the performance of the promisee, or the promise to perform, must have been given in exchange for the promise which the promisee is seeking to enforce.

The law does not ordinarily concern itself with actual motive or inducement in resolving consideration issues. If a wealthy individual teaches contract law because it is the most pleasant activity in the world, the rendition of this service is sufficient consideration to support the school's promise to pay even if in fact the pay was neither the motive nor the inducement to perform. Restatement, Second, section 81(2) provides:

(2) The fact that a promise does not of itself induce a performance or return promise does not prevent the performance or return promise from being consideration for the promise.

Assume that a parent wishes one of her children to have a valuable painting that hangs in her home. The simple method to accomplish this objective is to give the painting to the child. If the painting is delivered to the child with the intention of passing title, the gift is completed. Under the law of property, the painting now belongs to the child. No issue of contract law is involved.

However, assume that the parent wishes to retain possession of the painting for a period of time but wishes the child to have an enforceable right to receive the painting. The parent knows that a bare promise to give the painting to the child will not be enforceable. To avoid this result, she offers to sell the painting to the child for $100 and the child accepts this offer. This bargain should be enforceable.

Restatement, Second, section 81(1) provides:

(1) The fact that what is bargained for does not of itself induce the making of a promise does not prevent it from being consideration for the promise.

Restatement, Second, section 71(2) provides:

(2) A performance or return promise is bargained for if it is sought by the promisor in exchange for his promise and is given by the promisee in exchange for that promise.

Equality of values is not a prerequisite nor even a factor in determining whether sufficient consideration exists. (See § 59, *infra*.) However, if the parent offered the valuable painting to her child in exchange for the child's wornout, worthless shoe, the transaction appears to be a sham, and it is probable that a court will treat it as such and find consideration wanting. It would be erroneous to characterize this result as being predicated upon the old shoe not being the actual motive or inducement of the parent to make her promise, as actual motivation or inducement is not required. However, where the purported consideration is obviously without any value and the bargain is a sham, enforcement of the promise may be denied.

The exchange for which the promisor's promise is bargained may be either a return promise or a performance. The performance may consist of an act, a forbearance, or the creation, modification, or relinquishment of a legal right or relationship. Digging a ditch would be an act which could be the bargained consideration for a promise. Refraining from engaging in the shoe business in the City of Buffalo for one year would be a forbearance which could be a bargained consideration. Relinquishing the right to use the name "Shogun Restaurant" is the modification or foregoing of a legal right which could serve as consideration for a return promise.

A promise to act or forbear from acting or a promise to create or modify legal rights or relationships will also constitute sufficient consideration for a bargained exchange.

§ 48. Detriment, Benefit and Preexisting Legal Duty

A traditional formulation of the consideration requirement is that the promisee's act or forbearance which purports to be the bargained exchange must involve a legal detriment to the promisee or a legal benefit to the promisor. In all the cases in which there is a legal benefit to the promisor, there will also be a legal detriment to the promisee. However, a legal detriment to the promisee can exist with no benefit to the promisor. Therefore, the focus should be upon the presence or absence of legal detriment to the promisee.

A legal detriment is doing or promising to do that which one was not previously obligated to do or promising to forbear or forbearing from doing that which one had a legal right to do. "Legal detriment" is not synonymous with harmful. Refraining from smoking can be a legal detriment assuming one has a lawful right to smoke.

If one promises to do or does that which one was already legally obligated to do, this action is not sufficient to fulfill the consideration requirement. This concept has been labeled the preexisting duty rule.

A few examples will assist in exploring the reach of this concept:

(a) X is contractually obligated to construct a building for Y for $200,000. X requests or demands additional money for this work and Y agrees to pay $210,000. There is no consideration for the promise to pay an additional $10,000 because X's completion of the building was the performance of an act which X was already legally obligated to perform.

(b) D has a nasty habit of firing his rifle at birds in F's backyard in violation of a city ordinance. F offers to pay D $100 if D will refrain from this activity for a period of one year. D's forbearance is not a legal detriment because D has no legal right to engage in the activity in question. F's promise to pay D $100 is not supported by consideration.

(c) R, an on-duty police officer, apprehends a criminal for whom a reward has been offered. R has a preexisting duty to perform this activity and has incurred no legal detriment.

(d) R, an off-duty policeman vacationing in a neighboring jurisdiction, apprehends a criminal for whom a reward has been offered. Assuming R was aware of the reward offer, consideration is present because R has incurred a legal detriment by doing an act which he had no legal obligation to do.

(e) X has a contract with C whereby C is obligated to pave a dusty road. Wishing to make certain that the road is paved, a neighbor, N, promises to pay C an additional $1,000 if C will pave the road, and C performs the requested act. There has been considerable conflict among the decisions and the writers as to the correct result and the proper explanation of those decisions.

Under the given facts, C is a party to a valid enforceable contract with X. Thus C has a legal duty to pave the road. A further promise to pave or the act of paving is not a legal detriment in that C is only doing that which he was already legally obligated to do. This leads to the conclusion that there is no consideration to support N's promise to pay $1,000 to C and the promise cannot be enforced.

There are several avenues of assault upon this analysis. One position suggests that if C made a promise to N to pave the road, then N has the right to enforce C's promise, and in the event C defaults, N has a legal remedy. Thus N is obtaining a legal benefit which can be the basis for finding consideration. This theory is the product of circular reasoning in which the presence of a valid contract is assumed for the purpose of determining whether a valid contract exists.

Another approach is to inquire into the potential for a rescission of the C–X contract. If in fact C and X might have mutually agreed to rescind their contract, then it could be found that N was bargaining for C to forego this legal right to negotiate a rescission agreement. Thus C has given up a legal right and has incurred a detriment.

If the C–X transaction was simply an offer for a unilateral contract made by X to C, then C would have no preexisting legal obligation owing to anyone since only C's performance would conclude the bargain. If N made an offer to C for a unilateral contract, the performance by C of the act of paving the road could be a valid acceptance of both offers and there would be consideration to support each promise.

The most sweeping assault upon this phase of the preexisting duty problem would be to exclude from its application duties owing to third persons. Only a legal duty owed to the promisor would constitute a preexisting duty which would preclude a new promise or an act from constituting consideration. This is the position which the Restatement, Second, has taken. Section 72 provides: "Except as stated in Sections 73 and 74, any performance which is bargained for is consideration." The portion of the referenced sections which is relevant to this discussion is in section 73 which provides in part: "Performance of a legal duty owed to a promisor which is neither doubtful nor the subject of honest dispute is not consideration . . ."

The comments in the Restatement indicate that "legal duty owed to a promisor" includes legal duties owed to an individual as a member of the public by public officials. Thus the Restatement rule would reach the same results described above in the hypotheticals involving police officers collecting reward offers. Presumably legal duties owed would include the duty to refrain from committing a tort or a criminal activity which harms the person or property of the promisor. Thus there would be a legal duty owing to the promisor not to fire a rifle in his backyard in hypothetical (b) above, and the same result would be reached under the Restatement rule.

§ 49. Compromise of Disputed Claims

From the principles outlined in the preceding sections, it should be apparent that a mutual agreement to compromise a validly disputed claim is supported by consideration. When D agrees to pay $10,000 for the settlement of P's negligence action, P's dismissal of the suit or release of his claim is a legal detriment which is being incurred as a bargained exchange for D's promise.

So long as there is a valid dispute which is being compromised, no novel issues are presented. Problems arise where P brings an action to enforce a promise to pay $10,000 which D made in settlement of a claim which may have been invalid. Assume that D seeks to defend by proving that under the facts and the applicable law, D could not have been liable for negligently causing P's damages. Assume further that D seeks to prove that P knew that there was no valid action for negligence against D or did not have a good faith belief that there was a valid action. The problems presented here require analysis of different policy considerations.

There are strong public policy factors supporting the voluntary settlement of disputes. It is inappropriate to place impediments in the path of persons seeking to compromise their differences. One must also note that in claims in which liability is disputed, it is self-evident that there is a possibility that the defendant is not liable. If the odds in favor of finding liability are no better than 50–50, one might find P settling what is reasonably considered to be a $20,000 loss for $10,000. Where liability is tenuous, P might be willing to settle a $100,000 loss for $10,000. However, if D can force the litigation of the disputed issue in order for P to enforce the promise to pay $10,000, then P has no motive to enter a settlement agreement. If the resolution of disputes by voluntary settlement is to be fostered, it is apparent that contract law must accommodate the enforcement of proper settlement agreements.

To accommodate these policy considerations within the rules of consideration, courts hold that the surrender of a validly disputed claim or the release of a validly asserted defense is sufficient consideration for a return promise. A claim is validly disputed if there is factual or legal uncertainty as to its merits. Where the facts and the law establish that the claim is definitely without foundation, some jurisdictions still treat the release of the claim as valid consideration so long as the person who asserted the claim had a good faith belief in its validity. It is often stated that this "good faith belief" must have some foundation in fact or law, but courts in these jurisdictions generally find consideration unless there is a factual determination that the assertion of the claim was made in bad faith. Similar rules can be applied to the surrender of a defense.

§ 50. Substituted Performance; Accord and Satisfaction

An agreement by which a debtor promises a new performance different from the one owing as a bargained exchange for the creditor releasing the existing obligation is supported by sufficient consideration. If D owes $100 to C and promises to paint C's wagon (or paints C's wagon) instead of paying the $100, there is sufficient consideration to support C's discharge of the duty to pay the $100. The bargain is the performance of an act or a promise to perform an act which constitutes a legal detriment to D which is being undertaken as a bargained exchange for C's release of his legal right to receive $100. The transaction produces a substitute contract or an accord and satisfaction (§§ 181 and 182, *infra*).

§ 51. Partial Payment in Exchange for a Discharge

If D has a present duty to pay C $100, C's agreement to discharge the entire $100 in exchange for D's payment or promise to pay $75 is not supported by consideration. Promising to pay the lesser amount is not a legal detriment because the party is simply doing that which he is already legally obligated to do. Fulfilling a portion of a duty of immediate performance cannot provide consideration for the creditor's promise to release the balance. It was a holding to this effect in the case of Foakes v. Beer (1884), which is credited with providing modern case law foundation for the preexisting duty concept. The *Foakes* case involved an agreement by which a judgment debtor paid the principal owing on the judgment in exchange for the creditor agreeing to forego her right to collect the interest then due. The court held that the promise to forego interest then due was unenforceable because the debtor incurred no legal detriment. The debtor had a present legal duty to pay the entire amount.

The principle of the *Foakes* case remains the law in almost all jurisdictions, but various exceptions have been recognized.

(a) If the obligation in question is not yet due and owing, pre-payment of a lesser sum is sufficient consideration to support an agreement to discharge the whole. Payment at a place other than the place where payment is due has also been suggested to be a performance different from the duty which was owing and thus can serve as valid consideration under the preceding section on substituted performances. Note in this regard, however, that Restatement, Second, section 73 provides in part: ". . . a similar performance is consideration if it differs from what was required by the duty *in a way which reflects more than a pretense of bargain.*"

(b) If the matter arises out of a transaction in goods, U.C.C. section 2–209(1) permits good faith modification of contracts without new consideration. This would appear to permit a seller of goods to agree to take a lesser sum in satisfaction of a greater sum which was due.

(c) Some states have statutes in addition to the U.C.C. which permit contract modification without new consideration in all types of transactions. Some provide that payment of a smaller sum can support a discharge of a greater sum which is presently owing. Some provide that a written release by a creditor needs no consideration.

(d) All jurisdictions recognize that an existing contract can be mutually rescinded by the parties and a new contract can thereafter be formed. The fact that the new contract is identical with the old one but for one party assuming an added burden or being relieved of a burden does not raise a pre-existing duty issue. Some states have used this rescission and new contract reasoning in situations where the facts do not support it. A few courts simply purport to find a rescission despite the absence of any factual basis. Other courts admit that they are using a legal fiction to accomplish what they consider to be a just result (§ 68, *infra*).

(e) All jurisdictions recognize that while a gratuitous promise may be unenforceable, a completed gift is irrevocable. This opens a door to finding that one party gratuitously released the other from his preexisting duty and that the gift is complete.

(f) There is authority for the proposition that a debtor who is insolvent and contemplating bankruptcy may incur a legal detriment by foregoing his right to seek a discharge of his obligations in bankruptcy. This has been found to serve as a bargained exchange for a creditor's promise to accept a lesser sum in satisfaction of a larger debt presently due and owing.

(g) At least one state supreme court has simply announced, albeit by way of dicta, that Foakes v. Beer will not be followed. (Rye v. Phillips (1938).)

(h) If one creditor agrees to take less than what is due in satisfaction of the whole obligation in consideration for other creditors agreeing to do the same, then consideration is present. Likewise, a promise to pay or payment by X to C of a portion of the obligation owing from D to C in exchange for C's agreement to release the balance of the obligation is sufficient consideration (§ 183, *infra*).

§ 52. To Whom and From Whom Consideration Must Be Given

In determining whether a promise is enforceable, there is no requirement in American law that the return promise or performance which constitutes the bargained exchange need come from the promisee. Likewise, there is no requirement that the promise or performance which constitutes the bargained exchange need be made to or rendered for the promisor.

Consideration can be found in each of these examples:

X offers to pay Y five dollars if Y will cut Z's hair. (Or if Y will promise to cut Z's hair.)

S offers to deliver a book to N if D will promise to pay $25 to S.

S offers to deliver a book to N if D will promise to pay $25 to G.

R offers to paint C's house if S will agree to repair C's porch without charge. (The bargained exchange is between R and S, but it matters not whether S renders the performance to R or to C.)

In the foregoing examples, the person who will be seeking to enforce the promise is not a party to the contract and enforcement will be dependent upon establishing rights as a third party beneficiary (§§ 160–162, *infra*). Cases decided under English common law as well as early American cases denied enforcement by thu :! parties because they were persons "from whom no consideration flowed" or because there was no "mutuality of obligation." However, with the general recognition in the United States of enforceable rights in third party beneficiaries, the notion that the plaintiff had to incur some legal detriment as part of the bargained exchange has been rejected.

§ 53. Condition to Gift and Bargained Exchange Compared

A gratuitous promise may be conditioned upon the promisee doing something to place himself in a position to receive the gift.

If a professor wished to give a hornbook to a student, the professor might state: "Come to my office after class, and I will give you a copy of Farnsworth on Contracts." This communication contains a promise and a request that the promisee perform an act. The act of the promisee is certainly legal detriment in the technical sense of the term because the student is being required to do an act which he was not previously legally obligated to do (§ 48, *supra*). However, there is no consideration because there is no bargain (§ 47, *supra*). Coming to the office to pick up the book is simply a reasonable means to make it possible to complete the gift.

Assume that a professor needs the copy of Farnsworth on Contracts which she left in her office. The professor states to a student: "Go to my office and get my Farnsworth on Contracts, and I will give it to you when I am finished using it." This communication also contains a promise and a request that the promisee perform an act. The act again involves legal detriment as the student is being asked to do an act which he was not previously legally obligated to do. While the legal detriment is no different from that in the preceding hypothetical, here it is possible to find a bargain.

When a transaction involves legal detriment to the promisee but has gratuitous overtones—the appearance of being a gift—there are some questions which one can ask to determine whether a court is likely to find a bargain. Is the act which was requested of the promisee something which was necessary or convenient to facilitate making a gift from the promisor to the promisee? Will the promisor benefit from the promisee's act?

Assume that a party with an empty house says to a relative: "Move here. You can stay in my empty house for a few years." Without additional facts, this appears to be a gift, and moving is simply a condition to that gift. Moving to the place where an empty house is located is a necessary act to place oneself in a position to receive the free gift of occupancy, and there is no apparent benefit to the promisor.

Assume that an uncle states to his niece: "If you go to law school and brief all of your cases, I will pay for your tuition." This would appear to be a bargain. A gift of law school tuition requires that the niece go to law school, but the additional requirement that the niece brief all of her cases is not a necessary condition to a gift.

§ 54. Alternative Promises

A contract may permit one party to elect between alternative performances. If X contemplates selling one of his two cars, Y may offer to buy "whichever one you decide not to keep" for a stated price. If X accepts this offer, there is a valid bargain. X has a choice to make, but X is obligated to deliver one car or the other and either performance constitutes consideration for Y's promise to pay.

Where a purported bargain gives one party a choice among alternatives, each alternative must be analyzed to determine whether it would constitute consideration for the return promise. Assume that S agrees to sell and B agrees to buy between 400 and 600 tons of fertilizer in installments as ordered by B. There is consideration for S's promise because B must order and pay for at least 400 tons of fertilizer.

Assume that A owes B an undisputed debt of $5,000 payable in five years. A makes a subsequent promise that he will either pay $4,000 at the end of the first year or pay the debt at maturity; in return B promises to accept the $4,000, if paid at the end of the first year, in full satisfaction of the debt. A's subsequent promise is not consideration for B's return promise since the alternative of performing his legal duty is not consideration. (Illustration number 6 in Restatement, Second, section 77.)

§ 55. Illusory Promises

A promise cannot serve as consideration for the return promise of the other party if it is in fact illusory. Promises that are subject to a condition the occurrence of which is within the control of the promisor must be examined with care to determine whether they are in fact illusory.

X promises to pay Y $20 for cutting X's lawn and Y promises to cut the lawn if he feels like it. There is no consideration for X's promise. Y has not made a binding commitment. Y's promise is illusory as he has a "free way out." Y's duty to perform is dependent upon his mood or whim.

The result would probably be the same if Y agreed to cut X's lawn unless Y decided to go to the football game. Unless one assumes some additional facts that make attendance at the football game a significant event, it would appear that Y has preserved discretionary control over whether he will become obligated to cut the lawn or not. One could view attendance at the football game as an alternative promise by Y, however, it seems readily apparent that this alternative is not a promise for which X has bargained. Attendance at the football game is not an alternative performance of the contract but rather an event that will prevent Y from having to perform. It is thus a condition to Y's duty that is within Y's control leading to the probable conclusion that Y's promise is illusory.

Professor who lives in New York has been offered the position of dean at a school in New Mexico. B promises to buy Professor's house in

New York for a stated price and Professor agrees to sell the house provided she accepts the position in New Mexico. There is consideration for B's promise. Professor's promise to sell is subject to a condition that is within her discretionary control, however, her promise is not illusory. She does not have a "free way out." The decision to accept or reject the offered position is one that will be made based upon many factors other than the house sale contract. It is going to occur or not occur based upon these other factors. If the position is accepted, the duty to convey the house will arise.

S owns and operates a widget factory. B promises to buy and S promises to sell for a stated price all of S's output of widgets for a period of two years. S has a duty to act in good faith (see U.C.C. section 2–305(1)), but it is possible for S to terminate production of widgets and avoid any obligation on the promise to B. Despite the fact that S may be free to sell or close the plant or otherwise terminate widget production, there is consideration for B's promise to buy. The obligation is subject to an event that is within S's control, but the owner of a widget factory may not terminate production simply to avoid the contract with B. (See § 57, *infra*.)

The presence of a condition within the control of one party creates a more difficult problem when that condition is related to the contract performance. Assume that A promises to pay B a stated sum for transporting A's goods from New Orleans to Puerto Rico for a period of five years, and B promises to haul A's goods if B decides to buy a certain ship. If the ship would be used primarily or exclusively to haul A's cargo, it would appear that there is no consideration for A's promise. B's decision to purchase or not purchase the ship would not reflect B's evaluation of independent factors but would be primarily determined by whether B wanted to perform or avoid B's agreement with A.

Assume that X promises to deliver gravel to Y and Y agrees to order and pay for the gravel unless Y notifies X in writing within 60 days that Y does not wish to perform. Y's duty to perform is subject to a condition within Y's control which has no significance independent of this contract. Y is free to avoid any obligation by simply giving written notice of intent not to perform. Proper analysis leads to the conclusion that there is no consideration for X's promise to deliver gravel. One might find that there is an open offer from X to Y, but X is free to revoke that offer. However, after the 60 days has expired and the right to cancel is gone, there is a binding contract between the parties.

Some court opinions have analyzed situations such as the gravel hypothetical above in terms of alternative performances. (See § 54, *supra*.) One can indulge in the reasoning that Y has a choice between two performances, ordering and paying for gravel or writing a letter stating none will be ordered. Of course, writing a letter does involve doing something that Y was not previously obligated to do and could thus be seen as a legal detriment. However, it is not a bargained for detriment. The parties were not agreeing to a bargain which involved X promising to deliver gravel in exchange for Y's writing a letter stating that Y would not perform.

§ 56. Implied Promise to Use Best Efforts or Act in Good Faith

In determining the presence or absence of a firm undertaking, a court is not limited to the express terms of the agreement. What appears on the surface to be an illusory promise may be properly characterized as a firm undertaking if one can infer that the parties intended an implied promise.

L agreed to give to W the exclusive right to place L's endorsements on the designs of others, to market L's own designs, and to license others to market them. W agreed to pay L one-half of all profits and revenues. The agreement was for one year and renewable thereafter unless canceled. W made no express promise to do anything beyond his promise to account to L monthly for monies received and pay one-half of the profits to L, duties which would never arise if he never did anything. The court found that a promise by W to use reasonable efforts in marketing L's name and products was fairly implied, and held that there was consideration to support L's promises. (Wood v. Lucy, Lady Duff-Gordon (1917).) The fact that W possessed a business organization suitable for the purposes of the agreement assisted the court in reaching the decision that the parties had intended an implied promise by W that reasonable efforts would be applied to the task. Possibly more important, however, is the apparent fact that the parties intended to enter an agreement which would have business efficacy and that this manifested intention could be effectuated only by concluding that the parties intended that there be a commitment by W.

U.C.C. section 2–306(2) provides:

(2) A lawful agreement by either the seller or the buyer for exclusive dealing in the kind of goods concerned imposes unless otherwise agreed an obligation by the seller to use best efforts to supply the goods and by the buyer to use best efforts to promote their sale.

It has been suggested that the provisions of U.C.C. section 1–203, which imposes an obligation of good faith in every contract arising under the U.C.C., may permit a court to find enforceable obligations in circumstances in which the undertakings of the parties appeared to be inadequate to find a present contract. For example, at common law an "agreement to agree" was found to be too indefinite to be a contract. The provisions of the U.C.C. may induce courts to find an enforceable duty to meet and negotiate in good faith where such an "agreement to agree" has been made. (See §§ 40, *supra* and 95, *infra*.)

§ 57. Requirements Contracts and Output Contracts

S agrees to sell and B agrees to buy all of B's requirements of olive oil for $12 per gallon. Requirements contracts such as this appear to give the buyer the opportunity to reduce the contract quantity and his obligation to zero or increase the quantity to a great amount depending upon B's choice of future conduct. Because of the apparent illusory nature of B's promise and the problem of certainty of terms, early common law courts had difficulties enforcing contracts in which quantity was measured solely by the requirements of the buyer or the output of the seller.

With respect to the consideration issue, courts came to the position that if B had an established source of requirements, his promise to buy was not illusory. If B had a salad dressing factory or a Greek restaurant, his promise to buy his requirements of olive oil was not illusory because he had an alternative of buying oil or going out of business. Some court opinions view this situation as involving two alternative performances both of which involve a legal detriment. However, the seller could not logically be found to have bargained for a promise to sell in exchange for B's detriment of terminating his business. The better explanation of this result is that B's alternative of terminating his business has substantial significance to him independent of the olive oil contract. The availability of this alternative does not make his promise illusory; it does not afford him a free way out. (See §§ 54 and 55, *supra*.)

The interpretation of rights and duties in requirements and output contracts is now controlled in part by U.C.C. section 2–306.

§ 58. Consideration Based Upon Voidable Promises

Certain promises are voidable or legally unenforceable due to factors such as the status of the person making them, the improper inducements used by the promisee, or the failure to comply with a requirement for a writing. Despite the fact that a promise may be unenforceable for one of these reasons, it may still provide sufficient consideration to support a return promise for which it was bargained. A minor may be immune from liability upon his promises, but this fact does not preclude his promise from serving as consideration, thus permitting him to enforce the contract. A person with diminished mental capacity may have the right to avoid his obligations under a contract, but the promise can still serve as consideration.

The same result is reached when a promisor has the right to avoid his obligations due to the promisee's misrepresentations, or because of mistake, or because the statute of frauds requires his promise to be in writing. Promises made by persons totally lacking in capacity are void and would not serve as consideration to permit enforcement on behalf of the incapacitated person.

The expression "mutuality of obligation," while frequently used or abused, does not accurately reflect a requirement of the law of contracts. There are situations in which a concept referred to as mutuality of remedy may have an effect upon the remedy which a court might make available to one party, but the validity of a contract is not dependent upon both parties being obligated.

§ 59. Adequacy of Consideration

The fairness or equivalence in the values exchanged is not a factor in determining the presence or absence of consideration. The presence or absence of an equal exchange can have great significance in determining the availability of certain defenses or the availability of certain remedies. For those purposes, it will be appropriate to discuss "adequacy of consideration" referring to amount or value. For purposes of determining whether a bargain exists with the requisite consideration, the appropriate vocabulary is "sufficiency of consideration" referring to legal sufficiency rather than fairness or adequacy.

While benefit to the promisor is often included as an alternative to detriment to the promisee in the traditional definition of what constitutes sufficient consideration, no actual benefit to the promisor need be found. Undoubtedly, most persons who make promises as part of a bargained exchange do so because they anticipate a benefit for themselves, but the requirement of consideration leaves to the promisor the determination of what constitutes a satisfactory bargain. Thus P may promise to pay $500 to X if X will quit smoking; or if X will start studying; or go to church; or paint the church. The question of benefit to P is not relevant to the discussion of consideration in any of these examples.

The enforcement of P's promise is not predicated upon the gratification that P is receiving from the performance of the requested acts. Adoption of the notion of psychological benefit as a basis for promise enforcement would logically extend to gratuitous promises and cause one to conclude that they, too, are given for bargained consideration. Such is not the case.

§ 60. Non-bargained Detriment

The making of a gratuitous promise may stimulate or induce various types of responses in the promisee. If X offers to let Y use X's ladder to reach the apples on Y's tree, it is not uncommon that Y will say thanks and volunteer a few free apples for X's family. Gratuitous promises may induce all manner and means of action in reliance thereon. Despite the presence of a "detriment" on the part of both parties, there is no bargained exchange present. While detrimental reliance may be available as a basis for asserting some contract rights (§ 69, *infra*), it is important to distinguish that theory from the enforcement of bargained exchanges.

To have consideration, it is not enough that the making of the promise induced conduct on the part of the promisee. There must be a concurrence of these two elements to create a bargained exchange. Objective manifestations of inducement and bargain are sufficient. There is no inquiry into the undisclosed intention or "true motive" of either or both parties. (See Restatement, Second, section 71, comment b.)

§ 61. Recitals of Consideration; Shams

While consideration is often viewed as a formalistic requirement, most courts have resisted the argument that a false recital of consideration in a writing should be sufficient to make a promise enforceable. Most jurisdictions permit the promisor to go behind the document to attempt to prove that the recital was in fact a sham to create the appearance of a bargain where none was in fact present.

In the case of the consideration necessary to support an option contract, there is some authority for the proposition that a sham recital of consideration is sufficient to show an intent to create an enforceable obligation which the law should respect. One court indicated that if the promisor had not received the consideration for the option, he could sue for it. The Restatement, Second, section 87, comment c states: "In view of the dangers of permitting a solemn written agreement to be invalidated by oral testimony which is easily fabricated, therefore, the option agreement is not invalidated by proof that the recited consideration was not in fact given." In view of the numerous instances in which the Restatement, Second, embraces rules which permit oral evidence to alter or terminate the legal effect of written instruments, solemn or otherwise, it is perhaps more likely that the authors were influenced by the other reason given, which is: "The signed writing has vital significance as a formality, while the ceremonial manual delivery of a dollar or a peppercorn is an inconsequential formality."

The Restatement, Second, also takes the position in section 88 that a mere recital of consideration is enough to support a promise to be surety for the performance of a contractual obligation.

It is suggested that there is no doctrinal reason or logic in the common law to relax the requirements of consideration for option contracts or guarantee contracts. Most courts continue to deny enforcement where the recital of consideration is proven false.

§ 62. Subsequent Promises to Perform Unenforceable Contracts

Sections 63 through 67 deal with the limited circumstances in which courts will enforce a new promise to perform an obligation that was originally not enforceable or has become unenforceable or has been discharged. In order to be bound by the new promise, the promisor must know or have reason to know the essential facts of the previous transaction, but there is no requirement that he have knowledge of the legal effect of these facts.

In these circumstances there is no bargained consideration and the basis for enforcement of the new promise can be said to be the moral obligation of the promisor. However, use of moral obligation as a basis for enforcement of a promise is almost always limited to the situation described in the following sections.

§ 63. Debts Enforceable but for the Statute of Limitations

An express or implied promise to pay a debt barred by the statute of limitations is enforceable. Many jurisdictions require the new promise to be in writing. A new promise may be implied from a part payment of the debt or other acknowledgment so long as these acts are not qualified so as to negate or limit the implication of a promise to pay. The new promise or acknowledgment must be communicated to the creditor. A mere notation by the debtor in his records that he owes the amount is insufficient, as would be a statement to a stranger that the creditor is owed the money.

It should be noted that the primary purpose of statutes which limit the time within which legal actions may be brought is to avoid stale claims and permit people to discard old records. If a debtor has acknowledged an obligation and impliedly promised to pay it, then it is not a stale claim in the sense that it is old and forgotten by the parties.

Thus, the purpose of the statute is not defeated by enforcing claims which debtors acknowledge to be unsatisfied and impliedly promise to pay.

§ 64. Debts Discharged in Bankruptcy

Common law permits the enforcement of a new promise to perform an obligation which was discharged in bankruptcy or which is in the process of being discharged in an existing bankruptcy proceeding. Unlike stale claims, the issue here is not one of recollection and available records, thus, a mere acknowledgement of the validity of the claim and the fact that it has not been satisfied is not significant. However, an express and specific promise to perform all or part of a preexisting obligation discharged in bankruptcy is enforceable under contract law despite the absence of any new consideration.

This problem is the subject of specific legislation in the Federal Bankruptcy Reform Act of 1978. The statute requires, among other things, that the agreement to repay the debt contain a conspicuous statement that the debtor may rescind the agreement within a specified time frame and that under certain circumstances the court approve the agreement as not imposing an undue hardship on the debtor and is in the best interest of the debtor.

§ 65. Obligations Unenforceable Due to Statute of Frauds

If an obligation was originally unenforceable because the statute of frauds was not satisfied, and

thereafter the obligor signs a memorandum sufficient to satisfy the statutory requirement, the obligation becomes enforceable. The consideration is
found in the original oral contract. Some cases
discuss the enforcement of the "new" promise contained in the writing and find consideration or a
substitute for consideration in the unenforceable
oral agreement.

§ 66. Promise to Perform Obligations That Were Voidable

If an original obligation was unenforceable because the promisor lacked capacity, a new promise
made after the promisor has attained capacity will
be enforced although there is no mutual assent or
new consideration to support it. This same rule
applies to other cases where a promisor had a
defense, such as misrepresentation, mistake or undue influence. If after the facts are known or the
disability has been removed the promisor promises
to perform, this new promise can be enforced although there is no mutual assent or new consideration. A common example is found where a minor
enters a voidable contract and then reaffirms the
obligation after attaining the age of majority.

§ 67. Promise to Pay for Benefits Previously Conferred

The law of restitution recognizes an obligation
under certain limited circumstances to pay for
benefits conferred where there was no express or
implied contract. The basis of the legal right is in

many cases labeled "quasi-contract" or "unjust enrichment." Examples may include benefits conferred by mistake such as a debtor accidentally paying to a creditor more than is owing, or benefits conferred with the expectation of compensation in an emergency such as a doctor treating an unconscious accident victim. (See § 70, *infra*.)

If X has received a benefit from Y for which Y has the legal right to recover under the law of restitution, a promise by X to pay a certain sum that Y agrees to accept in satisfaction of the claim is legally enforceable. The bargain is easy to find. Y is sustaining the legal detriment of giving up Y's valid claim against X in exchange for X's promise to pay a specific sum.

If X has received a benefit from Y and Y honestly believes that Y has a right to recover from X for the reasonable value of this benefit, a promise by X to pay a certain sum of money that Y agrees to accept in settlement of this disputed claim is legally enforceable. (See § 49, *supra*.) Y is giving up the right to pursue the claim against X in exchange for X's promise to pay the agreed sum.

Assume that F's prize bull escaped and found its way to B's farm. B fed the bull until its owner was found and reclaimed it. F promised to pay a certain sum for the feeding of the bull and this promise was held to be enforceable. (Boothe v. Fitzpatrick (1864).)

In Webb v. McGowin (1935), Webb sustained serious injuries while performing an emergency act which saved McGowin from death or serious injury. McGowin's subsequent promise to pay Webb $15 every two weeks for life was found to be enforceable. The court compared the act of saving McGowin's life to the act of feeding the bull in the Boothe case (above) stating: "Such service would have been far more material than caring for a bull." On this basis the court found that McGowin was obligated to Webb on the basis of quasi-contract. The court also stated that a basis for enforcing McGowin's promise was the moral obligation owing from him to Webb. The unanswered question is whether "moral obligation" alone would have been a sufficient basis for enforcing McGowin's promise if the court had found no obligation owing for services rendered.

At least one case has enforced a promise made "in consideration of" a benefit previously conferred even where no cause of action for quasi-contract or restitution existed. In re Schoenkerman's Estate (1940), the court enforced a promise to pay $1,500 for services rendered while holding that the plaintiff did not have the right to recover for the full value of the services rendered which was found to be $4,610.

Restatement, Second, section 86, provides:

Sec. 86. Promise for Benefit Received

(1) A promise made in recognition of a benefit previously received by the promisor from the

promisee is binding to the extent necessary to prevent injustice.

(2) A promise is not binding under Subsection (1)

(a) if the promisee conferred the benefit as a gift or for other reasons the promisor has not been unjustly enriched; or

(b) to the extent that its value is disproportionate to the benefit.

Subsection (1) appears to state a broad rule enforcing promises for benefits previously conferred. However, subsection (2)(a) limits this enforcement to situations where there was a legally enforceable obligation owing in restitution based upon unjust enrichment. This section thus does not appear to provide any authority for enforcing promises beyond that discussed above.

§ 68. Modification of Existing Contracts

Agreements to modify existing contract obligations are generally subject to the preexisting duty rule. A promise to perform an existing legal duty under a binding contract is not sufficient consideration to support the other party's promise to do more or pay more. For example, A agrees to hire B to work for one year starting in September at $200 a week. In December, A and B agree to modify the employment contract, setting B's salary at $250 a week. A's promise to pay the additional $50 a week is not enforceable if B is merely doing what he is already obligated to do. B is incurring no detriment in exchange for the promise to pay more. While a majority of jurisdictions have followed this rule, they have also recognized it as an impediment to enforcement of modifications to which parties have freely agreed. Many courts have avoided the rule's application by making exceptions to the rule or by construing the facts so that the problem is removed.

(1) Some courts have found an implied agreement of rescission of the preexisting contract followed by the formation of a new agreement. If such a rescission is found, the new contract is supported by consideration under standard bargained exchange principles.

(2) Another exception has been used when one party has already broken the contract. An additional promise by the other to secure the actual performance of the work contracted for in place of a right to sue for damages has sometimes been found to be supported by consideration and enforceable.

(3) A number of jurisdictions will uphold the modified agreement if it was made after unforeseen and substantial difficulties were encountered which were not known or anticipated when the contract was entered into and which cause an additional burden upon a party's performance. Of course, if the unforeseen difficulties are such as would excuse performance, then there is in fact no preexisting duty to perform. (See §§ 176 and 177, *infra.*)

(4) Some cases suggest that an agreement to modify is supported by consideration since a party gives up his legal right to breach the original contract, thereby suffering detriment.

A few states, including New Hampshire and Minnesota, have taken a more direct approach by discarding the rule altogether with the result that consideration is not required for the modification of an executory agreement. Statutes in some states have made a signed writing a substitute for consideration to support a modification.

The Restatement, Second, section 89(a), provides for the enforcement of modification agreements not fully performed in the following circumstances:

(a) if the modification is fair and equitable in view of circumstances not anticipated by the parties when the contract was made; or

(b) to the extent provided by statute; or

(c) to the extent that justice requires enforcement in view of material change of position in reliance on the promise.

The U.C.C. has abandoned the requirement of consideration for modifications of contracts for the sale of goods. The official comment to section 2–209 states: "This Section seeks to protect and make effective all necessary and desirable modifications of sales contracts without regard to the technicalities which at present hamper such adjustments."

Legislative reform and abandonment of the pre-existing duty rule as related to the modification of a contract may still reflect a minority position. However, courts increasingly search for exceptions to enable them to enforce such agreements and thereby not frustrate the expectations of the parties who have negotiated a desired modification in good faith.

The enforcement of an agreement to modify a contract is subject to the usual contract defenses. Since modifications are sometimes forced upon one party, the defense of duress is the most common concern. (See § 105, *infra.*) All agreements to modify contracts governed by the U.C.C. must meet the good faith test to be effective. Contract modifications frequently involve issues relating to the statute of frauds (§ 98, *infra*).

B. DETRIMENTAL RELIANCE (PROMISSORY ESTOPPEL)

§ 69. Enforcement of Promises That Induce Reliance

"A promise which the promisor should reasonably expect to induce action or forbearance on the part of the promisee or a third person and which does induce such action or forbearance is binding if injustice can be avoided only by enforcement of the promise. The remedy granted for breach may be limited as justice requires." (Restatement, Second, section 90(1).)

Reliance upon a promise is a distinct basis for creation of contract rights and duties. It is not dependent upon finding any agreement nor any bargained exchange consideration. Legal historians have found reliance upon a promise to be a historical basis for an action of assumpsit. During the nineteenth century, the bargained exchange became the source of contract rights and duties. However, in the latter part of that century, decisions were reached in the United States in which gratuitous promises were found to be enforceable by one who had incurred substantial detriment by reasonable and foreseeable reliance thereon. Since estoppel was the handiest concept available to explain the enforcement of promises which were not part of a bargained exchange, the phrase "promissory estoppel" was frequently applied to describe the basis for the rights and duties recognized in these cases. It was not uncommon for a court opinion to state that the promisor was estopped from asserting the lack of consideration for the promise. Today many courts use the term "detrimental reliance" to describe this theory of liability. While neither phrase is erroneous, "detrimental reliance" is preferred because it avoids an imprecise analogy to "estoppel" and avoids the incorrect notion that detrimental reliance is a "substitute" for consideration.

Detrimental reliance must not be confused with legal detriment. Legal detriment need not be harmful, can be of any magnitude, and must be bargained for. Detrimental reliance must involve significant adverse consequences and does not arise out of a bargained exchange.

Providing some measure of recovery to one who has reasonably and foreseeably relied upon the promise of another is an appealing concept. The apparent logic and fairness of this proposition together with its appearance in the First and Second Restatements and in all major works on the subject of contracts would lead one to believe that it enjoys acceptance in all quarters. Such is not the case.

Detrimental reliance is a uniquely American concept. Only one English case recognizes the concept and that case limits its use to providing a defense. Some jurisdictions limit the application of detrimental reliance to intra-family transactions and to philanthropic subscriptions to educational, charitable or religious organizations. These jurisdictions also permit enforcement of promises in which a bailor relies upon a promise of a bailee in connection with the insurance or care of the entrusted property. However, these jurisdictions exhibit a reluctance to extend the enforcement of promises on the basis of reliance into other relationships and appear particularly reluctant to extend it into business relationships.

An example of this judicial attitude is found in James Baird Co. v. Gimbel Brothers (1933). A general contractor, after receiving a supplier's bid on linoleum, used the latter's figures in making its bid on a job with a state government. The supplier was clearly bargaining for the general contractor's promise to pay for the materials, but the supplier also made a gratuitous promise not to revoke its offer. The general submitted its bid and posted a forfeitable bond with the government. Thereafter, the supplier revoked its offer. The general contractor did not withdraw its bid, and the government awarded it the contract. The general contractor then tried to accept supplier's bid, contending that the use of the supplier's bid in computing the general's bid constituted a change of position in reliance on the promise not to revoke which made the supplier's offer irrevocable. The court rejected this argument, holding that the supplier's offer was one for a bargained exchange; hence, the doctrine of promissory estoppel or detrimental reliance does not apply. Much of the court's opinion is devoted to the evident points that the general contractor did not by its reliance become contractually bound to purchase the linoleum and that the supplier did not intend to deliver linoleum in exchange for the general contractor's reliance. At the end of the opinion the court did consider the fact that the supplier had made a gratuitous promise not to revoke upon which the general contractor did apparently rely to its detriment. The thought that this detrimental reliance could provide a basis for making the promise not to revoke enforceable was dismissed with the observation: "There is not the least reason to suppose that the defendant meant to subject itself to such a one-sided obligation. True, if so construed, the doctrine of promissory estoppel might apply, the plaintiff having acted in reliance upon it, though, so far as we have found, the decisions are otherwise."

In other jurisdictions, the application of the concept of detrimental reliance is not so limited to particular classes of transactions. A leading case which enforced a gratuitous promise in a commercial setting quite similar to that discussed above is Drennan v. Star Paving Co. (1958). In *Drennan,* the subcontractor did not expressly promise not to revoke its bid but such a promise was found to be reasonably implied. The general contractor relied upon this implied promise not to revoke by using the subcontractor's price in computing its own bid to a school district. The court found this detrimental reliance upon the subcontractor's promise sufficient to make that promise enforceable. Thus, the subcontractor was bound by its implied promise not to revoke its offer until the bids to the school district had been opened and the general contractor had had reasonable time and opportunity to accept the subcontractor's offer. Simply stated, reasonable and foreseeable reliance upon a promise not to revoke an offer is sufficient to create an option contract.

The period of irrevocability is brief. If the general fails to accept the subcontractor's bid promptly after the general is awarded the contract, the subcontractor is no longer bound. Any further negotiation or counter-offer by the general would permit the subcontractor to revoke. As thus qualified, the *Drennan* position has gained substantial acceptance.

The result of the *Drennan* case was expressly adopted and perhaps expanded in the Restatement, Second, section 87(2) which provides:

> An offer which the offeror should reasonably expect to induce action or forbearance of a substantial character on the part of the offeree before acceptance and which does induce such action or forbearance is binding as an option contract to the extent necessary to avoid injustice.

This subsection is not expressly limited to situations in which the offeror expressly or impliedly promises not to revoke the offer. One might reason that the offeror would not "reasonably expect" the offer to "induce action or forbearance of a substantial character" in the absence of at least an implied promise not to revoke.

So long as the only available remedy for detrimental reliance was enforcement of the promise, the courts recognized rights only where there was substantial detriment incurred in reliance upon the promise. A further expansion of the application of detrimental reliance was made possible by decisions which recognized an alternative remedy for only reliance damages. Relief can be granted in a greater number of cases if courts have the alternative of limiting the remedy to compensation for the reliance interest, for restitution, or for such other remedy as may be appropriate. The alternative of granting relief other than expectancy damages is recognized in the Restatement, Second, which modified the language of the Restatement, First, by adding this sentence in section 90: "The remedy granted for breach may be limited as justice requires." The requirement that reliance produce "substantial" detriment was deleted.

The most far-reaching application of detrimental reliance has been recognized in a few cases in which a right of action has been found to arise where a party was reasonably induced to rely on general statements and indefinite promises. This has occurred in a commercial setting in which both parties contemplated entering into a binding bargain. During the course of negotiations, one party made promises which were not sufficiently certain to constitute the basis for an enforceable bargain. However, the promises were sufficient to induce the other party to change position in reasonable reliance. When this foreseeable reliance occurred, an enforceable right was found to exist. Since the promise in question was too uncertain to be the basis of an agreement, the available remedy was for damages incurred in reliance rather than the loss of the value of the unfulfilled promise.

Detrimental reliance has been used as a basis for enforcement of a charitable subscription where the facts of reliance were questionable at best. It might be concluded from these cases that the policy factors in favor of enforcing charitable subscriptions are sufficiently strong that minimal or tenuous reliance will be sufficient to permit enforcement of the promise. Cases also exist in which the act of getting married is found to be sufficient proof of reliance upon a gratuitous pre-marital promise. The Restatement, Second, section 90(2) takes the position that no proof of reliance is necessary in charitable subscription or marriage settlement cases.

Prevention of injustice is the stated underpinning of detrimental reliance cases. In determining whether it might be applicable in a given fact situation, it is necessary to determine whether injustice will result if the remedy is withheld.

When you have completed your study of this chapter, you may wish to analyze questions 10–17 at the end of this book and compare your analysis with the one given there.

III. QUASI–CONTRACT
(RESTITUTION)

§ 70. Quasi-Contract

Quasi-contract is generally viewed as merely a part of a broader area of substantive law generally referred to as restitution or unjust enrichment. Restitution is not explored in any depth in contracts courses because it is commonly offered as an advance course in most law schools. Restitution encompasses a number of different areas of law that create substantive rights or remedies or both including quasi-contract, rescission, constructive trust, equitable liens, accounting for profits, subrogation, indemnity and contribution. Some authors also include replevin and ejectment within this subject.

Legal rights and remedies in the areas of restitution may arise out of the commission of a tort, the formation or attempted formation of a contract or fact situations which involve neither tort nor contract. Coverage in this work will be limited to certain aspects of the subject of quasi-contract which are frequently touched upon in contracts casebooks.

Quasi-contracts are not true contracts. The right of action is not based upon an enforceable bargain to which the parties have mutually agreed. The term "quasi-contract" is used because the right of action is in some ways analogous to a contract action and the remedy given is similar to one of the remedies that might be allowed for breach of contract.

Because of the breadth and flexibility of quasi-contract recovery, hard rules are nonexistent and generalizations are difficult. One general rule might be: Where one supplies goods or renders services with the expectation of compensation and the recipient who benefits from those goods or services would (presumably) have promised to pay for them if able to do so or should have promised to pay for them by the minimum standards of the community, courts may recognize a right to recover in quasi-contract for the reasonable value of the goods delivered or services rendered.

Examples of quasi-contracts are numerous. The following list is by no means exhaustive, but merely illustrative of the problems encountered:

1. BENEFITS CONFERRED BY MISTAKE—A, who contracted with X to paint X's house, painted B's house next door by mistake and without B's knowledge. B, who had previously put the house on the market, raises the asking price of the mistakenly painted house. Some cases permit A to recover from B in quasi-contract, for the reasonable value of the painting job, as reflected by the increase in value of the house. As discussed later, A's recovery is less likely if B is not in the process of selling his house.

2. AID RENDERED IN EMERGENCY—Where Dr. A comes upon the scene of an accident and renders necessary medical aid to B, who is unconscious, Dr. A has a quasi-contractual claim against B for the reasonable value of services rendered. The ambulance company that drove the unconscious B to the hospital at the insistence of Dr. A likewise has a quasi-contractual claim against B. Where C accidentally drove his car into a ditch in the midst of a rainstorm and left it to seek help, the tow truck company that pulled his car out of the ditch just before it was inundated may recover the reasonable value of the services rendered. Assume that D hired a carpenter to repair the stairs in D's mountain cabin. While performing this work, the carpenter noticed that the roof of D's cabin was about to cave in due to a recent snowfall. If the carpenter was not able to contact the owner and proceeded to perform reasonably necessary services by affixing support beams to the roof, the carpenter may recover for the reasonable value of the services rendered.

3. NECESSITIES OF LIFE SUPPLIED—Dr. X happens to notice that the foot of C, a minor child is swollen and blue. Dr. X inquires and finds that an injury occurred over a week ago and the foot is broken. However, C's parents have refused to do anything about the injury and when Dr. X asks permission to treat the foot, they refuse. Dr. X treats the foot anyway. Despite the recalcitrance of the parents, the doctor might be entitled to

payment for the reasonable value of the services rendered. This result is based on quasi-contract and on the duty of a parent to care for a child. It is illustrative of the difference between quasi-contract and contract, in that a disavowal of assent does not necessarily preclude quasi-contractual recovery.

4. WORK PERFORMED UNDER AN UNENFORCEABLE CONTRACT—A orally agrees to hire B for 18 months, payment to be made after completion of the work. B performs for 16 months, after which A fires him. B cannot sue under the contract, as it is an oral contract not to be performed within a year in violation of the statute of frauds. However, B may recover the reasonable value of services performed based on quasi-contract. The oral contract is not enforceable, but the wage which the parties agreed upon can usually be introduced as evidence of the reasonable value of the services rendered.

5. DISCHARGE OF A DUTY OWED BY ANOTHER—T, tenant under a long-term lease of landlord L who is vacationing in Europe, pays taxes on the property in order to prevent foreclosure. T may recover that money from L based on quasi-contract.

In these situations, it has been found appropriate to recompense one party despite the lack of a contractual relationship. The legal (as opposed to equitable) solution to the problem is derived from the common law form of action called *indebitatus assumpsit.* The traditional explanation for allowing recovery of a contractual nature is that in these situations the defendant should have or would have promised to pay the plaintiff for the services rendered and therefore, the court will impose that promise on the defendant.

The modern rationale for quasi-contractual recovery is the prevention of unjust enrichment. As the words themselves indicate, there are two equally important facets to the doctrine: (a) There must be an enrichment of the defendant. In other words, the defendant must somehow have benefited. His assets must be increased in value, or he must somehow be better off. Note, however, that the estate of the deceased can be liable in quasi-contract for an unsuccessful effort by a doctor to save the deceased. Liability can be found even when the cause of the need for medical attention was attempted suicide. (b) The enrichment must be unjust. This is a judgment call by the court, but example (1), *supra*, illustrates the principle. If B's house were not on the market, there might be little justice in requiring B to pay for a paint job that he did not want or possibly could not afford. There is no question that B has been enriched; the question is whether it is unjust enrichment.

The plaintiff must have actually expected compensation at the time the services were rendered or the services will be seen as a gift rendered as a mere volunteer. Thus, Attorney Y who did pro bono work for an impoverished client cannot subsequently recover the reasonable value of the services even if the client unexpectedly received a million dollar inheritance.

One who is an officious intermeddler will be denied recovery. For example: A, an independent painting contractor, is out driving on a Sunday and notices B's house, which is badly in need of a paint job. Without consulting B, A shows up the next day with a full crew and paints B's house while B is at work. A will be denied any recovery in this situation; there is no reason to say that B should have or would have promised to pay, nor could A reasonably have expected B so to promise. B is the lucky recipient of a windfall; A is an officious intermeddler. A more difficult example involves the situation in which X left his horses in a barren corral with no food. After repeated requests made to X and unsuccessful efforts to secure help or action from governmental agencies and the SPCA, Y fed the horses. One court denied Y recovery despite the fact that the situation was so extreme that X was convicted on a charge of cruelty to animals.

Another outgrowth of the traditional viewpoint is the requirement that the one performing the services must be a proper person to be performing. This is a corollary of the reasonable expectation of payment requirement, and another aspect of the prohibition against actions by officious intermeddlers or volunteers. For instance, where the state law requires a school district to transport the children to school and the district refuses to do so, a parent who transported the children was permitted to recover from the district under quasi-contract, but a person who picked up the children as they hitchhiked to school did not recover damages.

§ 71. Measure of Recovery in Quasi-Contract

The measure of recovery in restitution cases including quasi-contract is usually stated to be the value of the benefit conferred. Literally applied, this directs the inquiry to the dollar value of the actual benefit which the defendant received as distinguished from the cost which the plaintiff incurred or the reasonable value of the plaintiff's services. However, after stating that the proper measure of recovery is the benefit of the defendant, courts in fact often look to the reasonable value of the goods supplied or services rendered and conclude that this is the value of the benefit conferred.

When a physician renders necessary emergency treatment to an unconscious accident victim, the court's opinion will usually state that the victim is liable for the benefit conferred. If this were the case, one might expect that the victim whose life was saved would be liable for extensive damages whereas the estate of the victim who died despite the care rendered would owe little if anything. In fact, the court will measure the "benefit conferred" on the basis of the reasonable value of the services rendered by the doctor. In like manner, the carpenter who saved the cabin from collapse (example

2 in § 70, *supra*) will recover the value of the services rendered, not the value of the cabin saved. In these examples, the remedy actually awarded in quasi-contract cases is more analogous to the usual contract remedy than it is to a restitution. The court is fixing damages as the sum that the defendant might reasonably have agreed to pay had there in fact been a true contract.

IV. STATUTE OF FRAUDS

A. CONTRACTS WITHIN THE STATUTE

§ 72. Statute of Frauds; History

In 1677, the English adopted "An Act for the Prevention of Frauds and Perjuries." This legislation contained provisions on a number of subjects including two sections which imposed the requirement of a writing for certain types of contractual obligations. These two sections provided:

Sec. 4. . . . no action shall be brought (1) whereby to charge any executor or administrator upon any special promise, to answer damages out of his own estate; (2) or whereby to charge the defendant upon any special promise to answer for the debt, default or miscarriages of another person; (3) or to charge any person upon any agreement made upon consideration of marriage; (4) or upon any contract or sale of lands, tenements or hereditaments, or any interest in or concerning them; (5) or upon any agreement that is not to be performed within the space of one year from the making thereof; (6) unless the agreement upon which such action shall be brought, or some memorandum or note thereof, shall be in writing, and signed by the party to be charged therewith, or some other person thereunto by him lawfully authorized.

128

Sec. 17. . . . no contract for the sale of any goods, wares and merchandises, for the price of ten pounds sterling or upwards, shall be allowed to be good, except the buyer shall accept part of the goods so sold, and actually receive the same, or give something in earnest to bind the bargain, or in part payment, or that some note or memorandum in writing of the said bargain be made and signed by the parties to be charged by such contract, or their agents thereunto lawfully authorized.

Except for Louisiana, all American states have substantially copied section 4 with Maryland and New Mexico adopting it by judicial decision. A comprehensive list of these state statutes can be found in Restatement, Second, Chapter Five, Statutory Note.

The provisions of section 17 found their way into the Uniform Sales Act with $500 being substituted for 10 pounds sterling. With some significant modifications, this law is now embodied in section 2–201 of the U.C.C. While England repealed almost all of its writing requirements in 1954, there is no apparent movement for repeal in the United States. The recent trend in many states is to extend the writing requirement to additional types of transactions.

A requirement of a writing can serve three functions: evidentiary, cautionary, and channeling. The original purpose of the requirement of a writing for the enforcement of certain contracts was

undoubtedly evidentiary, to provide evidence of the
existence and terms of the contract. Incorporation
of the requirement in sections of an act adopted
"for the prevention of frauds and perjuries" is a
fair indication of such purpose and historians have
indicated that there is no evidence of any other
purpose. However, courts now permit enforcement of contracts within the statute based upon
oral testimony of the existence of a lost writing
(§ 83, *infra*), and it is apparent from this and other
accepted methods for avoiding the application of
the statute that it does not always fulfill an evidentiary purpose today. The requirement of a signed
writing undoubtedly has a cautionary purpose
guarding the promisor to some degree against ill-
considered promises. The requirement no doubt
also serves what has been characterized as a channeling function by providing a form or format by
which people undertake binding obligations for
such transactions as the sale of real property. In
the process of reducing an oral agreement to writing, people might naturally be expected to cover
more details and refine their agreement in more
precise terms. By requiring a writing, those agreements intended to be binding are distinguished
from those which were intended as tentative or
exploratory expressions of intention.

What purpose or function the statute of frauds is
designed to serve is a significant inquiry when an
attempt is made to formulate rules permitting its
avoidance.

§ 73. Contracts Within the Statute of Frauds

While all common law jurisdictions in the United States have adopted writing requirements roughly paralleling the original statutory enactments, the details of the coverage varies from state to state. Most states have also adopted a substantial number of additional writing requirements. These tend to be scattered in many different statutes relating to varied subject matter running from government contracts to consumer protection statutes.

An example of one state's basic statute of frauds section is found in section 1624 of the California Civil Code which includes:

(1) An agreement that by its terms is not to be performed within a year from the making thereof;

(2) A special promise to answer for the debt, default or miscarriage of another . . .;

(3) An agreement made upon consideration of marriage, other than a mutual promise to marry;

(4) An agreement for the leasing for a longer period than one year, or for the sale of real property, or of an interest therein; and such agreement, if made by an agent of the party sought to be charged, is invalid, unless the authority of the agent is in writing, subscribed by the party sought to be charged;

(5) An agreement authorizing or employing an agent, or broker, or any other person to purchase or sell real estate or to lease real estate for a longer period of one year, . . . for compensation or a commission;

(6) An agreement which by its terms is not to be performed during the lifetime of the promisor, or an agreement to devise or bequeath any property, or to make any provision for any person by will;

(7) An agreement by a purchaser of real property to pay an indebtedness secured by a mortgage or deed of trust upon the property purchased, unless assumption of said indebtedness by the purchaser is specifically provided for in the conveyance of such property.

To this list must be added the writing requirements from the U.C.C. which include:

1. A contract for the sale of goods for the price of $500 or more (sec. 2–201);

2. A contract for the sale of securities (sec. 8–319);

3. A contract for other personal property to the extent of enforcement by way of action or defense beyond $5,000 (sec. 1–206); and

4. An agreement which creates or retains a security interest in personal property, timber to be cut, or fixtures which are not in the possession of the creditor [sec. 9–203(1)(a)].

In addition, different states have additional classifications of agreements which are the subject of writing requirements which may include:

1. An agreement by which a principal appoints an agent to execute a contract which is itself within a provision of the statute of frauds (a so-called "equal dignities" rule);

2. Promises to pay debts, the enforcement of which was barred by the statute of limitations;

3. Promises to pay debts discharged in bankruptcy;

4. Numerous types of consumer transactions including sales warranties, contracts for vehicle repairs, detailed data relating to loans and other consumer transactions; and

5. Specific writing requirements in some states in particular areas of law relating to everything from contractors' bids on government construction projects to offers to purchase nuts from persons engaged in the production of nuts.

Once one has assembled a list of contracts within the statute of frauds writing requirement, it is necessary to explore what specific interpretations or exceptions have been judicially developed in determining the applicability of specific provisions.

§ 74. A Contract That, by Its Terms, Cannot Be Performed Within One Year

The one year period referred to in this section begins to run from the time of the making of the agreement, not from the date performance is scheduled to begin.

If A enters into an oral contract on June 1 to work for X for one year commencing July 1, the contract is unenforceable. If performance were to begin immediately, the contract would be enforceable.

The true test is whether the contract by its terms can possibly be performed within one year. Most courts ask simply whether the terms of the contract preclude performance within one year. The statute does not preclude enforcement of an oral contract to build the Empire State Building or the Grand Coulee Dam unless the express terms of the contract preclude completion of performance within one year. Suppose X Co. orally agrees to insure A's house against loss by fire for three years. A court could find that the contract is capable of performance within one year since the house may burn tomorrow. Likewise, an agreement to pay an annuity for life is capable of performance within one year since the promisee may die at any time. However, a contract to support a sixteen year old minor until the attainment of age twenty-one is within the statute of frauds since full performance cannot be had unless the minor lives five more years. An early death by the minor would merely constitute a discharge of performance. Tantalizing questions arise where the promise is to support the sixteen year old for life or until age twenty-one, whichever is shorter.

§ 75. A Promise to Discharge the Duty of Another; Exceptions Thereto

The statute of frauds writing requirement applies to a promise made by a surety or guarantor to a creditor or obligee to pay the debt or perform the obligation of the principal debtor or obligor if the creditor has reason to know of the surety relationship. In many jurisdictions a similar statute of frauds requirement protects executors or other personal representatives who promise to pay out of their own funds the obligations of the estate which they represent.

In order for there to exist a "promise to pay the debt of another," there must be a principal debtor who is primarily liable. If R says to E, the owner of a shoe store, "Sell a pair of shoes to X, and I will pay you," there is no writing requirement. The promise of R is the primary promise, not a guarantee of any obligation of another. If R said to E, "Sell X a pair of shoes, and if he does not pay you, I will," the promise of R is collateral to the primary liability of the principal debtor, X. R is a surety or guarantor, and his promise is within the statute of frauds.

The writing requirement does not apply to the promise to pay the debt of another where the promisor's main purpose is to obtain an immediate and direct economic benefit or advantage for himself. Assume that X, a contractor, has a substantial obligation owing to Lumber Co. (L) for prior purchases and that L denies further credit to X.

To hasten completion of his home that X is building, Homeowner (HO) phones L requesting that X be given additional credit and promising to guarantee X's obligations. This promise is not within the statute of frauds because HO's main purpose is to obtain a direct economic benefit for himself.

The writing requirement of the statute of frauds does not apply to a promise to pay the debt of another where the promisor is promising to pay with funds which belong to the debtor or funds which the promisor holds for the purpose of paying the debtor's obligations.

If the creditor accepts a promise in satisfaction of the previously existing obligation of a third party, this does not involve a suretyship arrangement and is not within the statute of frauds. Thus, if the new owner of a business promises to pay the rent in exchange for the landlord agreeing to release the former tenant from his remaining obligations, this is not within the statute of frauds. It is a novation and not a suretyship agreement. (See § 183, *infra*.)

§ 76. A Contract in Consideration of Marriage

Contractual promises made in consideration of marriage, other than mutual promises to marry, must be in writing. Hence, A's oral promise to marry B need not be in writing, whereas D's promise to pay $50,000 to A if A marries B is within the statute.

§ 77. A Contract for the Sale of an Interest in Realty

The critical element of this section is the analysis of what does and does not constitute an "interest in real property." Promises to sell legal or equitable interests in real property are within the statute. However, the following are not within the statute. (1) An agreement to share profits from the sale of real property; (2) A partnership agreement to deal in real property; (3) Agreements settling boundary disputes which have been implemented by marking or use of the land; (4) A promise to sell cultivated crops annually; (5) A license, even though irrevocable because of improvements. A determination must be made as to whether an interest is a profit, a license or an easement, for all but the license fall within the statute.

§ 78. An Oral One-Year Lease

Most jurisdictions include within the statute of frauds leases of an interest in land with a duration of more than one year. Assume that L and T enter into an oral contract for a one-year lease to commence on the first day of the following month. This contract does not involve an interest in real property of more than one year's duration, but it is a contract that is not capable of being performed within one year of the day of making. Some jurisdictions, probably the majority, hold that the dominant nature of the agreement is an interest in land, and since it does not come within the statute of frauds as an interest lasting beyond one year, there is no writing requirement. Other jurisdictions, e.g. California, hold that since the contract cannot be performed within one year, it comes within a section of the statute and a writing is required.

§ 79. A Contract That Cannot Be Performed During the Lifetime of the Promisor

This provision is included in the statute of frauds in a minority of jurisdictions. It provides the estate of a decedent with some measure of protection against oral claims. For example, if R orally promises to pay E $5,000 if E attends R's funeral, the statute requires a writing since R's duty to perform will not arise until after his death. Note that in these jurisdictions, a contract to devise realty receives double coverage under the statute, since it is both a contract to transfer an interest in realty as well as a contract which, by its terms, cannot be performed during the lifetime of the promisor.

B. SATISFACTION OF THE WRITING REQUIREMENT

§ 80. Sufficiency of the Written Memo

Restatement, Second, section 131 provides:

Sec. 131. General Requisites of a Memorandum

Unless additional requirements are prescribed by the particular statute, a contract within the

Statute of Frauds is enforceable if it is evidenced by any writing, signed by or on behalf of the party to be charged, which

(a) reasonably identifies the subject matter of the contract,

(b) is sufficient to indicate that a contract with respect thereto has been made between the parties or offered by the signer to the other party, and

(c) states with reasonable certainty the essential terms of the unperformed promises in the contract.

U.C.C. section 2–201 requires only that the writing be sufficient to indicate that a contract for sale has been made between the parties but it limits enforcement to the quantity shown in the writing and thus, a quantity term must be included.

The writing need not be a single document, but may consist of several writings including unsigned writings which are clearly referable to those which are signed. The writings need not be made for the purpose of memorializing the contract and need never have been delivered to or come into the possession of the party who is seeking to enforce the contract. The writing need not be made at the time the contract is consummated. An intra-company memorandum to the production department advising of a contract with X for 100 widgets could serve as a writing sufficient to satisfy the statute.

Oral testimony can be used to establish the existence of a lost writing which satisfies the statute of frauds. This enforcement of contracts where the writing cannot be produced clearly derogates from the evidentiary function of the statute.

§ 81. The Signature

A signature may include any symbol executed or adopted by a party with present intention to authenticate a writing. This could include letterhead stationery or a firm logo on a purchase order. Since "writing" is defined in U.C.C. section 1–201(39) to include "printing, typewriting or any other intentional reduction to tangible form," it would appear that dictating the terms of a contract onto a tape could constitute a writing. If self-identification by name and the use of voice print for identification can be found to satisfy the signature requirement, a signed writing can be found to result.

The writing need only be signed by the party to be charged. The fact that only one party is bound does not preclude enforcement. The U.C.C. provides that between merchants, failure to object within ten days to the contents of a written memo which is good as against the sender makes the memo good as against the recipient even though he does not actually sign it (section 2–201(2)).

C. AVOIDANCE OF THE WRITING REQUIREMENT

§ 82. Effect of Part Performance; Sale of Goods

The statute of frauds does not prevent enforcement of contracts for the sale of goods to the extent that payment has been made and accepted or the goods have been received and accepted. Pre-U.C.C. statutes provided that part performance made the entire contract enforceable, but the U.C.C. makes the contract enforceable only to the extent that performance has been tendered and accepted.

The U.C.C. also provides that the writing requirement does not preclude enforcement of a contract for specially manufactured goods not readily resalable in the ordinary course of the seller's business, once the seller has made a substantial beginning on their manufacture or commitments for their procurement [2–201(3)(a)]. The party seeking to enforce the contract must establish circumstances reasonably indicating that the goods were intended for the buyer.

§ 83. Effect of Part Performance; Real Property

Failure to comply with the statute of frauds will not preclude enforcement of a contract for the sale of land where there has been a change of possession referable to the sale and the buyer has made permanent improvements on the real property. This is referred to as "part performance" despite the fact that the critical element, making improvements, is not really part of the performance called for in the contract. Some jurisdictions will accept part performance in lieu of the required writing where the buyer has made rather minor improvements or paid a portion of the purchase price in addition to taking possession. Case law in different states varies widely as to what acts of part performance are sufficient to make an oral contract for an interest in real property enforceable.

§ 84. Full Performance; One-Year Provision

Part performance does not make enforceable an oral contract which cannot by its terms be performed within one year. However, once one party has completed full performance, the one-year provision does not prevent enforcement of the return promise.

If a transaction involves an offer for a unilateral contract to be accepted by performance of an act that will take more than one year, the one-year statute of frauds provision is generally held not to be applicable. If one adopts the theory that the unilateral contract is not formed until performance is completed, then the contract is not incapable of being performed within one year from the time of its making.

§ 85. Reliance as a Basis for Avoiding the Statute of Frauds

A well established line of cases has permitted enforcement of oral contracts within the statute of frauds where the party seeking enforcement has changed position to his detriment in reliance upon some representation by the party against whom enforcement is sought. These cases ordinarily indicate that the party who would assert the statute of frauds as a defense is estopped from doing so because of the representation which he made and upon which the other party reasonably relied. Estoppel has been found where there was reliance on a representation that a writing will be executed; that a writing has been executed; that the statute of frauds will not be asserted as a defense or that the statute of frauds is not applicable to the transaction in question. The ultimate question is whether an estoppel arises if the other party simply relied upon the making of the oral contract itself.

The Restatement, Second, provides:

Sec. 139. Enforcement by Virtue of Action in Reliance

(1) A promise which the promisor should reasonably expect to induce action or forbearance on the part of the promisee or a third person and which does induce the action or forbearance is enforceable notwithstanding the Statute of Frauds if injustice can be avoided only by en-

forcement of the promise. The remedy granted for breach is to be limited as justice requires.

(2) In determining whether injustice can be avoided only by enforcement of the promise, the following circumstances are significant:

(a) the availability and adequacy of other remedies, particularly cancellation and restitution;

(b) the definite and substantial character of the action or forbearance in relation to the remedy sought;

(c) the extent to which the action or forbearance corroborates evidence of the making and terms of the promise, or the making and terms are otherwise established by clear and convincing evidence;

(d) the reasonableness of the action or forbearance;

(e) the extent to which the action or forbearance was foreseeable by the promisor.

Except for one word which does not appear to be of consequence, subsection (1) restates the elements of Restatement, Second, section 90(1). (See § 69, *supra*.) The comments state: "Like Section 90 this section states a flexible principle, but the requirement of consideration is more easily displaced than the requirement of the writing." Referring to subsection (2), the comment states: "Each factor relates either to the extent to which reliance furnishes a compelling substantive basis for relief in addition to the expectations created by the promise or to the extent to which the circumstances satisfy the evidentiary purpose of the Statute and fulfill any cautionary, deterrent and channeling functions it may serve."

Analysis of existing case law indicates that most courts have been unwilling to find that a party is estopped from asserting the statute of frauds as a defense where the other relied upon nothing more than the existence of the oral contract. The apparent cause of the courts' reluctance to accept this position is that it may be viewed as a virtual judicial repeal of the statute of frauds as a defense. Most estoppel cases purport to be based on reliance upon some additional statement or promise as discussed at the start of this section.

One can make a credible argument that in all of these estoppel cases, the person who changes position in reliance is in fact relying upon the oral contract itself rather than some ancillary promise or representation relating to a writing. The Restatement, Second, now provides authority for courts to recognize such reliance on the oral contract as sufficient to preclude a statute of frauds defense. There appears to be a small but growing body of case law that takes this position.

§ 86. Effectiveness of the Unenforceable Oral Agreement

While many state statutes describe the contract which is not in a signed writing as being "void", such contracts have considerable legal force. Only a party to a contract or his successor in interest can assert the statute of frauds to challenge the enforceability of the contract. Thus an oral contract to buy a house can give the buyer an insurable interest which the insurance company cannot challenge on the basis of the statute of frauds. The tort of interference with contractual relationships can exist despite the fact the contract is oral. The existence of an unenforceable oral agreement may be introduced into evidence in any action for purposes other than its enforcement.

§ 87. Enforcement of Admitted Oral Contracts Under the U.C.C.

The U.C.C. provides that a party who admits the making of an oral contract cannot rely upon a statute of frauds defense. Section 2–201(3)(b) provides:

(3) A contract which does not satisfy the requirements of subsection (1) but which is valid in other respects is enforceable . . .

(b) if the party against whom enforcement is sought admits in his pleading, testimony or otherwise in court that a contract for sale was made, but the contract is not enforceable under this provision beyond the quantity of goods admitted . . ..

When you have completed your study of this chapter, you may wish to analyze questions 18–22 at the end of this book and compare your analysis with the one given there.

V. CONTRACT INTERPRETATION

A. GENERAL INTERPRETATION PROBLEMS

§ 88. Basic Considerations; Whose Meaning

One purpose of contract law is to protect the reasonable expectations of persons who have become parties to a bargain. This may be referred to as the expectation interest. A second purpose is to compensate people for damages resulting from reasonable reliance upon the promise of another. This may be referred to as the reliance interest. In order to determine such things as the reasonable expectations of a party or the reasonableness of reliance, it is necessary to interpret the communications which have passed between the parties.

A fundamental question which should be resolved before one attempts to interpret the terms of a contract is: Whose meaning should prevail? Consider the following hypothetical.

M sold his dairy farm which had a barn on it. M bought a new farm with an old dilapidated barn. M sent a letter to X offering $1,000 "if you will tear down my old barn." Not knowing of the sale of the dairy farm, X tore down the barn on that property while the new owner was at church. Litigation follows between M and X, and the court faces the task of interpreting M's communication.

It is not uncommon to find a court stating that it will apply the "plain meaning" rule to interpret M's letter. There is nothing wrong with "plain meaning" and it may be a satisfactory answer to interpretation questions in some cases, but the problem may be more difficult than this expression indicates. Does the court look to general usage of language in the nation or the particular locality? Should consideration be given to meanings attached to words by people in a particular occupation, religion or ethnic group? Which meaning should be used if M and X are not members of the same group? Should this question be resolved on the basis of which party had superior knowledge, making him aware of the meaning that the other might attach?

If one is seeking a standard that relates to the reasonable expectations of the parties, should one not look for the meaning that the person to whom the manifestations are addressed might reasonably give to them? Should one ask what X reasonably understood M's letter to mean? X's reasonable understanding will take into consideration matters of which X is aware. Is it fair to hold M to that standard, or should we inquire as to the meaning which the party employing the words (M) should reasonably have understood that they would convey to the other party? M's reasonable understanding will take into consideration matters of which M understood X to be aware. This may be different from what X actually did know or should know.

With some oversimplification, it has been stated that Williston and the Restatement, First, sought to apply an objective standard as the first step in contract interpretation. Thus Williston might have focused upon M and asked what meaning the party making the manifestation should reasonably have expected the other party to place upon it. (Focusing upon X and asking what a reasonable person in X's shoes would have interpreted M's letter to mean is also a utilization of an objective standard.) Using this approach, it is theoretically possible to find a contract with terms different from what M intended to say and different from what X intended to accept since Williston was not concerned with the subjective understanding of either party at this point. This possibility of finding contract terms which neither party subjectively wanted has been a great source of criticism of the objective theory, but Williston thought it a small price to pay for the certainty and predictability of an objective standard. Use of an objective standard also permits the court, rather than the jury, to interpret contract writings. This is designed to reduce the uncertainty in contract interpretation.

Since Williston's approach placed primary concern upon what reasonable persons should have expected or understood, it was essential for his scheme that rules of construction be utilized to determine this "legal" meaning of the parties' communications. Thus Restatement, First, section 230 provides:

> The standard of interpretation of an integration, except where it produces an ambiguous result, or is excluded by a rule of law establishing a definite meaning, is the meaning that would be attached to the integration by a reasonably intelligent person acquainted with all operative usages and knowing all the circumstances prior to and contemporaneous with the making of the integration, other than oral statements by the parties of what they intended it to mean.

To help resolve the questions which one would encounter interpreting section 230, the Restatement, First, also included the so-called "primary rules of construction" found in section 235 which provides:

> The following rules aid the application of the standards stated in Secs. 230, 233.
>
> (a) The ordinary meaning of language throughout the country is given to words unless circumstances show that a different meaning is applicable.
>
> (b) Technical terms and words of art are given their technical meaning unless the context or a usage which is applicable indicates a different meaning.

(c) A writing is interpreted as a whole and all writings forming part of the same transaction are interpreted together.

(d) All circumstances accompanying the transaction may be taken into consideration, subject in case of integrations to the qualifications stated in Sec. 230.

(e) If the conduct of the parties subsequent to a manifestation of intention indicates that all the parties placed a particular interpretation upon it, that meaning is adopted if a reasonable person could attach it to the manifestation.

Where the meaning to be given to an agreement or to acts relating to the formation of an agreement remains uncertain after the application of the standards of interpretation stated in sections 230, 233, with the aid of rules stated in section 235, then section 236 is applicable:

(a) An interpretation which gives a reasonable, lawful and effective meaning to all manifestations of intention is preferred to an interpretation which leaves a part of such manifestations unreasonable, unlawful or of no effect.

(b) The principal apparent purpose of the parties is given great weight in determining the meaning to be given to manifestations of intention or to any part thereof.

(c) Where there is an inconsistency between general provisions and specific provisions, the specific provisions ordinarily qualify the meaning of the general provisions.

(d) Where words or other manifestations of intention bear more than one reasonable meaning an interpretation is preferred which operates more strongly against the party from whom they proceed, unless their use by him is prescribed by law.

(e) Where written provisions are inconsistent with printed provisions, an interpretation is preferred which gives effect to the written provisions.

(f) Where a public interest is affected an interpretation is preferred which favors the public.

Utilizing standards of interpretation such as these diminishes the incidents in which one will conclude that terms are ambiguous. Where ambiguity was found, Williston turned to a subjective approach. He directed that courts inquire whether one party knew or had reason to know of the ambiguity and the other did not. If so, the contract would be interpreted in accordance with the meaning given to it by the latter party. (This approach would presumably resolve the question as to which barn M and X contracted to demolish.) Where neither party knew or had reason to know or where both knew or had reason to know of the ambiguity, then a contract was created only if both attached the same meaning to the terms employed. This meaning would naturally prevail.

In summary, one can say that the approach advocated by Williston and incorporated into the Restatement, First, used every available step to interpret the contract terms without resort to the actual subjective meaning that the parties attached to the terms. Only when these steps failed to provide an interpretation would one turn to inquiring as to the subjective meaning or understanding of the parties. This approach has the virtue of being efficient and lends itself to greater certainty in the interpretation of written documents. The meaning of documents will be determined by the judge utilizing established legal rules of construction. The obvious criticism is that when the system works in its intended fashion, it ignores the actual intentions or understandings of the parties. It also effectively removes most questions of interpretation of documents from the province of the jury, which is one method by which it promotes certainty.

Corbin's approach and that adopted by the Restatement, Second, has some basic differences from that advanced by Williston. With a bit of oversimplification, one can say that the first step in Corbin's approach is to determine what the parties subjectively intended. This requires inquiring into their subjective meaning or understanding and could be a factual question for the jury to resolve. Where both had the same subjective intent, that becomes the proper interpretation. Where one party (X) knew of the subjective intent of the other

(Y) and Y did not know of the subjective intent of X, then Y's subjective meaning would control. If subjective intent fails to establish an interpretation of the contract, then Corbin would turn to objective standards to determine the proper interpretation. This approach has the virtue of placing the initial focus upon finding what the parties actually intended and thus permitting enforcement of a contract that reflects their true expectations. In achieving that end, certainty and efficiency are sacrificed to some degree.

Corbin's views on this and other subjects tend to be complex, but his writings are quite lucid and thoughtful. Students should indulge themselves in the luxury of reading some of his works.

Restatement, Second, sections 201, 202 and 203 may be a reasonably accurate reflection of Corbin's views in this area. Section 201 provides:

(1) Where the parties have attached the same meaning to a promise or agreement or a term thereof, it is interpreted in accordance with that meaning.

(2) Where the parties have attached different meanings to a promise or agreement or a term thereof, it is interpreted in accordance with the meaning attached by one of them if at the time the agreement was made

(a) that party did not know of any different meaning attached by the other, and the other knew the meaning attached by the first party; or

(b)   that party had no reason to know of any different meaning attached by the other, and the other had reason to know the meaning attached by the first party.

(3) Except as stated in this Section, neither party is bound by the meaning attached by the other, even though the result may be a failure of mutual assent.

It should first be noted that section 201 makes the subjective intention of the parties the initial inquiry in contract interpretation. This would apparently involve allowing each party to testify as to what he understood the communications to mean. The jury rather than the court would be primarily involved in this process, and some lessening of predictability of results would no doubt be a price which must be borne.

Subsection (1) is a change from the objective theory of contracts although it is hard to find a case in which both parties understood and intended the same meaning but the court chose to apply an objective standard to reach a different meaning. This subsection does, however, establish subjective intention of the parties as the primary inquiry.

It would appear that most disputes as to contract interpretation will come within the provisions of subsection (2)(b) which frames the question in terms of what meaning the respective parties had reason to know the other might attach to the contract. Since this is an objective standard, it becomes essential to determine what rules or methods will be utilized to determine what each party "had reason to know."

Restatement, Second, section 202 provides:

(1) Words and other conduct are interpreted in the light of all the circumstances, and if the principal purpose of the parties is ascertainable it is given great weight.

(2) A writing is interpreted as a whole, and all writings that are part of the same transaction are interpreted together.

(3) Unless a different intention is manifested

(a) where language has a generally prevailing meaning, it is interpreted in accordance with that meaning;

(b) technical terms and words of art are given their technical meaning when used in a transaction within their technical field.

(4) Where an agreement involves repeated occasions for performance by either party with knowledge of the nature of the performance and opportunity for objection to it by the other, any course of performance accepted or acquiesced in without objection is given great weight in the interpretation of the agreement.

(5) Wherever reasonable, the manifestations of intention of the parties to a promise or agreement are interpreted as consistent with each other and with any relevant course of performance, course of dealing, or usage of trade.

Section 203 provides:

In the interpretation of a promise or agreement or a term thereof, the following standards of preference are generally applicable:

(a) an interpretation which gives a reasonable, lawful, and effective meaning to all the terms is preferred to an interpretation which leaves a part unreasonable, unlawful, or of no effect;

(b) express terms are given greater weight than course of performance, course of dealing, and usage of trade, course of performance is given greater weight than course of dealing or usage of trade, and course of dealing is given greater weight than usage of trade;

(c) specific terms and exact terms are given greater weight than general language;

(d) separately negotiated or added terms are given greater weight than standardized terms or other terms not separately negotiated.

§ 89. Interpretation Against Drafter; Adhesion Contracts

It is often stated that in choosing among reasonable meanings, a contract will be interpreted against the interests of the party who drafted it. It is assumed that the party responsible for drafting the contract will provide for his own interests and will have reason to be conscious of uncertainties and obscure provisions. Thus there is a certain justice in interpreting the contract against the interests of that party in cases of doubt. If the drafter created an ambiguous agreement, it is reasonable to hold that party to the meaning that the other party attached to the ambiguous provisions. This rule has no application where the contract terms were the product of the joint efforts of the two parties.

Adhesion contracts are those which are drafted by one party and usually reduced to a form which is presented to the other party under circumstances in which there is no realistic opportunity to negotiate. A typical situation exists where the adhering party is dealing with an agent who possesses no authority to modify the terms of the contract form but can only say "take it or leave it."

Adhesion contracts are not per se objectionable. One could not get through the typical day if it were necessary to negotiate every transaction starting with the price of coffee, particularly where the coffee is purchased from the owner of a vending machine. However, adhesion contracts are subjected to greater judicial scrutiny than other types of contracts. Provisions such as interpretation against the interests of the draftsman certainly apply, and if unconscionable terms are present, a court may take appropriate action. (See § 119, *infra.*)

The Restatement, Second, makes the following observations about adhesion contracts in comment b to section 211:

> b. Assent to unknown terms. A party who makes regular use of a standardized form of

agreement does not ordinarily expect his customers to understand or even to read the standard terms. One of the purposes of standardization is to eliminate bargaining over details of individual transactions, and that purpose would not be served if a substantial number of customers retained counsel and reviewed the standard terms. Employees regularly using a form often have only a limited understanding of its terms and limited authority to vary them. Customers do not in fact ordinarily understand or even read the standard terms. They trust to the good faith of the party using the form and to the tacit representation that like terms are being accepted regularly by others similarly situated. But they understand that they are assenting to the terms not read or not understood, subject to such limitations as the law may impose.

The text of section 211 provides:

(1) Except as stated in Subsection (3), where a party to an agreement signs or otherwise manifests assent to a writing and has reason to believe that like writings are regularly used to embody terms of agreements of the same type, he adopts the writing as an integrated agreement with respect to the terms included in the writing.

(2) Such a writing is interpreted wherever reasonable as treating alike all those similarly situated, without regard to their knowledge or understanding of the standard terms of the writing.

(3) Where the other party has reason to believe that the party manifesting such assent would not do so if he knew that the writing contained a particular term, the term is not part of the agreement.

It is apparent that the authors of the Restatement, Second, wish to encourage courts to follow those cases which interpret adhesion contracts to contain those provisions that the reasonable person signing such a contract would anticipate. Provisions that a reasonable person would not anticipate and to which a reasonable person would not willingly agree are not considered part of the bargain. (Steven v. Fidelity & Casualty Co. (1962).)

§ 90. Usage of Trade (Custom); Course of Dealing; Course of Performance

Under such designations as "custom," "custom and usage" or "usage of the trade," common law courts have recognized the necessity of learning how people usually talk and what they usually mean by their language before one interprets their contracts. Where by trade custom two packs of shingles of a certain size are referred to as "1,000 shingles," then a contract for 4,000 shingles will be fulfilled by delivering eight bundles of the designated size even though the actual count of shingles in the eight bundles is 2,500. If the custom of the local rabbit raisers considers 100 dozen rabbits as constituting a thousand, then a contract with a price per thousand will mean that delivery of 19,200 rabbits results in payment for sixteen thousand. Special trade usages which depart from dictionary definitions are always "strange" when we first learn of them, and "obvious" when we have dealt with them for a long period of time. Anyone who has worked with lumber knows that a finished two by four is not two inches by four inches but approximately one and three-fourths inches by three and five-eighths inches.

At early common law, "trade customs" were required to exist from "time immemorial" and had to be universally observed. This is no longer the case. The U.C.C. defines "usage of trade" as "any practice or method of dealing having such regularity of observance in a place, vocation or trade as to justify an expectation that it will be observed with respect to the transaction in question." (U.C.C. section 1–205(2).) This definition reflects modern common law decisions.

Usage of trade is thus found not in the terms of the contract nor in prior discussions or dealings of the parties but rather from community practices. One basic problem is describing or defining the appropriate place, vocation or trade. If the place is Remote County in Isolated State, more usages will exist and they will be more readily proven than if the place is the entire U.S. The next burden which must be overcome to establish a usage of trade is to show the specific usage or meaning and show that it is observed with the requisite regularity. The fact that it is "usually" done that way is not enough. It must be a usage which is observed in virtually all cases except where it is expressly disavowed or altered.

An additional problem with proving usage involves the situation in which one of the parties is not a member of the trade or vocation or a resident of the place where the practice is observed. Where one party is an "outsider" and unaware of local usages, it may not be justified to expect that a usage of trade will be observed in a transaction with that person.

The U.C.C. defines "course of dealing" as "a sequence of previous conduct between the parties to a particular transaction which is fairly to be regarded as establishing a common basis of understanding for interpreting their expressions and other conduct." (U.C.C. section 1–205(1).) It might be appropriate to look upon course of dealing as the parties own private usage of trade which they have developed for themselves in their prior dealings with each other to control their transactions. Since it is thus personalized, an established course of dealing will control a usage of trade where the two are in conflict.

A third factor which can be looked to for interpretation of a contractual agreement is course of performance. The U.C.C. provides in section 2–208(1): "Where the contract for sale involves repeated occasions for performance by either party with knowledge of the nature of the performance and opportunity for objection to it by the other, any course of performance accepted or acquiesced in without objection shall be relevant to determine the meaning of the agreement." Thus "course of performance" refers to a pattern of performance of the contract which is the subject of the dispute, as contrasted to "course of dealing" which refers to the pattern of performance in prior contracts between the same parties. Section 2–208(2) provides: "The express terms of the agreement and any such course of performance, as well as any course of dealing and usage of trade, shall be construed whenever reasonable as consistent with each other; but when such construction is unreasonable, express terms shall control course of performance and course of performance shall control both course of dealing and usage of trade (Sec. 1–205)."

While the above quoted provisions are from the U.C.C., their application to general contract law is not inappropriate.

B. PAROL EVIDENCE RULE

§ 91. When the Parol Evidence Rule Applies

The parol evidence rule is applicable to contracts, wills and deeds. Because of the nature of this work, the following discussion will be limited to the application of this concept to contracts.

The term "parol evidence rule" is a misleading expression. This topic does not involve a single rule nor even a single concept. It involves questions regarding the admissibility and exclusion of written as well as "parol" evidence. It is a substantive rule of contract law and not a rule of evidence.

Parol evidence rule issues can arise where parties to a contract have reduced at least part of their agreement to a writing or writings and one party seeks to use evidence of prior agreements to add to or modify the terms of the writing. The party who wishes to exclude this extrinsic evidence will attempt to invoke the parol evidence rule to establish that the prior agreement is not, as a matter of law, part of the legally enforceable contract between the parties. Usually there is a single writing involved, but the "writing" may in fact include more than one document.

When faced with a question of interpretation of a writing or a question of the applicability of the parol evidence rule, the court must first determine whether the writing of the parties constituted a final expression of the parties' agreement at the time it was adopted. At this stage, the court is simply attempting to determine whether the writing was intended to be merely a tentative draft of their agreement or whether it was intended to be an operative expression of their contract. If the writing is in fact a final expression of at least a portion of the parties' agreement, the court must next determine whether it is a partial integration or a complete integration. As the name implies, a complete integration is a writing which the court finds to have been adopted by the parties as a complete statement of the terms of their agreement.

Where the court finds that the parties have expressed their contract in a completely integrated written agreement, neither party may offer evidence of extrinsic agreements made prior to or contemporaneously with the signing of the writing for the purpose of adding to or modifying its terms.

If the writing is found to be a final expression but not a complete statement by the parties of their agreement, it is identified as a partial integration. Where the court finds that the parties have expressed their contract in a partially integrated written agreement, a party may offer evidence of extrinsic agreements made prior to or contemporaneously with the signing of the writing. This evidence of the extrinsic agreements will be limited, however, to terms that are consistent with the writing and are either supported by separate consideration or are such terms as might naturally be omitted from the writing even though the parties intended these terms to be a part of their contractual agreement. In determining what might naturally be omitted from the writing, one considers what might be expected of similarly situated parties entering into an agreement of a similar nature.

Specific observations can be made as to when a parol evidence issue is probably raised.

(1) There can be no application of the parol evidence rule unless there is a written contract. The concept is applicable only where there is a writing which the court concludes to have been intended by the parties as the final expression of their agreement or of some portion thereof.

(2) Despite the misnomer "parol," the rule applies to all evidence of extrinsic agreements made prior to the signing of the writing, whether oral or written. The rule also applies to oral statements or agreements made contemporaneously with the signing of the writing or writings. It is not difficult to justify the notion that prior agreements which were omitted from the final writing must have been omitted because they did not constitute a part of the bargain at which the parties ultimately arrived. However, statements which are made or agreements which are reached during the process of executing writings present a different issue than those made prior to the signing process. It is more difficult to justify the conclusion that agreements expressed contemporaneously with the signing of the writing were not intended to be part of the "final" agreement. Nonetheless, that is the position which the courts take with regard to contemporaneous *oral* agreements.

Contemporaneous writings are handled differently from oral agreements. It is usually possible for the court to construe two or more contemporaneous writings to be a single agreement. Thus contemporaneous writings are usually not barred by the parol evidence rule.

(3) The rule applies to use of prior or contemporaneous extrinsic agreements which are offered for the purpose of adding to or modifying the terms of the writing. The rule has no application to extrinsic evidence which is offered to prove a defense such as misrepresentation, mistake, duress, lack of capacity or undue influence, nor does it apply to extrinsic evidence offered to establish facts from which unconscionability, violation of public policy or illegality might be found. The majority of court opinions find that the rule has no application when extrinsic evidence is being offered to show that a writing which appears to be a contract was not intended to create contractual obligations or was intended to become effective as a contract only upon the happening of some contingency. The rule does not preclude use of extrinsic evidence offered for the purpose of lending meaning to contract terms (§ 137, *infra*). The use of extrinsic evidence to establish usage of trade, course of dealing or course of performance is not barred by the parol evidence rule. The reason the rule does not apply in the situations described is simply that they do not involve evidence of an extrinsic agreement offered for the purpose of adding to or modifying the terms of the writing. Course of performance, course of dealing and usage of trade are part of the parties' agreement by implication. They are

not the subject of any extrinsic agreement between the parties. (See U.C.C. section 1–201(3).)

(4) The parol evidence rule does not preclude a party to a written contract from proving the existence of a separate distinct contract between the same parties. Nothing precludes people from having two contracts with each other, and proof of the existence of a written contract does not, in itself, bar proof of another contract. However, both contracts must be sufficient in and of themselves to constitute valid enforceable contracts, e.g. the "separate agreement" must be supported by "separate" consideration. While there is case authority for the proposition that the consideration for the promise in the collateral contract could be the promisee agreeing to enter into the written contract, this is not a generally accepted principle.

Attempting to prove a separate contract when an integrated written contract exists between the parties can present other problems. If the separate contract was entered into before the execution of the integrated writing and is inconsistent with its terms, then the execution of the writing will be found to discharge the prior contract. If the subsequent contract is found to be a complete integration, it will logically be found to indicate the parties' intent to discharge all prior agreements involving subject matter within its scope.

(5) The parol evidence rule does not bar evidence which establishes the modification of a contract. Evidence of agreements made subsequent to the

signing of a written contract are not subject to the parol evidence rule. The underlying assumption of the parol evidence rule is that where the parties adopted a completely integrated writing, what was left out of the writing was not intended to be part of their total bargain. However, the parties to a contract remain free to modify it at a later time (§ 98, *infra*) and the writing could not be expected to contain modifications that were agreed upon after the writing was adopted.

(6) The parol evidence rule does not preclude proof of usage of trade, course of dealing or course of performance when offered to add a consistent additional term to a written agreement. It is generally stated that these items cannot contradict an express term of the written agreement, but they can be used to interpret the contract language and course of performance can be used to show a modification of the contract or waiver. (See U.C.C. section 2–208 and § 98, *infra*.)

§ 92. Determining the Question of Integration

As discussed in the preceding section, the court must decide whether a writing is a complete integration or only a partial integration. One item of evidence which the court must consider is the writing itself. The completeness and specificity of the writing may reasonably indicate that it is intended by the parties as a final expression of their agreement thus constituting at least a partial integration. The terms contained in the writing may further indicate that it is a full and complete or "complete and exclusive" statement of terms thus constituting a completely integrated agreement. Another item of evidence that a court may consider is the nature and terms of the prior extrinsic agreement that one of the parties seeks to prove to assist in determining whether the writing was intended to express the complete agreement between the parties.

In many jurisdictions courts apparently still follow the "face of the document" rule pursuant to which a document which appears "on its face" to be a complete integration will be held to be a complete integration. It is sometimes stated that the document is taken "by its four corners" to determine whether it appears to be a complete integration or a partial integration. The hallmark of this approach is that the court purports to make the decision as to the integration or non-integration of the writing without considering the extrinsic evidence which a party is offering nor the specific additions or modifications which a party seeks to make to the written contract.

In what would appear to be a majority of jurisdictions, questions concerning the admissibility of parol evidence cannot be resolved without going beyond the "face of the document" and considering the nature and scope of the extrinsic evidence which is being offered. The court must consider the extrinsic evidence which a party is attempting to prove as well as the contents of the writing to determine whether the writing should be found to be a complete or only a partial integration. There are differing views concerning how this decision is to be reached or how the test is to be articulated.

The Restatement, First, section 240(1)(b) provides:

(1) An oral agreement is not superseded or invalidated by a subsequent or contemporaneous integration, nor a written agreement by a subsequent integration relating to the same subject matter, if the agreement is not inconsistent with the integrated contract, and

(a) is made for separate consideration, or

(b) is such an agreement as might naturally be made as a separate agreement by parties situated as were the parties to the written contract.

This approach is stated somewhat differently in comment 3 to U.C.C. section 2–202 which provides: "If the additional terms are such that, if agreed upon, they would certainly have been included in the document in the view of the court, then evidence of their alleged making must be kept from the trier of fact."

Restatement, Second, section 209(3) provides:

(3) Where the parties reduce an agreement to a writing which in view of its completeness and specificity reasonably appears to be a complete agreement, it is taken to be an integrated agreement unless it is established by other evidence

that the writing did not constitute a final expression.

Application of these standards requires consideration of the nature of the written contract and of its terms and the proposed terms which are being offered. One must also consider the parties, the circumstances under which the writing was prepared, and such matters as whether the writing was a standard form or a hand-tailored writing.

§ 93. Merger Clauses

A writing may contain language to the effect that the writing is intended to be the complete expression of the agreement between the parties or that there are no understandings or agreements between the parties other than those contained in this writing. Such provisions in the writing indicate the parties' intent that all prior communications are "merged" into the written agreement. Many cases take the position that such a clause is conclusive as to the issue of integration and must be enforced in the absence of a showing of fraud, mistake or other personal defense which would establish that the clause did not express the parties' intent.

Some cases distinguish between merger clauses contained in writings negotiated by the parties which are ordinarily given full effect and merger clauses contained in standard form or adhesion contracts where the clause is less likely to be given literal meaning. Parol evidence issues arise with some frequency in cases where the parties used standard form contracts. These contracts usually do not lend themselves to convenient modification to include special terms to which the parties agreed, and for this reason, a court is less likely to hold a form contract to be a complete integration.

§ 94. Use of Extrinsic Evidence to Aid in the Interpretation of the Contract Language

Evidence is admissible to show the background and circumstances in which a contract was negotiated as well as such matters as the identity of the parties. Such facts can add meaning to a contract. The sale of "100 bundles" takes on meaning if one learns that buyer and seller are engaged in the business of buying and selling shingles which are sold by the bundle.

Where a court is unable by the usual methods of judicial interpretation to establish the meaning of contract language, then the contract is ambiguous. In this situation, in addition to the general evidence relating to background facts and circumstances, parties may introduce evidence of specific statements and agreements to show intended meaning of contract terms. The general application of this principle is rather narrow, however, because it is usually found to be applicable only where the court is unable to interpret the contract. Where the court is able to decide which of two available meanings is the "proper" one, the contract is plain and unambiguous, and evidence will not be admitted to assist in its interpretation.

In Pacific Gas & Electric Co. v. G.W. Thomas Drayage & Rigging Co. (1968) the California Supreme Court established the principle that evidence of an extrinsic agreement or understanding as to the meaning of contract language can be admitted to assist in the interpretation of a written contract so long as the evidence is being offered to prove a meaning to which the language of the writing is reasonably susceptible. This represents a significant expansion of the use of extrinsic evidence to prove the intended meaning of contract terms because it is not dependent upon finding the contract language ambiguous. Use of extrinsic evidence to show the parties' intended meaning is consistent with the Restatement, Second, approach to contract interpretation. (See § 88, *supra*.) If the actual meaning attached to contract language is a primary concern, then one must logically admit evidence of the parties' understanding as to the meaning of contract language.

C. GOOD FAITH AND FAIR DEALING

§ 95. Duty of Good Faith and Fair Dealing

Restatement, Second, section 205 provides: "Every contract imposes upon each party a duty of good faith and fair dealing in its performance and enforcement." U.C.C. section 1–203 provides: "Every contract or duty within this Act imposes an obligation of good faith in its performance or enforcement." Numerous common law decisions impose similar requirements.

The obligation of good faith or good faith and fair dealing as defined above arises with the creation of a contract. It becomes an implied term in all contracts. There is no general obligation of good faith or fair dealing owing prior to the making of a contract. This does not mean that there are no minimum standards applicable to the parties during contract negotiations, but the obligation of good faith and fair dealing is not generally applicable to the contract negotiation process.

The standards imposed upon parties during the negotiation process are primarily found in the law dealing with contract defenses. The law may permit the victim to avoid a contract where the victim's consent was the product of duress (§ 105, *infra*), where a party took advantage of another's trust and confidence or weakened mind (§ 104, *infra*), where one party was attempting to take advantage of the other's mistake (§ 111, *infra*), where one party misrepresented facts or failed to disclose that which he had a duty to disclose (§§ 115–118, *infra*), or where one party obtained the other's consent to an unconscionable bargain (§ 119, *infra*).

The key point to remember is that misconduct in the negotiation process is not properly handled by simply stating that the miscreant violated an obligation of good faith and fair dealing because the law does not recognize such a general obligation

during the negotiation process. Successful assertion of a legal right based upon misconduct in the
bargaining process will ordinarily require application of the law relating to some recognized contract
defense.

Where there is already an existing contract with
its attendant obligation of good faith and fair dealing, this standard of conduct can be applied to
further negotiations between the parties. The following are examples.

    1. Where the parties have an existing con-
tract, the obligation of good faith and fair dealing will apply to negotiations to modify that
contract.

    2. Where the parties have a general contract
or master agreement pursuant to which they
negotiate specific contracts such as contracts for
deliveries or shipments, there is an obligation of
good faith and fair dealing applicable to the
secondary transactions. An example would be a
dealership or franchise agreement which would
impose a duty of good faith in the negotiation of
specific orders.

    3. Where parties have reached an agreement
in principle in which they have agreed to attempt to negotiate a valid enforceable contract,
some courts have found an obligation to meet
and negotiate in good faith. For example, a
letter of intent executed by a shopping center
owner and a prospective tenant may not be sufficiently definite to enforce as a lease agreement,

but it may create an obligation to meet and attempt in good faith to negotiate a lease. Thus the landlord could be in breach of the good faith obligation if the property is rented to another without first attempting to negotiate a lease with the first prospective tenant. A limitation upon this theory is the difficulty in determining an appropriate remedy, but the aggrieved party should at least be able to recover reliance damages. (See § 130, *infra.*)

§ 96. Interpretation of the Good Faith and Fair Dealing Obligation

Section 1–201(19) of the U.C.C. defines good faith as "honesty in fact in the conduct or transaction concerned." This is a minimal standard sometimes referred to as the "pure heart and empty head" approach to good faith. It does not require reasonableness or fairness or observance of reasonable commercial standards but only honesty. This is the only U.C.C. standard that applies to transactions within that act other than sales or leases of goods. It is thus the only standard that controls such things as the conduct of a banker in dealings with customers. Many cases dealing with such questions as the proper interpretation of the good faith obligation of parties such as bankers conclude that honesty in fact is all that is required. Other cases have expanded the definition to include some measure of reasonableness despite the Code definition.

For example, assume that Depositor wrote a check for $5,000 payable to "cash." The check was stolen by a thief who presented it for payment to the bank on which it was drawn. The thief had no identification and additional facts should have indicated to a reasonable banker that something was wrong, yet the bank payed on the check and debited Depositor's account. While the bank may not have followed reasonable commercial standards, there is no indication that the bank employees were not acting honestly. Since the Code provides that good faith is defined as honesty in fact, the bank did not act in bad faith.

If a contract is governed by U.C.C. Article 2 (sale of goods) or 2A (leasing of goods), there is a higher standard of good faith that is applicable to parties who come within the code definition of "merchants." In addition to honesty, merchants are required to observe "reasonable commercial standards of fair dealing in the trade." (U.C.C. sections 2–103(1)(b) and 2A–103(3).)

Common law cases generally interpret the obligation of good faith to mean more than simple honesty in fact, however a precise definition of the term is often not attempted in court opinions. Unlike the U.C.C., the common law also provides that contracts impose an obligation of fair dealing as well as good faith. California cases describe the obligation as follows: There is an implied covenant of good faith and fair dealing in every contract that neither party will do anything which will impair the right of the other to receive the benefits of the agreement.

Comment d to section 205 of the Restatement, Second, gives these examples of bad faith: evasion of the spirit of the bargain, lack of diligence and slacking off, willful rendering of imperfect performance, abuse of a power to specify terms, and interference with or failure to cooperate in the other party's performance. Most of these examples of bad faith would constitute breaches of a contract even if no obligation of good faith were recognized. In fact, most court opinions that discuss the obligation of good faith and fair dealing involve fact situations in which a breach of contract is present and has already been identified in the court opinion. In these circumstances, discussion of bad faith does not add anything to the resolution of the contract action. However, there are some circumstances where the requirement of good faith does permit a court to find a breach where one might not otherwise readily be found. Examples of these situations will be noted in context in the chapter on performance, *infra*.

§ 97. Bad Faith as a Tort

Numerous cases have identified a tort founded upon a bad faith breach of contract. This is a rather recent development in the law that started in California in the 1950's with cases involving insurance carriers acting in bad faith in the settlement of claims involving their insureds. (See

Comunale v. Traders & General Ins. Co. (1958).) Subsequent cases in some jurisdictions have found this tort arising out of contracts involving matters such as employment and even in purely commercial contexts such as contracts between a corporation and its bank.

Most courts have exhibited a cautious approach toward finding a tort arising from bad faith breach of contract in transactions other than insurance obligations. The California Supreme Court in a closely divided case has held that the bad faith breach of an employment contract is not a tort. This decision apparently limits the tort action to bad faith breach of insurance contracts. (Foley v. Interactive Data Corp. (1988).)

When you have completed your study of this chapter, you may wish to analyze question 23 at the end of this book and compare your analysis with the one given there.

VI. CONTRACT MODIFICATION

§ 98. Common Issues Encountered in Contract Modification; Waiver Distinguished

Parties who have the capacity to make a contract have the capacity to modify a contract. The basic requirements for modification of a contract are no different from those required to create a contract. Thus there is no special law or particular rules applicable to contract modification which are different from general contract law. However, contract modifications tend to present a typical group of problems and it may be helpful to set them forth in one unified presentation.

Contract modifications may result from an express agreement (usually involving an identifiable offer and acceptance) or from an implied agreement. Where both parties incur a new legal detriment, there is usually no difficulty finding a bargain. However, in many instances, a modification is made to accommodate the needs of only one of the parties, and one may be faced with the problem that there is no consideration for the other party's promise to render a new or different performance. (See §§ 48 and 68, *supra.*)

Contract modifications are sometimes the result of threats made by one of the parties. Where such threats have been made, an issue may be presented

181

as to whether the purported modification should be found to be unenforceable as the product of duress (§ 105, *infra*) or breach of the obligation of good faith and fair dealing (§ 95, *supra*).

Written contracts frequently contain a clause which provides that all modifications must be contained in a signed writing. Some jurisdictions have sections in their statutes of frauds which require a writing to modify a written contract. Where such a requirement is present and there is no signed writing evidencing the modification, one must determine whether there is some means of enforcing an oral agreement to modify.

Where a contract modification is freely negotiated, there is every reason to assume that the parties intend to be bound by its terms and justice is not served by imposing technicalities to defeat this intention. Many court opinions evidence a conclusion that refusing to enforce an otherwise valid modification because of the absence of new detriment to one party is such a technicality. In some cases there are statutes which dispense with the requirement of consideration for a contract modification. These matters were discussed in § 68, *supra*.

If the law successfully dispenses with the requirement of consideration for a contract modification, then it becomes all the more important that the courts review carefully whether the purported agreement to modify was the result of improper threat or violation of the obligation of good faith and fair dealing. As discussed in § 106, *infra,* care must be exercised in determining what is an improper threat. A threat to breach a contract may be improper when it is made for no "good" reason other than a desire to force the other party to pay more money for the performance to which he is already entitled. The same threat may be found to be not improper where it is made by a party who has sustained increased costs or encountered unforeseen difficulties for which he seeks additional compensation to avoid serious loss or possible insolvency. Comment 2 to U.C.C. section 2–209 states in part: ". . . (M)odifications . . . must meet the test of good faith imposed by this Act. The effective use of bad faith to escape performance of the original contract terms is barred, and the extortion of a 'modification' without legitimate commercial reason is ineffective as a violation of the duty of good faith. Nor can a mere technical consideration support a modification made in bad faith. The test of 'good faith' . . . may in some situations require an objectively demonstrable reason for seeking modification. But such matters as a market shift which makes performance come to involve a loss may provide such a reason even though there is no unforeseen difficulty as would make out a legal excuse from performance. . . ."

The writing requirement may be treated differently depending upon whether it is imposed by state statute or by the terms of the existing contract. Statutes which impose a writing requirement for the modification of a written contract frequently make an express exception for executed oral agreements. In this case, the oral modification may become enforceable when performed by one side. Otherwise, compliance with or avoidance of the requirement is handled in like manner as other statute of frauds compliance problems. (See §§ 80–87, *supra.*) Where the writing requirement is imposed by the terms of the contract, the same methods of compliance or avoidance are available. In addition, it is possible to find that the parties agreed to waive the writing requirement if it is self-imposed. Such a waiver will become irrevocable when relied upon by the other party.

An attempted modification of a contract that is unenforceable because of failure to comply with a writing requirement or consideration requirement may be effective as a waiver. This result can be reached under the common law or the U.C.C. (section 2–209(5)). Waiver does not require mutual assent or consideration and waivers are not subject to any writing requirement. However, one must appreciate the limitations that the law places upon the concept of waiver.

One can waive most conditions in a contract (§ 152, *infra*). One cannot waive an essential part of the bargain, such as the return performance due. Thus, generally speaking, one cannot waive a promised performance. Likewise, one cannot waive a condition that is a fundamental part of the bargain. In a fire insurance contract, destruction of the property by fire is a condition to the insurer's liability. Such a fundamental condition cannot be waived.

Assume that X is to deliver to Y 100 tons of hay on December 1, for which Y has already paid $90 per ton. X advises Y that X can only deliver 80 tons to which Y responds, "That's OK. I'll take 80 tons." Y has waived his right to have a complete tender of the entire 100 tons (§ 159, *infra*) and will be obligated to accept 80 tons. However, Y has not waived the *promise* to deliver 100 tons, and X will be liable for breach for failure to deliver the full amount.

Assume the same facts except that X advised Y that X could not deliver until Dec. 15 and Y stated that this was OK. Y has waived the condition of prompt delivery and must accept the hay if it is tendered on December 15. Y may still recover for any damages resulting from the delay.

Assume the same facts except that Y advised X that Y needed the hay by November 20 and X stated he would deliver it by that date. If this is not an enforceable contract modification, then it is not effective to change the contract terms. Y cannot impose upon X a new duty to deliver by November 20 under the concept of waiver. Waivers involve giving up the right to insist upon full compliance with contract terms and cannot be used to impose new obligations that did not previously exist.

A further distinction between contract modification and waiver is that waivers may be revocable. Some cases, principally those dealing with contracts of insurance, state that waivers are irrevocable. Most case authority finds that waivers are revocable unless the other party has changed position in reliance. Retraction of a waiver must be accomplished in sufficient time to give the other party a reasonable opportunity to comply with the condition. To the extent that a party has changed position in reliance upon the other party's waiver, courts will find the waiver to be irrevocable or state that the waiving party is estopped from retracting the waiver.

Some decisions permit waiver of a condition after it has already failed. These cases usually involve contracts of insurance. The insurance company that continues to negotiate a settlement of a claim after the insured has failed to make a timely filing of a proof of loss will be found to have waived that condition. Ordinarily it is not possible to find a change of position in reliance upon a waiver that occurs after the event. Where a court finds a waiver in this circumstance, it is held to be irrevocable. The better analysis of this situation is that the insurance company has elected not to assert the condition precedent to its liability. Such an election is irrevocable.

If the purpose of the statute of frauds is viewed as solely evidentiary, then the thrust of this subsection will be appreciated. However, whatever cautionary, deterrent or channeling functions the statute of frauds provides are destroyed by this code provision that makes oral contracts enforceable against all honest people.

VII. DEFENSES

A. DEFENSES AFFECTING ASSENT

§ 99. Defenses Affecting Assent to Be Bound

The sections that follow deal with the subjects of capacity, undue influence, duress, mistake, and misrepresentation. Each of these matters, when present, has a direct bearing upon whether the parties in fact assented to any agreement or to what agreement they consented.

An analysis of these defenses could appropriately be included in the chapter dealing with contract formation because they impact directly upon the agreement process. However, the approach that most people use to determine the presence or absence of an enforceable contract is to consider first whether there are sufficient manifestations and conduct by the parties from which one can find apparent assent to a bargained exchange. Only when it is established that there is a plausible case for finding a contract do we turn to the matter of searching for facts which will support a defense to the contract or a basis for altering its interpretation and meaning.

The sections relating to the agreement process dealt in substantial measure with objective intent. The subject of defenses affecting that assent frequently requires analysis of the subjective intent of the parties. We are dealing here with the qualifications upon the law of contracts which permit subjective intentions to be considered in appropriate circumstances to avoid injustice which might otherwise result from an approach which considers nothing but what was objectively manifested. Most of these defenses were originally recognized in the law of equity and they have the general effect of introducing elements of basic fairness and justice that might otherwise be lacking in the law of contract formation.

Some authors have chosen to include these and other topics under headings such as "policing the bargain," and in a sense, they do serve such functions. Others have attempted to restate contract defenses under a single heading or concept such as fairness. We feel that a student will pass more exams and attorneys will win more cases if they have a grasp of each of the different defenses and can appreciate and articulate the circumstances in which courts will grant relief. This requires that one avoid generalized combined treatment of contract defenses.

§ 100. Capacity to Contract

Capacity is the legal power to do what normal adult persons have the power to do. The absence of capacity may be total, in which case a person is unable to enter into any contractual obligations, and any manifestation of intent to do so is void. A person whose property is under legal guardianship by reason of an adjudication of a mental defect is totally lacking contract capacity. While such persons may have quasi-contractual liability, they will not be liable in contract.

Lack of capacity to contract may be partial, in which case the contracts may be voidable rather than void. Rights and duties involving persons whose capacity is impaired will depend upon the nature of the transaction and the circumstances surrounding its making.

§ 101. Infants (Minors)

Most states have statutes which establish the age at which people have full capacity to contract. Persons below this age are termed "infants," and their contracts are generally held to be voidable. At early common law the age was twenty-one, but most states have lowered it to eighteen, or in some cases, nineteen. Unless the statute provides otherwise, the required age of majority is reached on the day before the birthdate in question. State statutes commonly provide for the enforcement of certain types of infants' contracts, in some cases with the requirement of prior court approval. Considerations of public policy also dictate the enforcement against infants of some types of agreements, such as a promise to support an illegitimate child.

A contract entered into by an infant may be avoided by his guardian or by the infant until he attains the age required for contracting and for a reasonable period thereafter. This disaffirmance may be made by act or declaration disclosing an unequivocal intent to repudiate. This right of an infant may be lost by failure to disaffirm within a reasonable time after reaching majority. The infant may also ratify after he attains the required age, thus making the contract no longer voidable.

Disaffirmance by the infant revests title to any property received in the party from whom the infant obtained it. If the property has been consumed or destroyed or transferred to a good faith purchaser for value, this may not result in satisfactory restitution. Some jurisdictions have required the minor to compensate the other party for the fair value of property that cannot be returned or to pay restitution for services or other benefits received.

An infant is not precluded from disaffirming his contract because he misrepresented his age, although some cases permit use of such misrepresentation as a basis for imposing a requirement of restitution. While a tort action cannot be brought against an infant if it is basically an action arising out of the breach of a contract, cases do exist in which minors are held liable for the tort of deceit arising out of misrepresentation of age.

Infants can be held liable in quasi-contract for the reasonable value of necessities furnished to them or their spouses or children. The purpose for this exception is to permit minors to obtain necessities of life which would be more difficult if they could not make an enforceable contract. The question of what constitutes necessities may depend upon whether the minor is still being supported by the parents or has been emancipated. The liability may be measured by the value of the goods provided or services rendered rather than the agreed upon contract price.

§ 102. Parties With Mental Defects or Illness

Mental defects which partially impair a person's thought processes may be a basis for contract avoidance. The law must balance the interest in protecting the mentally ill with the interest in pursuing their right and freedom to contract and the interest in protecting the rights of the other party to the bargain.

Many cases distinguish between mental conditions that impair a person's cognitive ability—the ability to understand the nature and consequences of a proposed transaction—and mental conditions which impair a person's motivation or ability to act reasonably. Where a party to a contract lacks cognitive ability or understanding, the contract may be voidable without regard to whether the other party knew or had reason to know of the mental impairment. Where a party has impaired motivational control, the contract is usually held to be voidable only if the other party knew or had reason to know of the mental impairment. There is a significant minority position which permits avoidance of the contract even where the other party had no reason to know of the mental disability if the status quo can be restored.

A person seeking to avoid a contract has the burden of proof of the requisite facts. If the contract is still executory, the appropriate remedy is rescission. If the other party to the contract was not taking advantage of an apparent mental weakness and if the contract is not otherwise unfair, the right of avoidance may be lost to the extent that the contract has already been performed.

The defense of incompetency or lack of contract capacity is often raised in conjunction with other contract defenses. To the extent that there is evidence which tends to establish an impairment of the cognitive or motivational type, this may properly be considered in determining whether relief should be granted on the grounds of mistake, misrepresentation or duress. The presence of mental impairment is of particular significance in cases involving undue influence.

§ 103. Persons Under the Influence of Drugs or Intoxicants

As previously noted, the law in this area attempts to accommodate two conflicting goals: (1) to protect reasonable expectations and provide stability in commercial transactions, and (2) to protect those who have mental impairment. When one considers these policy factors, it becomes apparent why the cases distinguish sharply between those who are voluntarily intoxicated or under the influence of drugs and those who are under medical care or are somehow involuntarily drugged or intoxicated.

Persons who voluntarily drink or take drugs to the point that they lose cognitive ability or motivational control will be permitted to avoid their contracts only where the other party knew or had reason to know of the degree of impairment. In practice, courts exhibit little sympathy for the party who claims intoxication as a defense, and contract avoidance is permitted only where it is apparent that the other party was taking advantage of an apparent incompetent.

Persons who are under medication or who are involuntarily drugged or intoxicated are treated in the same manner as persons with mental defects or illnesses (§ 102, *supra*).

§ 104. Undue Influence

Undue influence may be available as a defense where a person entered an unfair transaction induced by improper persuasion. This involves finding that the victim was prevented from exercising free choice in the transaction due to the other party taking conscious advantage of a weakened mental state.

Undue influence can be viewed as filling the niche between incapacity and duress. The victim may not be so lacking in capacity as to be able to assert a defense on that ground (§ 100, *supra*) and the misconduct of the other party may not be sufficient to establish duress (§ 105, *infra*), but the combination of the victim's weakness and the other party's conscious taking advantage of that condi-

tion is sufficient to provide a defense to the enforcement of an unfair bargain. The weakened
state of mind can result from illness, advanced age,
immaturity of youth, recent death of a spouse, use
of alcohol or drugs, or any other circumstances
that tend to deprive a person of the ability to make
sound decisions.

A common basis for asserting an undue influence
defense is breach of a fiduciary relationship. A
fiduciary relationship exists where one party occu-
pies a position of trust and confidence with respect
to the other. These are commonly found in intra-
family and in professional-client relationships, but
a fiduciary status may exist in any circumstances
in which it can be found that one party has imposed trust and confidence in another and come to
rely upon the judgment of that other person.

If a contract between fiduciaries is found to be
unfair to the dependent person, it will be set aside
on the grounds of undue influence. No additional
wrongdoing such as a conscious taking advantage
of the dependent person need be shown. Entering
an unfair bargain with the dependent person is the
only misconduct required.

§ 105. Duress; What Must Be Threatened

An apparent manifestation of assent may be
defeated and the resulting contract avoided if assent was obtained by coercion which constitutes
duress. A finding of duress requires an improper
threat of sufficient gravity to induce the other

party to manifest assent to an agreement and assent must have in fact been induced by this threat.

The threat may be express, implied or inferred from words or conduct and must communicate an intention to cause harm or loss to the other party. Many threats are quite proper. An auctioneer spends the entire auction threatening everyone in attendance that if they do not bid quickly, he will sell the goods to someone else.

Historically court opinions have stated that to constitute a basis for the defense of duress, there must be a threat to do something unlawful or wrongful. Actually, this is still the law, however many current writers express the opinion that it is too narrow a test because the circumstances in which the courts find duress today have been expanded. There has in fact been no change in the law of duress but rather the law has expanded its notions as to what conduct is wrongful and unlawful. There follows a list of some types of threats which have been held to provide a basis for a finding of duress justifying rescission of a contract. As will be noted, each item can be classified as constituting a threat to engage in wrongful or unlawful conduct.

(1) A threat to commit a criminal act which will injure the person, family or property of the victim is a basis for duress and is by definition a threat to engage in an unlawful act.

(2) A threat to commit a tortious act which will injure the person, family or property of the victim is a basis for duress and is wrongful.

(3) A threat to institute criminal action is viewed as using the criminal justice process for private gain and is criminal activity in virtually all jurisdictions.

(4) A threat to commence a civil action in circumstances where the use of the civil process of the courts would be characterized as an abuse of process is in fact a tort and thus can properly be characterized as wrongful.

(5) Threats not to engage in business dealings with the victim either by refusing to sell goods or refusing to purchase output in particular circumstances may constitute duress. Where such activity has been found to constitute duress, it was also apparently a violation of state or federal antitrust or trade laws and was thus criminal.

(6) A threats to disclose embarrassing facts to other parties or to the community is a crime commonly called blackmail.

(7) A bad faith threat not to perform a contract and intended to extract an economically unjustified modification or collateral contract from the victim will support a claim of duress. Comment 2 to U.C.C. section 2–209 states "the extortion of a 'modification' without legitimate commercial reason is ineffective as a violation of the duty of good faith." This ground for duress is one that is frequently cited as evidence that duress is not limited

to threats of conduct which are unlawful or wrongful. However, it is generally accepted that acts or
threats which constitute bad faith in the performance or enforcement of a contract are wrongful and
may in fact be treated as an intentional tort (§ 97,
supra).

(8) A threat to terminate the terminable-at-will
employment contract of the victim or some relative
or close acquaintance of the victim unless the
victim consents to some agreement not connected
with the employment contract can constitute duress. It is recognized in many cases today that an
employer may not terminate a terminable-at-will
employee for improper reasons (e.g., Sheets v. Ted-
dy's Frosted Foods, Inc. (1980)). Thus, a threat to
discharge for refusal to manifest assent to an unre-
lated transaction is very possibly a threat of a
wrongful breach of contract or a tort. As with a
bad faith refusal to perform to force assent to a
modification, this is not an exception to the requirement that duress be based upon a wrongful or
unlawful act but is an example of modern expansion of the notion of what conduct is wrongful and
unlawful.

Subtle variations of this fact situation can produce difficult cases. Assume an employer is invited to the home of his employee's mother. While
there, the employer admires an antique mantle
and offers $500 for it. After mother rejects the
proposal, the employer notes what a healthy impact upon her son's employment relationship could

be effected if she would only reconsider. When mother agrees to sell for $500, the resulting contract may be avoidable on grounds of duress. The individual facts of each case concerning the reprehensible nature of the offending party's conduct and the apparent strength of will of the party who succumbed to the threats will have a significant impact upon the outcome (§ 106, *infra*).

(9) Duress may be based upon threats that are shockingly immoral or wrongful and result in purported bargains that are unconscionable. While this type of activity is sometimes labeled "duress", it is properly a matter of unconscionability and is treated in § 119, *infra*.

The Restatement, Second, utilizes the term "improper" to characterize threats which can provide a basis for the defense of duress, and it provides in section 176(2):

(2) A threat is improper if the resulting exchange is not on fair terms, and

(a) the threatened act would harm the recipient and would not significantly benefit the party making the threat,

(b) the effectiveness of the threat in inducing the manifestation of assent is significantly increased by prior unfair dealing by the party making the threat, or

(c) what is threatened is otherwise a use of power for illegitimate ends.

§ 106. Duress; Sufficient Gravity to Induce a Manifestation of Assent

"If a party's manifestation of assent is induced by an improper threat by the other party that leaves the victim no reasonable alternative, the contract is voidable by the victim." (Restatement, Second, section 175(1).)

The degree of compulsion which must be established is highest in cases in which the threatened conduct is in the category sometimes referred to as "economic duress," such as threatened refusals to deal. Even where the threatened activity involves an obvious criminal act, it will not provide a basis for duress unless it threatens sufficient harm or damage to the victim as to justify finding that it would induce and did induce a manifestation of consent which he would not otherwise have given.

§ 107. Misrepresentation, Duress or Undue Influence by a Third Party

If a party to a contract knows or has reason to know that the other was induced to enter the contract as the result of misrepresentation, duress or undue influence committed by a third person, then the victim may avoid the contract. There is also authority for the proposition that where the other party has no reason to know of the improper conduct, the victim may still avoid the transaction unless the other party has materially relied upon the transaction or given value.

§ 108. Mistake Defined

As used in the law of contracts, the term "mistake" refers to a belief that is not in accord with the facts. It must relate to a present factual matter existing at the time the contract is made. Mistake is generally considered to be a contract defense whereby a person can avoid an otherwise valid contract. However, it can also be the basis for revising or reforming a contract with the result that the court will alter the rights and obligations of the parties. Proof of the existence of a mistake does not, in itself, afford a basis for relief from a contract or revision of the contract. It is simply the first step in establishing a right to avoid or reform a contract.

If a party contracts on Tuesday to purchase a commodity whose price declines sharply on Thursday, one might be inclined to state that the buyer made a mistake, but this is actually an error in judgment or an error in prediction. There were no facts existing on Tuesday, when the contract was made, about which either party was mistaken, and thus there can be no mistake.

A party may contract to move a pile of dirt for a certain price thinking that the pile contains 800 yards of dirt. If the pile in fact contains 1,000 yards of dirt, there was a mistake of fact. If there is in fact only 800 yards of dirt but the actual cost of moving the dirt exceeds the contract price, there is no mistake of fact but rather an error in judgment.

Assume that two people contract for the sale of a horse for $4,000 thinking the horse is sound and can win races. If the horse in fact has a broken bone in its leg, there is a mistake of fact. If the horse has no broken bones but has run its last good race and never wins again, there is no mistake of fact. The mistake is one of judgment or prediction as to what the horse will do in the future.

Early common law cases often took the position that relief could not be granted where one or both parties were operating under a mistake of law. It was often stated that everyone is presumed to know the law which may have been an appropriate assumption in days when laws were less complex than they are today. Modern cases treat a mistaken understanding of the law as a mistake of fact and thus such an error can provide the basis for relief if the other requirements are met.

The law of mistake arose in courts of equity at a time when common law courts were disposed to enforce all bargains without regard to the "equities" of the situation. Today the law of mistake is part of the general law of contracts, but it is still applied and interpreted as a matter of equity. Concepts of fault, good faith, unconscionability and general fairness can be quite relevant in determining the proper disposition of a mistake issue, and all of the general rules that have come to be accepted in this area are subject to overriding considerations of what is fair under the circumstances. In applying the law of mistake, one must keep in mind that contracts are made to be performed and that relief from contracts on grounds such as mistake is the exception.

§ 109. Mistakes That Prevent Formation of a Contract

The existence of a mistake of fact may prevent the formation of a contract. This can occur where there is a mistake as to parties or other fundamental error by one party which is known to the other. It can also occur where there is a misunderstanding as to terms which the court cannot resolve.

If an offeror intends to make an offer to X but mistakenly makes that offer to Y who is aware of the error, Y cannot accept the offer. Assume that S intended to make an offer to the State Machinery Company in Connecticut. By inadvertence, S's employee addressed the offer to the Nutmeg State Machinery Corporation, an error that is understandable because Connecticut is the Nutmeg State. The communications from S referred to prior transactions between the parties. Nutmeg had had no prior transactions with S and thus had reason to know that S was operating under a mistake of identity. There is no valid offer and Nutmeg's purported acceptance did not produce a contract. If Nutmeg had no reason to know of the error, S would be bound to a contract on the terms of the objective manifestations made to Nutmeg.

If an offeree knows that in offer is the product of a mistake, there is no offer and there can be no acceptance. Assume that there is an established market for oranges with the price ranging from $2.60 to $2.65 per box. S sends what appears to be an offer to B by wire which states that S will sell a stated quantity of oranges for $2.00 per box. In the absence of unusual facts, B would have reason to know that the purported offer contained a mistake. There is no offer and B cannot form a contract by attempting to accept.

There is no contract resulting from an exchange of communications where the parties attach a materially different meaning to their communications and neither knows nor has reason to know the meaning attached by the other. This situation can arise where the language used by the parties is ambiguous or otherwise subject to more than one meaning and the court cannot find that either party should have known of the meaning intended by the other. Assume that A offers to sell and B agrees to buy for a stated price the ship "Peerless." Unknown to either party, there are two ships named "Peerless" and each intended a different ship. Assuming that there is no basis for finding that one party should have known that the other intended a different ship, there is no contract. In the unlikely event that both parties knew or had reason to know of the ambiguity yet did not resolve the question of which ship was intended, there would likewise be no contract. (Students of contract law will encounter a "Peerless" case with facts different from this hypothetical. It is suggested that in the actual case, the court overlooked various possibilities for finding an enforceable contract.)

§ 110. Mutual Mistake

Restatement, Second, section 152 provides in part: "Where a mistake of both parties at the time a contract was made as to a basic assumption on which the contract was made has a material effect on the agreed exchange of performances, the contract is voidable by the adversely affected party unless he bears the risk of the mistake . . ." Several elements are contained in this statement and each is important.

The mistake must relate to facts that exist at the time the contract is made. Events which occur later may provide a basis for avoiding the contract (see § 176, *infra*), but are not properly treated under the law of mistake.

The mistake must relate to a basic assumption upon which the contract was made. Earlier court opinions stated the requirement that the mistake must relate to the subject matter of the contract. Most modern cases focus upon whether the mistake goes to a basic assumption which is a more inclusive term.

Assume that in April a farmer contracts to sell for a fixed price wheat for delivery the following June after it is harvested. An error relating to the existing market price of wheat on a national exchange would likely be a mistake as to a basic assumption upon which a contract for the sale of wheat was made. An error as to the general market and harvest conditions for wheat would usually not be a basic assumption upon which the contract was made. (One might also contend that this is not an existing fact but a future projection. It might also be noted that this is a risk which has been allocated by the contract as discussed in § 177, *infra*.)

To provide a basis for relief, the mistake must have a material effect upon the agreed exchange. Mistakes as to facts that have a relatively minor impact on the transaction cannot serve as a defense or a basis for contract reformation. Merely showing that one would not have entered the contract if the true facts had been known is not necessarily enough to show materiality.

"Material effect" is a general concept not capable of precise definition. In determining whether a mistake produces an effect which is sufficiently material, a court can take into account the existing circumstances at the time the issue is raised and the nature of the relief that is sought or available. A mistake which might not be sufficiently material to avoid a contract might be sufficient to provide a basis for reforming a contract if there is a fair and equitable method to do so. If B and S negotiate for the purchase of a commercial lot on the basis of $2 per square foot and enter into a contract for $200,000 on the mistaken belief that the property contains 100,000 square feet, the fact that the property only contains 97,000 square feet might be an appropriate basis for reforming the contract by reducing the price by $6,000 even though the mistake was not sufficiently material to justify rescission of the contract.

The final element for a mutual mistake defense relates to allocation of the risk of mistake which is covered in § 112, *infra*.

The Restatement, Second gives this illustration. Assume that S, a violinist, contracts to sell and B, another violinist, contracts to buy a violin. Both believe that the violin is a Stradivarius, but in fact it is a clever imitation. The contract is voidable by B.

§ 111. Unilateral Mistake

This subject deals with a situation in which only one of the parties was mistaken. The first question one might pursue is whether the other party induced the mistake. If the non-mistaken party induced the mistake, one should explore the possibility that there is a defense of misrepresentation. (See §§ 115–118, *infra*.) If the defense of misrepresentation is not available then the party seeking relief is limited to proving unilateral mistake.

In order to obtain relief for unilateral mistake, a party must first prove all of the elements required for mutual mistake as set forth in § 110, *supra*. This includes proof that the mistake was made as to a basic assumption upon which the contract was made, that the mistake produces a material effect upon the agreed exchange, and that the mistaken party did not assume or legally bear the risk as to the mistaken fact.

In addition, to obtain relief on the basis of unilateral mistake, one must show that the other party knew or had reason to know of the mistake or that the resulting contract is unconscionable.

Unilateral mistake can arise in numerous situations, but a typical example is the case in which one party makes a mathematical miscalculation. An offer may be made to perform a task for a given price which the offeree accepts. Thereafter, the offeror discovers that there was an error in the calculation of the price and seeks to avoid the contract or have it reformed. To resolve this question, one must analyze each of the elements required for relief.

There was an error as to an existing fact at the time the contract was made. The error relates to price which would be a basic assumption upon which the contract was made. Whether the error is sufficiently material in terms of its effect upon the contract performance will depend upon the magnitude of the error in relationship to the total contract. Whether the offeror will be held to bear the risk of this error is a difficult question which is analyzed in § 112, *infra*. Finally, the party seeking relief must show either that the other party knew or had reason to know of the error or that the enforcement of the resulting contract would be unconscionable.

One must examine the specific facts of the case to determine whether the other party knew or had reason to know of the error. If the offeree had shopped prices to the point where he had knowledge of the amount that one would ordinarily expect to pay for the job in question, then he might be held to have reason to know of the fact that the offer was the product of a mistake. If he reviewed the offeror's figures and noted an error in addition, or noted that one item was omitted from the calculations, then he knew of the mistake.

It is sometimes stated that one cannot snap up an offer which he knows to be the product of a mistake. While this may be qualified to be limited to material mistakes, it is a reasonably accurate generalization. Where the offeree actually knew of the mistake, a court can be expected to be rather generous toward the mistaken party in finding the other necessary elements for a mistake defense. This whole subject is one in which the results are dictated by fairness and equity, and there is little fairness or equity in permitting the enforcement of a contract by one who knew that the offer was the product of a mistake. The basic objective of contract law of protecting the reasonable expectations of the parties does not suffer if we deny a party the benefits of a bargain which he knows to be the product of a mistake.

Where the party seeking relief for a unilateral mistake cannot prove that the other party knew or should have known of the mistake, relief will be granted only where enforcement of the contract would be unconscionable. Unconscionability is a difficult concept to define with any precision. In extreme cases, unconscionability is a defense in and of itself without proof of any mistake. (See § 119, *infra.*) Where one is seeking relief for unilateral mistake and has established the other necessary elements, a lesser level of unconscionability is ordinarily sufficient for relief. In the case of an offer that is the product of mathematical miscalculation as discussed above, courts will frequently inquire into whether performance of the contract as made will produce a net loss to the mistaken party. If the error results only in lower profit, the enforcement of the contract might be found not to be unconscionable. If the party would lose money from performance of the contract, that is usually sufficient to find that the requirement of unconscionability is fulfilled.

Cases dealing with this subject often inquire into additional factors. It is stated that relief will be more readily granted if the mistaken party discovers the error and seeks relief promptly. Court opinions sometimes inquire into the effect upon the non-mistaken party of granting relief. What additional burdens will the non-mistaken party now be required to bear if relief is granted? If performance has already begun so that simple rescission of the contract is no longer an available alternative, courts may be more reluctant to grant relief. Relief for mistake may also be denied because a third party has relied upon the transaction and would now be adversely affected by a rescission.

Assume that S, a violinist, contracts to sell and B, another violinist, contracts to buy a violin. S thinks it is a fine old instrument of unknown ancestry whereas B knows that it is a Stradivarius and thus worth far more than the contract price. The contract is voidable by S.

§ 112. Allocation of Risk of Mistake

When a party has assumed the risk of mistake with respect to the accuracy of certain facts existing at the time a contract is made, that party cannot obtain relief if those facts are incorrect. This allocation of risk is an overall control on the availability of mistake as a basis for contract relief. Thus, it is a matter that must be considered with great care.

People often enter into contracts for the purpose of shifting the risk of future events from the buyer to the seller. If a farmer is growing wheat to be harvested next June, the farmer has a risk that the price will go down before June. The farmer will profit if the price goes up before June. (Thus he bears the risk and rewards of price fluctuation.) If the farmer sells his wheat for June delivery in April for a fixed price, the buyer now bears the risk that the price may go down before June and will enjoy the benefits if the price increases. (Thus the contract has shifted the risk of price fluctuations from the seller to the buyer.)

A party may bear the risk of mistake as to certain factual matters because the contract allocated that risk to that party. In a sale of land, the contract may provide that the buyer has obtained information about the lawful use of the property and is relying completely upon his own investigation of this matter. If the buyer later seeks to avoid this contract on the grounds that the buyer was mistaken (or that both parties were mistaken) as to the zoning or the availability of a use permit for a given activity, the court might well conclude that the risk of such factual errors was allocated to the buyer in the contract.

In some construction contracts subsurface soil conditions are quite important. These contracts frequently contain provisions regarding which party has investigated these conditions. If responsibility for these matters was placed on the contractor, a court will deny relief for a later discovered mistake on the grounds that the contractor assumed this risk. Consideration must be given to the nature of the alleged mistake and the precise contract language to resolve this question.

Parties sometimes enter into contracts when they know that their knowledge of relevant facts is limited. Where these parties knowingly treat their limited knowledge as sufficient and proceed to enter into a contract, the risk of factual error will be allocated to the party who is harmed by a mistake.

Assume that Lumber Co. contracts to pay a stated sum to Landowner for the right to cut certain size logs on Blackacre. Prior to entering the contract, a representative of Lumber Co. walked across Blackacre and the parties discussed waiting until a detailed timber cruise could be performed to make a precise estimate of the quantity of timber available for cutting. However, Lumber Co. proceeded to enter into the contract without bothering to make a formal inventory of the trees. If Lumber Co. later learns that there is less timber than it assumed, no mistake defense is available. The risk that there is less (or perhaps more) timber than the parties assumed will likely be allocated to the aggrieved party.

The risk of mistake may also be allocated to a party on the grounds that it is reasonable to do so. Assume that a contractor reviews house plans and concludes that a given number of hours of labor will be required to perform the construction. The court will allocate to the contractor the risk that this calculation is erroneous. In many jurisdictions, in a construction contract risk as to unexpected subsoil conditions is allocated to the contractor as a matter of law even though the contract does not mention this matter. In a land sales contract, the risk that oil might be discovered under land after the contract is made is a risk that is allocated to the seller and no relief will be granted on the grounds of mistake.

Assume that S, a violinist, contracts to sell and B, another violinist, to buy a violin. Each knows that the instrument is old and is exceptionally good. Before concluding the contract, they discuss the fact that it could even be a Stradivarius. In fact, it is a Stradivarius. The contract should not be subject to avoidance as the seller was aware that he had limited knowledge as to the identity of the instrument but chose to treat his limited knowledge as sufficient.

Allocation of risks involves policy determinations. Assume that an injured party signs a release for all injuries, known and unknown, in exchange for a settlement of a tort claim. Despite contract language expressly allocating the risk to the injured party and despite the fact that the injured party may have been aware that he had limited knowledge at the time he signed the release, if it later develops that the injuries are far more extensive than was assumed, a court may review the facts carefully to determine as a matter of policy whether the risk of this mistake should be allocated to the victim.

§ 113. Fault in the Mistake Context

A party may be precluded from obtaining relief for mistake where the mistake occurred due to that party's fault. The mere fact that a party could have avoided the mistake had he been more careful is not sufficient to deny relief.

It is generally stated that "simple negligence" will not bar a person from relief, whereas "gross negligence" or the violation of a "positive legal duty" will bar relief. The problem with such vocabulary is that there is no workable definition of "gross" as distinguished from "simple" negligence, and such characterizations tend to patch over the uncertainty rather than providing definitive answers.

The Restatement, Second, takes the position in section 157 that fault will bar relief only where it amounts to a failure to act in good faith and in accordance with reasonable standards of fair dealing. Comment (a) contains the following:

> . . . The general duty of good faith and fair dealing, imposed under the rule stated in Section 205, extends only to the performance and enforcement of a contract and does not apply to the negotiation stage prior to the formation of the contract. See Comment c to Section 205. Therefore, a failure to act in good faith and in accordance with reasonable standards of fair dealing during pre-contractual negotiations does not amount to a breach. Nevertheless, under the rule stated in this Section, the failure bars a mistaken party from relief based on a mistake that otherwise would not have been made. During the negotiation stage each party is held to a degree of responsibility appropriate to the justifiable expectations of the other. The terms "good faith" and "fair dealing" are used, in this con-

text, in much the same sense as in Section 205 and Uniform Commercial Code Section 1–203.

So long as obvious illustrations are utilized, the "good faith" and "reasonable standards of fair dealing" tests can be applied, but they are of little help in the situation in which a party seeks relief from a "dumb, inexcusable" goof such as leaving out the cost of the roof in preparing an estimate for a construction contract. While imprecise, the "simple negligence"-"gross negligence" analysis may be as close as one can come to stating the question which the courts are attempting to resolve here. In jurisdictions which apply comparative negligence in tort cases, one may see an overt effort to compare negligence or fault in mistake cases.

§ 114. Mistake Resulting from Failure to Read

The basic rule is that one who assents to the terms of a writing is presumed to know its contents and is bound to what he would have discovered and known had he read it. With some exceptions in the area of adhesion contracts (§ 89, *supra*), this is the rule which is applied where the writing in question represents the offer and acceptance and is the only manifestation of the mutual assent of the parties. Thus, a party who signifies assent to a written proposal may not escape terms which would have been apparent had he read it.

A different problem is presented where parties have previously concluded an agreement and thereafter reduce it to written form or to a more formal writing. In this situation, a contract exists; the parties presumably know and understand its terms, and the purpose of the writing is to memorialize the agreement or reproduce it in a "cleaner" document. If the new writing does not accurately reflect the existing agreement between the parties, either can seek relief on the grounds of excusable mistake, and the failure to read or to read carefully does not necessarily bar relief.

§ 115. Misrepresentation That Prevents Formation of a Contract

No contract results when a person's purported consent is obtained by a misrepresentation that prevents the person from being aware of what he is doing. For example, a baseball player is signing autographs. A crowd of people is handing him programs and scraps of paper to sign. Someone hands the player a promissory note which he signs without any awareness of its contents. The misrepresentation can be labeled "fraud in the factum," and no legal obligation results.

These are relatively rare fact situations that are in some ways comparable to the mistake cases where no contract is formed (§ 109, *supra*). The party seeking to avoid the apparent obligation must establish that he neither knew nor had reasonable opportunity to know the nature of the document that he was signing. The apparent manifestation of consent does not result in a contract that can be avoided. It simply does not result in any contract at all.

The principal difference between an avoidable contract and no contract involves the rights which third parties may acquire. If one signs a voidable promissory note, the right to avoid it will be lost if the note is negotiable and is transferred to a holder in due course. If the note is void because of fraud in the factum, no one can acquire rights under it.

If Y acquires X's bike pursuant to a voidable contract, Y's right to recover the bike is lost if it is sold to a good faith purchaser for value. In this situation, however, X could lose his bike even if the purported contract was void. (For details, consult U.C.C. section 2–403.)

§ 116. Avoidance of Contract on Basis of Misrepresentation; Misrepresentation Defined

A misrepresentation is an assertion that is not in accord with the facts. Concealment is a form of misrepresentation. Failure to disclose is a form of assertion if there is a basis for finding a duty to disclose.

A party who seeks to avoid a contract on the grounds of misrepresentation must show that there was a misrepresentation which was either material or fraudulent and that he was induced to enter the contract as the result of reasonable or justifiable reliance upon the misrepresentation.

A misrepresentation is an assertion which is not in accord with the facts. An action which is designed to prevent or likely to prevent another from learning a fact is equivalent to an assertion that the fact does not exist. An example would be a seller painting over the water stains to hide the fact that the roof leaks. This is referred to as a concealment and requires an affirmative act or violation of a duty to disclose.

The law requires honesty but not necessarily candor. Nondisclosure does not constitute a misrepresentation unless there is some legal basis for imposing upon the party a duty to disclose the fact in question. Such a duty to disclose is recognized where there is a relationship of trust and confidence between the parties. There is a duty created by statute to disclose information in certain types of transactions. The duty also exists where disclosure is necessary to correct a previous assertion which, although not misleading when made, has become inaccurate due to a change in circumstances.

The duty to disclose may also exist where the party knows that the other party is operating under a mistake of fact, such as an error in arithmetic or an error as to the contents of a writing. While such a circumstance might give rise to a defense of mistake (§ 111, *supra*), that defense ordinarily requires a showing of materiality of the error and that the risk has not been allocated to the party claiming mistake. If basic standards of fair dealing require that the party who knew of the mistake should have disclosed it, then a defense of misrepresentation may be available to avoid the contract even though the error did not relate to a material matter. For example, a contractor who makes a minor error in calculating the price might be precluded from getting relief under the law of mistake. However, if the owner knew of the error, he would presumably be found to have a duty to disclose the mistake to the contractor. Given that duty, failure to disclose constitutes a misrepresentation which can then provide a basis for avoiding or reforming the contract.

A question regarding the duty to disclose is presented where one party knows that the other is mistaken as to a basic assumption on which that party is making the contract. For example, the first party knows about a certain fact which is material to the contract. The second party is unaware of this fact. Whether and to what extent there is a duty to disclose the true situation is a major policy question as to which courts are divided. Some require the seller to advise the buyer about such matters as the fact that there are termites in the house. Others assume that the buyer should ascertain such facts so long as the seller has not acted to conceal the defect. Where disclosure is required, it is usually a case in which one party has special knowledge or a special means of obtaining knowledge as to the facts in question. Some states have adopted statutes that impose higher duties to disclose than those recognized at common law.

A half-truth is a statement which is literally true with respect to the fact stated but which produces an implication which is false with respect to other facts. The statement: "I fed that dog just last night" is a half-truth and thus a misrepresentation if the dog was in fact so sick that it could not eat. In the absence of further disclosure to correct the false implications, such a half-truth is a misrepresentation.

The materiality or fraudulent nature of a misrepresentation and the reasonableness of the other party's reliance thereon are dealt with in the succeeding sections.

§ 117. Fraudulent Misrepresentation and Material Representations

One who seeks to utilize misrepresentation to avoid a contract must show that the misrepresentation was either material or fraudulent. Material misrepresentations can be divided into two categories. A misrepresentation is material if it would be likely to induce a reasonable person to manifest his assent to a bargain. A misrepresentation is material in a particular situation if the person who made it knew or should have known that it was likely to induce the particular person to whom it was made to manifest assent to a bargain. If a misrepresentation is material, it can provide grounds for avoiding a contract even if it was only a negligent or even an innocent misrepresentation.

In order to establish that a party's misrepresentation was fraudulent, one must prove that the misrepresentation was made with the intention of inducing the other party to rely on it and that it was made with knowledge of its falsity, or with knowledge that the party did not have the factual basis that he asserted or implied to support the assertion. In other words, the maker of the misrepresentation must know that it is false or must know that he doesn't know whether it is false or not. In matters of opinion, which are discussed in the next section, it is also sufficient if the maker of the misrepresentation believes that his assertion is false. This requirement of knowledge or belief in the inaccuracy or inadequate foundation of one's assertions is often labeled scienter. It is a required element in the tort of fraud in most jurisdictions. It is only an alternative element in the contract defense of misrepresentation and only need be established where there is inadequate evidence that the misrepresentation was material to the transaction. Since almost all decided contract cases do involve misrepresentations which are material, the question whether they were made fraudulently may not appear to be critical. However, it may have great practical significance in determining whether the finder of fact can be expected to find the reliance to have been reasonable or justified.

In contract cases involving the subject of misrepresentation, the terms "fraud" and "fraudulent" are often used rather loosely. So long as the misrepresentation was material, this imprecise usage of the term is of no great consequence. However, if materiality is not established, the requirement of scienter becomes critical if the misrepresentation is to serve as a basis for avoidance of the contract.

§ 118. Reasonableness of Reliance; Misrepresentations of Fact, Opinion, Law and Intention

A party cannot seek to avoid a contract on the basis of misrepresentation unless he relied upon it to the extent that it contributed significantly to his decision to enter into the contract. This reliance must have been to the party's detriment either in a pecuniary sense or in the sense that he has not received the bargain which he thought he was getting.

Reliance on the misrepresentation must be reasonable. What is or is not reasonable reliance is as complex as what constitutes negligent conduct in the field of torts, and all surrounding factors and circumstances in each case can be relevant. These would include the party's age, education, experience and other qualities. It would include the subject matter and nature of the transaction and the circumstances under which it is being made.

One critical factor in determining the reasonableness of the reliance is the source of the misrepresentation. One who concocts an elaborate scheme to defraud which is so bizarre that it should be obvious to any person with an ounce of common sense, will not be heard to complain that his victims should have known better than to fall into the trap he had laid. Conversely, a misrepresentation which is the product of an innocent or negligent mistake will not justify rescission of a contract where the party who relied is more at fault than the party who unintentionally misrepresented existing facts.

Reliance upon an expression of opinion presents additional considerations. Some opinions are non-factual and provide no basis for reliance; e.g., "Where we are standing on the porch of this cabin is the best view on the entire lake." This opinion is sufficiently devoid of factual basis that any reliance upon it would presumably be unreasonable. If the person to whom this statement is made is blind, however, it might be reasonable for the blind party to rely upon the opinion being honestly held. The statement of opinion is an expression of fact as to what the speaker believes it to be true. Thus, a dishonest statement is a misstatement of fact, and if the blind person is found to have reasonably relied, rescission for misrepresentation should be available.

Many expressions of opinion clearly infer that the speaker knows facts upon which the opinion is based or at least that he does not know facts which are incompatible with that opinion. The statement, "You should be able to grow good tomatoes on this ground," infers that the speaker knows that the soil is compatible with tomatoes or at least that he does not know that the ground will not grow tomatoes. As in the case of other misrepresentations, surrounding facts and circumstances will determine whether reliance upon this representation was reasonable.

An expression of opinion by one who possesses or appears to possess superior knowledge may justify reasonable reliance. This is particularly true where the parties have some relationship of trust and confidence or where other facts exist from which one might justify reliance upon such an expression. The seller who makes his living as a mechanic and who tells his sister-in-law that the car which he is selling her has a "good engine" expresses an opinion which could become the basis of justified reliance and provide grounds to rescind a contract if erroneous.

It is sometimes stated that one cannot rely on a misrepresentation as to domestic law because all persons are presumed to have equal access to the law. There are still cases which appear to take the position that reliance upon a representation as to the law is not justified. The better approach is to subject the assertion to the same inquiries as are applied to other representations. The representation may be one of fact, e.g., "I just read the new law and it states that it does not go into effect until next January." The representation may be a completely nonfactual opinion, e.g., "Now that the composition of the Supreme Court has changed, that statute will be held to be unenforceable." Reliance may be justified because the person who expressed the opinion has or appears to have superior knowledge. Misrepresentations as to matters of law are not fundamentally different from misrepresentations of fact and should be resolved in the same manner.

Statements of future intentions do not ordinarily provide a basis for reasonable reliance by the other party to a contract. It is apparent that intentions may change and the future intentions of one party are not ordinarily deemed to be of significant concern to the other, thus they are not the proper basis for reliance. The classic example of this principle and of the exception to the rule involves the buyer who misstates his intended use of the property which is the subject of the sale. Stating that he wants the property for a pasture when he plans to build an oil refinery is ordinarily not the proper basis for a misrepresentation action. However, if the seller is selling only a portion of his property and would be harmed or offended by the construction of the refinery next to his remaining holdings, then the misrepresentation by the buyer of his present intention may justify such reliance as to provide a basis for rescission of the contract.

B. DEFENSES BASED UPON POLICY

§ 119. Unconscionability as a Defense; Procedural and Substantive

The question of fairness to a bargain is frequently a relevant issue when a party asserts a defense of capacity, undue influence, duress, mistake or misrepresentation. (See §§ 99–118, *supra*.)

When one or more of these factors is present, a finding that the purported bargain is unfair to one party may be necessary to establish the right to relief. Court opinions discussing these defenses thus ordinarily also discuss unfairness and unconscionability.

In the absence of one or more of the above-mentioned defenses, courts have demonstrated a marked reluctance to deny enforcement to contracts simply because they are "unfair." It is generally deemed appropriate to leave the determination of what is and is not an appropriate bargain to the parties themselves. This reflects the notion that freedom of contract is important, and that courts should enforce agreements without passing judgment upon their substance.

Courts of equity traditionally withheld relief in the form of specific performance in the absence of an affirmative showing that the bargain was fair. Today, courts continue to require proof that the transaction was fair before specifically enforcing the obligation or enjoining its breach. Legal remedies as distinguished from equitable remedies are ordinarily granted without any inquiry into fairness. However, where the facts of a particular case are sufficiently egregious, enforcement of all or part of a contract can be denied on the grounds of unconscionability.

Prior to the adoption of the U.C.C., there were common law cases which refused to enforce a contract or a particular provision in a contract because it was too unfair or unconscionable. These cases are very few in number and the opinions do not articulate any standard beyond the vague notion that the contract shocked the conscience of the court. This general standard was incorporated into U.C.C. section 2–302 which provides:

Section 2–302. Unconscionable Contract or Clause

(1) If the court as a matter of law finds the contract or any clause of the contract to have been unconscionable at the time it was made the court may refuse to enforce the contract, or it may enforce the remainder of the contract without the unconscionable clause, or it may so limit the application of any unconscionable clause as to avoid any unconscionable result.

(2) When it is claimed or appears to the court that the contract or any clause thereof may be unconscionable the parties shall be afforded a reasonable opportunity to present evidence as to its commercial setting, purpose and effect to aid the court in making the determination.

All jurisdictions except Louisiana and California adopted this section and California later adopted a general law applicable to all contracts that contains identical language. The Restatement, Second, has adopted a provision (section 208) which parallels U.C.C. section 2–302.

This defense should not be confused with the duty of good faith which arises as a result of the making of the contract (U.C.C. section 1–203 and Restatement, Second, section 205). Good faith controls the conduct of the parties in the performance and enforcement of the contract after it is made. It is not generally applicable to the formation of the contract (cf. §§ 95 and 113, *supra*). However, some courts have identified bad faith in negotiations, indicating that its presence can fulfill the procedural element for a finding of unconscionability.

Unconscionability focuses upon the inception and not the performance of the contract. The doctrine of unconscionability was intended to prevent oppression and unfair surprise and not to relieve a party from the effect of a bad bargain. Recent decisions have provided some definitional parameters to identify what is unconscionable, distinguishing between procedural and substantive unconscionability. Procedural unconscionability has to do with how a term becomes part of a contract. It relates to factors bearing upon a party's lack of knowledge or understanding of the contract terms due to factors such as inconspicuous print, unintelligible legalistic language and a party's lack of opportunity to read a contract or ask questions concerning its terms and meanings. Illiteracy or lack of sophistication may be relevant here. Procedural unconscionability can also relate to a lack of voluntariness arising from great disparity of bargaining power which makes the stronger party's terms non-negotiable. These situations frequently involve an adhesion contract, which is simply a contract drafted by the dominant party and then presented to the other, the "adhering" party, on a take-it-or-leave-it basis. Adhesion contracts are not per se objectionable, but the presence of an adhesion contract and the attendant lack of any ability to negotiate may bear upon contract interpretation and defenses.

Substantive unconscionability is the term used to describe contracts or portions of contracts which are oppressive or overly harsh. In determining whether substantive unconscionability is present, courts have focused upon provisions which deprive one party of the benefits of the agreement or leave him without remedy for the nonperformance of the other; upon provisions which bear no reasonable relation to the business risk involved; or upon an excessively large disparity between the cost and the selling price of the subject matter of the contract. Some courts refer to contract provisions such as exculpatory clauses in terms of unconscionability, but such items are usually treated as mat-

ters of public policy or illegality which are discussed in the next section.

It is unlikely that relief will be granted on the
grounds of unconscionability unless some elements
of procedural and substantive unconscionability
are both present. So long as the contract is fair,
disparity of bargaining power, illiteracy, or other
factors relating to voluntariness of the agreement
will probably not provide a basis for avoiding the
contract terms. Conversely, almost every case that
has granted relief in a substantively unconscionable transaction has contained elements of procedural unconscionability. It is difficult to justify
relieving a party from a contract on the grounds of
fairness where none of the factors relating to procedural unconscionability are present.

It should not be assumed that this defense is
available only to those who are unsophisticated
and economically deprived. In fact, most of the
cases appearing in the appellate reports involve
contracts between business entities or other relatively sophisticated parties.

§ 120. Public Policy or Illegality as a
         Defense

The defenses discussed in §§ 99–119, *supra*, related to concerns for the protection of the promis-
or. Illegality or violation of public policy is a
defense which involves the public welfare and the
courts' reluctance to allow the judicial process to

become involved with the enforcement of certain transactions. In some cases there may be an additional motive to punish the promisee for making a bargain which is deemed antisocial even if the corollary is that the promisor will have the windfall benefit of escaping from his obligation.

In the Highwayman Case decided in 1725, a highway robber sued a fellow robber for failure to account for "partnership profits." The court dismissed the action and fined plaintiff's counsel for this scandal and impertinence. Denial of recovery was not predicated upon any notion of fairness or justice as between the parties. The concern in these cases is with protection of the court and not the defendant.

There is a general policy that freely made bargains should be recognized as valid contracts. This goal will be overriden when a court finds compelling public policy reasons to deny enforcement. The source of this public policy may be derived from case law or statutes, but not every violation of statute will create a policy concern strong enough to deny enforcement of an otherwise valid contract. Examples of terms which have been found by judicial decision to raise questions concerning enforceability include: (1) contracts requiring a performance that violates criminal laws; (2) contracts requiring a performance which is a tort; (3) contracts which involve a performance that will constitute a restraint of trade or interference with contractual relationships of another (which are also torts); (4) contracts to engage in conduct which, though not illegal, contravenes public morals; (5) contracts that impair family relationships; (6) contracts that interfere with the administration of justice; and, (7) contracts that purport to affect legal relationships in ways objectionable to the court, such as (a) agreements to be bound by the law of another jurisdiction where the apparent purpose is to avoid rules of law viewed as fundamental in the local jurisdiction, (b) agreements not to be bound by laws relating to such matters as usury or statutes of limitations or consumer protection legislation, (c) agreements not to hold a party liable for misrepresentation of fact, (d) exculpatory clauses which relieve a party from liability for harm caused by intentional or reckless conduct (§ 121, *infra*), and (e) contracts that are otherwise violative of a public duty.

Some statutes prohibit certain conduct and expressly provide that contracts made in violation of the statute are not enforceable. This is the case, for example, with some statutes which prohibit contingency contracts for lobbyists. A more complicated question arises where legislation has proscribed certain conduct with no clear indication whether violation of this legislation should preclude the enforcement of a contract. In this situation where no legislative intent is ascertainable, the court must resolve the question by analyzing whether the statute establishes a fundamental policy, violation of which should provide a basis to deny enforcement of a contract.

In determining when a violation of public policy will prevent enforcement of a contract, the courts must consider the closeness of the connection between the misconduct and the contract terms. There may be a direct connection where the contract performance itself is violative of public policy. The contract may involve no objectionable performance but have been obtained by improper methods such as by bribing an agent.

In cases in which the contract performance is not improper in itself but will further an improper purpose, it is ordinarily the case that only one party is directly involved with the intended improper activity. For example, a contract for the sale of a chemical may be legal, but difficulty arises when the person buying the chemical plans to use it to manufacture illegal drugs. The courts are concerned with the gravity of the threatened misconduct and the level of involvement of the "innocent" party. Of course, the party with the improper intent may not enforce the contract. If the other party has substantially performed, he will be permitted to enforce the contract unless he became actively involved in furthering the improper purpose or he knew of the intended use and that use involves grave social harm (Restatement, Second, section 182).

The seriousness of the violation of public policy is a factor which a court can be expected to weigh, along with the relative guilt or innocence of the parties. Minor violations and violations which resulted from ignorance or other relatively innocent conduct will ordinarily not preclude enforcement.

If a law or policy has been created to protect a class of persons of which the party seeking to enforce the promise is a member, then violation of that law or policy will not preclude enforcement. Thus wage earners can enforce contracts which were made in violation of minimum wage laws, but illegal immigrants have been denied the right to enforce contracts for wages. The minimum wage cases are examples of situations in which the parties are not in pari delicto, or not equally at fault. The employer being more at fault, could not enforce a below minimum wage contract, whereas the employee could enforce it and also recover the additional wages due under the law.

§ 121. Exculpatory Clauses

There is general agreement that a person may not enforce a contract term which would relieve him from liability for harm caused intentionally or recklessly. Exculpatory clauses that relieve a party from liability for harm caused by simple negligence are held to be unenforceable when they are asserted by an employer against an employee or by a public utility or other public service business in relationship to a harm which was caused in the course of the public utility or public service function. Thus a railroad could not use an exculpatory clause to avoid liability for negligent maintenance of its trains, but it might be able to enforce an exculpatory clause in a commercial lease of a warehouse owned by the railroad.

Exculpatory clauses have enjoyed a mixed response from the courts when used by landlords to exculpate themselves from liability to their tenants for defective premises; by amusement parks and other places of entertainment to avoid liability to patrons; and by such enterprises as horse rental concessions and golf cart concessions. Where the contract between a patient and a university research hospital relieved the hospital from vicarious liability for torts of its employees, the California Supreme Court held this contract term to be invalid, stating:

> In placing particular contracts within or without the category of those affected with a public interest, the courts have revealed a rough outline of that type of transaction in which exculpatory provisions will be held invalid. Thus the attempted but invalid exemption involves a transaction which exhibits some or all of the following characteristics. It concerns a business of a type generally thought suitable for public regulation. The party seeking exculpation is engaged in performing a service of great importance to the public, which is often a matter of practical necessity for some members of the public. The party holds himself out as willing to perform this service for any member of the public who seeks it, or at least for any member coming within cer-

tain established standards. As a result of the essential nature of the service, in the economic setting of the transaction, the party invoking exculpation possesses a decisive advantage of bargaining strength against any member of the public who seeks his services. In exercising a superior bargaining power, the party confronts the public with a standardized adhesion contract of exculpation, and makes no provision whereby a purchaser may pay additional reasonable fees and obtain protection against negligence. Finally, as a result of the transaction, the person or property of the purchaser is placed under the control of the seller, subject to the risk of carelessness by the seller or his agents. (Tunkl v. Regents of University of California (1963).)

§ 122. Violation of Licensing Requirements

Some statutes and ordinances which impose licensing requirements expressly provide that contracts made in violation of the terms of these laws are unenforceable by the party who was supposed to be licensed. Courts are bound to comply with such mandates although cases exist which demonstrate imaginative methods of providing some relief, such as permitting an unlicensed contractor to collect for the value of the materials consumed in a job for which the law denies a contract recovery.

Other license violation cases are generally divisible into two categories. Failure to possess a license which is required primarily to raise revenue is not a basis for denying enforcement of a contract made by one who does not possess that license. For example, a medical doctor who fails to obtain a city business license may still enforce a contract for professional services. Licenses which are designed primarily to protect the public by regulating access to a trade or profession are treated differently. Unlicensed persons are generally held not to be able to enforce contracts which are made in violation of the licensing statute. The attorney who is not admitted to practice law in a jurisdiction will not be able to enforce a contract for the rendition of legal services.

§ 123. Severability of Offending Provisions

If a contract is subject to being apportioned into corresponding pairs of performances which the parties apparently treated as equivalent exchanges and which are not interdependent for their value, then the contract may be treated as severable if this is consistent with the apparent intention of the parties (§ 155, *infra*). Where contract performances are severable and severance of a portion will cure the offense against public policy, the remaining portion of the contract may be enforced.

A contract may be unenforceable as written because it contravenes public policy, but a court may choose to enforce less than the entire contract, even when performances are not severable. An employment contract may contain a covenant not to compete which constitutes an unreasonable restraint of trade and is thus unenforceable. It would be anticipated that a court will still permit the employee to enforce the balance of the employment contract assuming that the employee is not guilty of wrongdoing. A more difficult question is presented if the employer seeks to enforce a part of the covenant which, standing alone, does not contravene public policy. For example, where a covenant not to compete extends to an area beyond that permitted by statute, some cases have permitted the plaintiff to restate the restriction by reducing the geographical area to which it is applicable, thereby making it valid.

§ 124. Restitution Where Public Policy Precludes Enforcement

A party who has not engaged in serious misconduct may withdraw from a transaction before the improper conduct has occurred and become entitled to restitution. Thus, one who advances money on account of a contract which is unenforceable, but not extremely shocking to the court's fundamental notions of policy and morality, may rescind the transaction before the improper purpose has been accomplished and obtain restitution of the monies paid.

Restitution is also granted in cases in which the court apparently views the question of non-enforceability as borderline. Thus relief may be granted where the party seeking restitution was unaware of the law, or where the denial of relief would result in a forfeiture disproportionate to the wrong, or where the misconduct is minor compared to that of the party against whom restitution is sought.

When you have completed your study of this chapter, you may wish to analyze questions 24–26 at the end of this book and compare your analysis with the one given there.

VIII. REMEDIES

A. REMEDIES AVAILABLE AT COMMON LAW

§ 125. An Overview of Possible Remedies for Breach of Contract

The subject of remedies is a broad topic. What follows is an introduction to some terms and concepts and a thumbnail description of when different remedies might be available. Most of these remedies relate simply to methods of calculating money damages but a few involve non-monetary relief.

EXPECTATION DAMAGES (Benefit of the bargain damages). The basic remedy for breach of contract in the Anglo-American legal system involves awarding damages to compensate the injured party for the loss of the benefits which that party would have received had the contract been performed. The formation of a valid enforceable contract creates an expectancy in each party to the contract which the law will protect. The right to the benefits that will be obtained from performance by the other party is in the nature of a property right. When the other party breaches, the victim is entitled to receive a judgment for that amount of money which will place the victim, as nearly as possible, in the position the victim would have occupied had the contract been performed.

In other words, the victim is entitled to the benefit of the bargain and should receive money damages to compensate for the loss of that benefit when the other party breaches (§ 126, *infra*).

RELIANCE DAMAGES. Where expectation damages cannot be proven or have not been proven, the non-breaching party may recover reliance damages. Reliance damages are measured by the amount of money necessary to compensate the innocent party for expenses or loss incurred in reasonable reliance upon the contract that was breached. Whereas expectation or benefit of the bargain damages are designed to place the victim in the position he would have occupied had the contract been performed, reliance damages are designed to place him in the position he was in before the contract was made. Reliance damages are designed to restore the status quo. The victim is not given any profit or benefit of the contract but is merely being made whole (§ 130, *infra*).

RESTITUTION DAMAGES. Restitution damages are designed to compel the defendant to disgorge the money value of the benefit that the defendant received from the breached contract. Thus, restitution damages are measured by the value of the benefit conferred upon the defendant. Whereas expectation damages are measured by the innocent party's loss of the benefits that would have been received had the contract been performed and reliance damages are measured by the expenses or loss incurred by the innocent party in reliance upon the contract, restitution damages focus upon the benefit conferred upon the other party.

In some cases, restitution damages and reliance damages will be the same. If X paid $500 as a down payment to Y and Y then breached the contract, in the absence of any additional facts, reliance damages (X's loss incurred in reliance) and restitution damages (Y's unjust enrichment resulting from partial performance prior to breach) will both be $500. However, frequently the expenses incurred by the innocent party and the value of the benefit enjoyed by the breaching party may be quite different. In that case, damages will be different depending upon which theory is applied.

Restitutionary damages are ordinarily awarded when there is no legally enforceable contract at the time the suit is brought. There are two typical cases: 1) The parties had a valid enforceable contract; the wrongdoer committed a material breach of that contract, and the innocent party elected to rescind the contract and sue for restitution. 2) The parties never had an enforceable contract but the plaintiff rendered performance which the defendant accepted and the defendant would be unjustly enriched if permitted to retain these benefits. (See §§ 71, *supra,* and 131, *infra.*)

STIPULATED DAMAGES (Liquidated damages). The parties to a contract may agree to a fixed sum of money or a formula for ascertaining a sum of money which will be due in the event of a breach of a certain nature. The contract may also expressly provide for certain remedies (such as the right of repair) or limitations on remedies (such as exclusion of any right to recover for consequential damages). When such contract terms are found to be valid and enforceable, the stipulated remedies will supercede whatever remedies might otherwise have been available to the innocent party. The critical question is when these agreements are valid (§ 132, *infra*).

INTEREST. Where the contract provides for interest and the sum specified does not violate local laws relating to usury, interest will be calculated in accordance with the contract terms and added to the damages awarded. Where there is no express provision in the contract, common law decisions typically allow recovery of interest from the time of the breach if the obligation in question was a "sum certain." For example, if the contract provided for the payment of $5,000 on April 1, and the defendant failed to pay this amount when due, the plaintiff is entitled to interest on $5,000 from April 1 until the date of judgment. Conversely, if the amount owing as a result of the breach of a contract is an unliquidated sum, that is, a sum that cannot be determined precisely until a court makes its findings of fact regarding damages, then most jurisdictions deny recovery of pre-judgment interest. The logic behind this rule is that when the obligation was a fixed sum of money or a sum that could be determined by mathematical calculation, the defendant should have paid it. However, if the sum is not ascertainable until it is fixed by the court, the defendant could not know how much was owing and could not be expected to have paid it. A growing number of jurisdictions have relaxed this rule and now permit the trial court to exercise discretion concerning the recovery of interest on unliquidated sums. The percentage rate of interest is usually provided by statute although some jurisdictions now permit flexibility in fixing pre-judgment interest rates.

All jurisdictions provide for interest on judgments from the time they are entered until they are paid. The percentage rate of post-judgment interest is typically fixed by statute.

PUNITIVE DAMAGES (Exemplary damages). Punitive damages are designed to punish the guilty party thereby making an example of him and discouraging similar conduct by him or other parties in the future. They are available only where the defendant is guilty of reprehensible conduct such as fraud, malice or oppression. They are not measured by the loss to the plaintiff nor the gain to the defendant but rather by the amount necessary to punish and to deter such conduct in the future. Thus calculation of the "proper" amount of punitive damages can include such matters as the wealth and income of the defendant.

In most jurisdictions, punitive damages are not available for breach of contract. However, wrongdoing in a contractual transaction might also involve the commission of a tort such as fraud in which case punitive damages might be appropriate. (See § 97, *supra*.)

SPECIFIC PERFORMANCE. Specific performance of a contract involves compelling the breaching party to complete the contract performance. In the Anglo-American legal system, common law courts could not specifically enforce a contract. Orders compelling a breaching party to perform could only be decreed by a court of equity and a court of equity would not act unless the remedy at law was inadequate. While courts of law and equity have been merged today, the requirements for obtaining specific performance have not been substantially changed. Thus specific performance is not available in most contract breaches because the money damage remedy at law is adequate to place the innocent party in the position he would have enjoyed had the contract been performed (§ 133, *infra*).

OTHER REMEDIAL RIGHTS. There are various other remedies that might be available to the innocent party when a contract is breached. As mentioned above, a material breach will permit the other party to invoke the remedy of rescinding the contract. Certain breaches by a seller will give the buyer the remedy of rejecting goods. Events which create reasonable insecurity may under the U.C.C. give rise to the remedy of being able to demand assurances of due performance by the other party. Delivery of defective goods may give rise to a right to have those goods repaired or replaced.

§ 126. Expectation Damages (Benefit of the Bargain)

When the defendant has breached a valid enforceable contract, the plaintiff is entitled to recover money damages in an amount sufficient to place the plaintiff in the position he would have been in had the contract been performed. This involves compensating the plaintiff for the dollar value of the benefits he would have received had the contract been performed less any savings that plaintiff was reasonably able to make by virtue of not having to perform his own obligations under the contract. In many cases this can be done by relatively easy calculations.

Assume Jane contracts to sell to Bob 1,000 shares of Ajax stock for $50,000. Bob breaches the contract by failing to pay after he has received the stock. Jane's loss resulting from Bob's failure to perform is $50,000. Her savings are zero as she has fully performed. Damages are $50,000.

Assume that Bob breached by repudiating the contract before Jane was to deliver the stock. Jane's loss resulting from Bob's failure to perform the contract is $50,000. Her savings are the market value of 1,000 shares of Ajax stock which she did not have to deliver due to Bob's breach. This must be reduced to a dollar figure in order to compute money damages.

Since the fair market value of all property varies from time to time, the law must fix a date for determination of that value. There are at least three logical possibilities: 1) The market value at the time when the stock was to be delivered to Bob (the time of performance). 2) The market value at the time Jane learned of Bob's breach which in this case would presumably be before the date of performance since Bob repudiated before the time of performance. 3) The price that Jane actually received when she resold the stock to someone else. This will be sometime after the breach. Assuming Jane resold in a reasonable manner and within a commercially reasonable time, the third alternative in fact is the most accurate measure of the actual damage Jane suffered due to Bob's breach. Most common law cases apply the second alternative. A few apply the first and some apply the third. If this were a transaction in goods, the U.C.C. would apply the third alternative if Jane had in fact resold the goods (section 2–706), and the first alternative if she did not resell (section 2–708). Jane's damages would thus be $50,000 minus the value of the 1,000 shares of Ajax stock, value being fixed by one of the three stated rules.

Assume that Harry contracts to build a home for Orpha for $175,000. Before Harry has done any work, Orpha breaches. Harry's damages are the dollar value of the performance he was entitled to receive which is $175,000, minus the savings that he was reasonably able to effect by not having to render his own performance. The latter figure will be established by evidence of what it would have cost Harry to build the house. If that figure were proven to be $160,000, then Harry's damages are $15,000 and that is what he should recover. (Note that Harry's "expectation" under the contract involved making a profit of $15,000 and that is exactly what he will recover.)

Assume that after Harry has partly performed and Orpha has paid $20,000 of the contract price, Orpha breaches the contract. Harry's damages will be the value of the performance he was to receive which is $155,000 (the $175,000 contract price minus $20,000 paid to date), less the dollar value of the savings that he is able to realize by virtue of not having to complete his own performance. Harry will have to produce evidence as to what his savings were. This can be quite complicated in some cases. It is not simply a matter of adding up what Harry has spent thus far and subtracting that figure from the total anticipated costs. Harry may have already rented equipment for which he has no use. He may have already contracted for specialized labor which cannot be profitably used on other jobs. Such factors will all receive proper consideration if one remembers that the figure to subtract is the actual amount that Harry was reasonably able to save by not having to complete performance. Assuming this figure proves to be $110,000, that sum should be subtracted from $155,000 and Harry's damages are $45,000.

In some situations, special facts may require some common sense modifications of the simple formula discussed above. For example, a breach of contract might leave the victim worse off than simply losing anticipated benefits of the bargain. Assume that Harry agreed to install new tile in the shower in Orpha's home for $3,000. Harry breached the contract by installing defective tiles which will now have to be removed at considerable cost. Orpha's loss includes not only the loss of the value of the tiling work (which might be proven by showing the cost of hiring another to do this work) but also the cost of removing the defective tiles. From this total figure Orpha must subtract her savings which would be whatever part of the $3,000 she had not paid.

Special facts might also establish some offsetting benefits to the injured party. If Orpha was able to resell the tiles that had to be removed for $100 scrap value, this offsetting gain which she was able to realize would have to be deducted from her recovery.

Different types of contracts create different specific problems, but the basic approach is the same. The first step is to establish the dollar value of the performance that the victim should have received but did not, the second step is to determine what deduction should be made for savings that the victim realized by not having to render her own performance.

Assume that Bill is wrongfully discharged from a one year employment contract. His damages are the wages he should have received which will not now be paid. His savings might include costs such as transportation and parking which can now be avoided because he does not have to go to work. Bill may also avoid damages by taking another job and reducing or eliminating his wage loss in that manner. What sort of employment Bill must accept and how hard he has to look for another job are matters relating to "avoidable consequences" or "mitigation of damages" which are discussed in § 129, *infra*.

Loss of the benefit of the bargain can produce other types of damages. Failure of a contractor to complete a movie theater on time will result in loss of use of the theater. Failure to deliver a machine or delivery of a defective machine may result in lost production. The basic rule is one can potentially recover for all damages that result from the breach of contract. Limitations on these types of damages are dealt with in the next sections.

§ 127. Limitations on Expectation Damages; The Requirements of Certainty and Foreseeability

Damages for breach of contract are not recoverable unless they are proven with a relatively high degree of certainty. When cases are carefully analyzed, it can be seen that courts demand evidence that clearly establishes that some damages of the nature claimed did in fact occur. Once the existence of some damage is proven with certainty, the precise amount of damages can be calculated in a reasonable fashion even though some estimation or approximation is required.

Assume that Sara and John contract to enter a partnership for the purpose of operating a restaurant. John is to be the chef and Sara the manager, and they agree to devote full time to the project for at least three years. Before the restaurant is opened, John gets a better offer and breaches his contract with Sara. Sara may be unable to recover any expectation damages or benefit of the bargain damages because the fact that such damages were suffered cannot be established with certainty. A large percentage of new restaurants lose money. It would be quite difficult for Sara to establish that the proposed restaurant would have been profitable. The frequency with which expectation damages are denied to new businesses has led some people to refer to this result as the "new business rule." There is no "rule" that a new business cannot recover expectation damages. But it does take strong facts to overcome the problem of showing damages with the necessary degree of certainty.

Assume that Sara and John operated their restaurant for one year with John serving as head chef. The business lost $2,000 during the first quarter of operation; broke even during the second quarter; made $6,000 in the third quarter, and made $9,000 during the fourth quarter. John now breaches the contract. Without its chef, the restaurant closes. Sara should be able to prove the fact of damages with certainty. Using evidence of profits and performance of other restaurants plus her own restaurant's history, she should then be able to prove a likely future profit for the remaining two years of their contract. Once the fact of lost profits has been proven with certainty, the law will permit her to recover future profits even though the precise amount of those profits is not actually certain. Sara's damage claim may be defeated or reduced if it is established that she could have replaced John with a comparable chef. (See § 129, *infra.*)

Recovery of contract damages is also limited by the concept of foreseeability. In determining what damages are within the scope of what the law deems to be foreseeable, a narrower range of foreseeability is used in contract than one finds in tort. There may be various reasons for this distinction. People select the parties with whom they contract. People enter contracts and make their decisions as to the bargain they are willing to make based in some part on the measure of risk that they are assuming in the event the contract is breached. Contracting parties may negotiate stipulated damages to be paid in the event of various types of breach. This is in sharp contrast with the usual tort case. One does not ordinarily pick one's tortfeasor nor negotiate with him. In most cases one does not embark upon an activity with conscious calculation of the exposure to liability for torts.

The standards of foreseeability in contract damages were established in the case of Hadley v. Baxendale (1854). This decision with its confused statements of facts was not rendered by a particularly distinguished court nor decided by any noted jurists, but it has had a profound impact upon the law relating to contract damages. The Hadley opinion divides contract damages into two categories: those that arise naturally in the usual course of events from the breach of a contract of the type in question, and those that arise due to special facts and circumstances existing in this particular case.

With respect to damages that are the natural and probable result of a breach of this type of contract, the breaching party could contemplate being liable for such damages when the contract was made. These damages have come to be referred to in contract law as "general" damages, and they may be recovered by the plaintiff without any further concerns as to foreseeability.

Damages which occur because of special facts and circumstances relating to the specific transaction will not be within the contemplation of the breaching party at the time the contract is made unless that person is aware of these special facts and circumstances. These damages have come to be referred to in contract law as "special" or "consequential" damages, and they may be recovered only if it is established that they were foreseeable to the breaching party at the time the contract was made.

The terms "general" and "special" damages are used with very different meaning in the law relating to pleading and in tort law. The definitions are not simply different, they are so different that they produce diametrically opposite categorization. For example, if one has already learned that pain and suffering damages are general damages and medical expenses are special damages in tort law and pleading, one must set that knowledge aside and learn a very different meaning of "general" damages and "special" or "consequential" damages for contract law. Since "special" and "consequential" have the same meaning in contract law, this confusion can at least be reduced if the term "consequential" is used in contract law.

Assume that Paul has a contract with the Government to deliver military uniforms. The contract provides for certain stipulated damages for each day of delay for late delivery. Paul contracts to pay $15,000 to Dan for delivery by a certain date of materials which Paul plans to use to make the uniforms. Thereafter, shortages of material develop in the marketplace and prices increase. Dan does not deliver. Paul uses reasonable efforts to secure another source of supply and after some delay is able to purchase replacement materials for $20,000. As a direct result of the delay, Paul becomes liable for $12,000 for late delivery of the uniforms to the Government.

Paul has two elements of damage in an action against Dan. He paid $5,000 above the contract price to obtain replacement material and he sustained a $12,000 loss due to the delay that was caused by Dan's breach. The first item is general damages. In a contract for the sale of goods, a natural and probable consequence of breach by the seller is that the buyer may have to pay more for the goods elsewhere. (There is no issue whether Dan could foresee this particular increase in price. Price changes of some sort are natural and probable.) Paul can obtain judgment for the $5,000 from Dan.

The $12,000 loss constitutes consequential damages because one must prove the special facts of Paul's particular situation to show how this loss was caused. Substantial loss on another contract is not a natural and probable result of a breach of a contract for goods. Therefore, Paul's ability to recover for this item is dependent upon showing that Dan was aware of the special facts that caused this loss at the time the Paul-Dan contract was made. Paul probably must show that Dan was aware that Paul had the contract with the Government; that this contract had a stipulated damage clause, and that delay in receipt of material would result in the inability to perform the other contract on time.

Justice Holmes devoted considerable efforts to making the law of contract damages even more restrictive. In lectures and court opinions (Globe Refining Co. v. Landa Cotton Oil Co. (1903)), Holmes advanced the "tacit agreement" test. Under the tacit agreement test, Paul could not recover the $12,000 consequential damages simply by showing that Dan was fully aware of all of the necessary facts. Paul must further show that Dan tacitly agreed to assume responsibility for consequential damages of this nature. While the twentieth century has seen concepts relating to recoverable damages in tort law steadily expanding, much effort in the field of contract damages during this century has been devoted to beating back Holmes' efforts to further restrict contract damages.

In comment 2 to section 2–715, the U.C.C. expressly rejects the tacit agreement test for the recovery of consequential damages. In common law decisions, language limiting damages to items for which the breaching party tacitly assumed responsibility is now encountered infrequently, and the tacit agreement test has probably been buried.

The distinction between general and consequential damages is important for another reason. Many contracts contain clauses expressly excusing liability for consequential damages. If this clause is legally enforceable, it requires the court to distinguish what damages are consequential and what are general.

Assume that Seller is in the business of producing and selling large computer systems for commercial application. These systems are not compatible with IBM equipment. Buyer has an existing IBM computer system. After extensive study of Buyer's business operations, Seller contracts to supply a new system for Buyer's business. The contract excludes liability for consequential damages. Seller's equipment fails to perform properly and is ultimately replaced by new IBM equipment. Buyer sues and proves damages resulting from: 1) the cost of converting the IBM records to the new system; 2) the loss of employee time while people sat idle with non-functioning machines; 3) the cost to reconvert all of the records back to IBM after the Seller's system was replaced.

A court found the second item to be general damages. In a contract for the sale of a computer system designed for commercial application, the loss of employee time resulting from the malfunctioning of the computer was viewed as a natural and probable consequence of the breach. No additional special facts need be proven to explain this loss. The first and third items were found to be consequential damages. They occurred only because of the special fact that Buyer had its existing records on IBM and went back to IBM when Seller's equipment failed. Given the facts of the case, Seller might have been liable for these consequential damages because all of the special facts were known to Seller before the contract was made. However, since the contract excluded liability for consequential damages, Buyer could not recover for these items. (See Applied Data v. Burroughs (1975).)

A breach of contract can cause emotional distress damages, but ordinarily such damages are not recoverable in a contract action because they are not foreseeable. In commercial transactions, emotional distress is not a natural and probable consequence of a breach nor does the breaching party usually know facts that would cause such damages to result. However, in specialized contracts, emotional distress might be foreseeable. A frequently cited example is a contract with a mortuary for funeral services. In fact, emotional distress is probably the only foreseeable damage resulting from breach of such a contract. One might develop a logical argument that emotional distress damages are also a foreseeable result of breach in such matters as employment contracts, but courts have demonstrated reluctance to permit recovery for this element of damage.

§ 128. Other Limitations on Expectation Damages

In many situations involving defective performance, the measure of expectation damages will involve a reduction in value of the subject matter of the contract resulting from the breach. Where a performance is incomplete rather than being completed in a defective manner, the loss in value will ordinarily be measured by the cost to complete. If a contractor builds a house but fails to install the doors, the loss of value will be measured by the cost to install doors rather than the diminished value of a house that is not habitable because it has no doors. This is a satisfactory remedy because it makes the innocent party "whole" in the sense that the damage recovery will provide an amount sufficient to complete the work called for in the contract.

Even in the case of incomplete performances, the innocent party may be denied the cost to complete where completion is viewed as economically wasteful. The classic example involves a contract in which one party is to remove material from the earth such as coal or sand and promises to restore the property to its natural grade when the removal is completed. Breach of the promise to restore may result in a situation in which the value of the property is diminished by only a small amount whereas the cost to complete the work is substantial. Assume that the property has a fair market value of $25,000 in its existing condition and would have a fair market value of $30,000 if it were restored to grade. If restoration would cost $45,000, some courts have held that the innocent party is limited to diminished value and can recover only $5,000. There is a sharp split of authority on this issue.

Another serious problem arises where the performance is defective rather than incomplete. Ordinarily, one might assume that if a performance is defective, the proper measure of damages should be the cost to correct the defect. However, if a house is built with a load-bearing wall one foot off from where it was supposed to be, the cost to correct this defect may be far greater than the diminution in market value resulting from the error. Where correction of the defect would be economically wasteful, the owner will ordinarily be limited to the diminished market value of the structure. If the defect affects the structural integrity of the building or otherwise involves safety of the occupants, then the cost to correct will be recoverable.

The innocent party may also recover the cost to correct rather than the diminished market value if the parties both understood that the contract performance involved highly personalized criteria. It is sometimes stated that anyone has the right to erect a monument to his folly. If the law school contracts for the erection of a statue of the dean in front of the school, construction of a statue that resembles John F. Kennedy rather than the dean should result in damages measured by the cost to correct even though the market value of the property might be more enhanced by Kennedy's likeness than the dean's.

Expectancy damages can also be denied where they are simply too large in relationship to the contract price. Breach of a contract to perform minor repairs on the furnace in a restaurant before a big weekend might result in very large consequential damages that were quite foreseeable. However, even though the innocent party proves substantial damages, recovery may be denied if the amount of damages is out of proportion to the contract price. Where recovery is denied, it is usually based upon the concept that liability for damages of this magnitude were not within the contemplation of the parties at the time the contract was made.

§ 129. Avoidance of Damages

One cannot recover for damages that could have been avoided with reasonable effort and without undue risk. It is thus stated that the victim of a contract breach is obligated to use reasonable efforts to protect his interests and prevent damages that could reasonably be avoided. This is frequently but inaccurately referred to as a "duty to mitigate" damages. For example, a buyer of goods cannot recover consequential damages resulting from non-delivery if there was a readily available source of substitute goods that the buyer could have purchased.

Interesting avoidance of damage issues can be presented when an employee is wrongfully discharged. The claim for damages for lost wages will be reduced by whatever wages the employee did earn or could reasonably have earned in another job. When the employee does not in fact obtain other employment, the court must determine whether the employee could reasonably have found or should reasonably have accepted another position.

In one famous case (Parker v. Twentieth Century-Fox Film Corp. (1970)), an actress (Shirley MacLaine) had contracted to perform in a musical movie in which she was to have certain artistic control. When the employer breached, she was allowed to recover her lost income even though she had refused the employer's offer to have her perform in another movie for the same salary during the same time period. The substitute movie was entitled "Big Country, Big Man." It was to be filmed in Australia, was not a musical, and MacLaine was to have no artistic control.

Generally speaking, courts will not require discharged employees to take positions that are demeaning or beneath their dignity. Courts may also consider geographic location of the new position, danger posed by the nature of the employment, competence required, impact upon future employment and career, and any other matters that bear upon the question whether this was a reasonable alternative employment for this plaintiff to have accepted.

§ 130. Reliance Damages

Reliance damages are that amount of money necessary to compensate the plaintiff for efforts expended or expenses incurred in reasonable reliance upon the contract. This measure of damages may be employed when benefit of the bargain or expectation damages are not proven.

Assume that Al contracts to build a commercial building for Mary for $190,000. Shortly after construction commences, Mary's principal tenant repudiates its lease and Mary repudiates her construction contract with Al. Of course, Al may prove anticipated costs and recover expectation of the bargain damages, but this may involve considerable effort and expense. As an alternative, Al may elect to recover reliance damages. This involves proof of all expenses reasonably incurred in preparing to perform and performing the construction work prior to the breach by Mary.

Assume that Al's estimator made serious miscalculations in preparing his figures and that the actual cost of construction of Mary's building was going to be $200,000. After Al had spent $6,000 in preparation and performance, Mary breached. Al elected to seek reliance damages of $6,000. If no evidence is introduced as to the total cost of the project, Al will recover $6,000. However, Mary may introduce evidence to prove Al's actual expectation damages which in this case are zero. (His expected benefit of the bargain was $190,000. His savings resulting from not having to complete his own performance were $194,000. Thus Mary's breach has in fact saved Al $4,000.) Since reliance damages cannot exceed expectation damages, Al cannot recover in this case.

Assume that Jane and Harry contracted to form a partnership to enter the restaurant business. After Jane had incurred expenses in the amount of $3,000 and before the restaurant was opened, Harry breached this contract. Jane may be unable to prove expectation damages because of her inability to establish the requisite certainty (§ 127, *supra*), but she can still recover her $3,000 as reliance damages.

§ 131. Restitution Damages

Restitutionary recovery is designed to force the defendant to disgorge the amount of money by which he has been unjustly enriched. The measure of damages in restitution is thus measured by the money value of the benefit that the defendant has received. It is distinguishable from reliance damages that are designed to compensate the plaintiff for the plaintiff's expenses or losses.

Restitution damages can be awarded where there is no contract to enforce. The right to recover in restitution can arise out of situations where the defendant committed a tort. Restitutionary recovery is often granted in patent infringement, copyright infringement or other intellectual property violation cases.

Restitution damages are awarded in quasi-contract cases where no actual contract exists (§ 71, *supra*). The doctor who treats the unconscious accident victim can recover in restitution despite the absence of any contract. The amount of the recovery will be the value of the benefit conferred which is measured by the ordinary fee charged in the community for the services rendered. The doctor does not recover reliance damages which would presumably be measured by the doctor's standard fee for her services. Thus if the doctor were a very high priced neurosurgeon who ordinarily received $500 per hour for her time, she would recover only the fee ordinarily charged in the community for services of the nature she rendered.

The right to restitution can arise where the parties erroneously believed they had a valid enforceable contract pursuant to which one conferred benefits upon the other. Quantum meruit is a common law term for the right to recover for the value of benefits conferred upon another. Assume that Buyer and Seller negotiated for the purchase and sale of Blackacre but did not reach an agreement sufficiently definite to be enforced. Thinking they had a valid contract, Buyer made a $20,000 down payment to Seller. Despite the absence of a contract, Buyer can recover $20,000 in restitution.

Historically a person who breached a contract after rendering part performance was denied restitution for the value of the benefits conferred. The enrichment of the other party was not deemed to be unjust because the claimant was guilty of breach. Numerous cases now permit recovery by the breaching party, particularly in employment contracts or other service contracts involving an individual rather than a large business. There is also statutory authority for permitting restitution to a breaching buyer in a transaction in goods (U.C.C. section 2–718(2)).

Assume that X and Y enter into an oral two year employment contract and X performs services for Y for one month. While the statute of frauds may prevent enforcement of the contract, X can still recover in restitution for the value of the services rendered.

§ 132. Stipulated Damages (Liquidated Damages)

The parties to a contract may negotiate contract terms providing for specific damages in the event of breach. Where this is effectively done, the stipulated damages or liquidated damages become the only damages that can be recovered for breach.

The major issue with stipulated damages is that in the Anglo-American legal system, there is a strong policy that contract damages must be only compensatory and not punitive. Thus, a stipulated damage will be found to be valid only if it results from an honest effort by the parties to anticipate probable damage consequences of a breach and provide for a sum which fairly reflects that amount of damages. Where the court concludes that liquidated damages were set at a high figure to compel performance, the provision for liquidated damages will be held to be void. Thus a measure of damages that appears to be punitive will not be enforced. This is in sharp contrast with other legal systems which generally permit the parties to negotiate very high liquidated damages to compel performance.

The fairness and reasonableness of a liquidated damage provision is analyzed on the basis of the facts known to the parties at the time the contract was made. The question is whether it appears to be fair and reasonable based upon the prospective damages that the parties might have anticipated as the result of a breach. However, there is some authority for considering whether the liquidated damage figure is reasonable in relation to the actual harm that resulted (U.C.C. section 2–718(1)).

Assume that Bob contracts to build a house for Charles and the contract provides that if the house is not completed within the time fixed in the contract, Bob will pay Charles $10,000. This stipulated damage clause is void. It is not an honest effort to estimate damages because it provides for a fixed sum without regard to the duration of the delay.

Assume the same contract with a clause providing for damages in the amount of $1,000 for every day of delay in completion. This clause is also probably void because the sum is so large that it appears to be designed as a club to compel timely performance rather than an honest effort to measure anticipated damages. People in the construction industry commonly refer to contract provisions for liquidated damages for delay as "penalty clauses." Attorneys must be careful not to use this phrase in court because if the judge decides it is in fact a "penalty clause," it will not be enforced.

Because of the preference for actual compensatory damages rather than stipulated damages in our legal system, some jurisdictions have a further limitation upon the validity of such contract terms. These states limit the use of stipulated damages to situations in which at the time the contract is made, it is evident that in the event of breach, damages will be very difficult or impossible to ascertain. Many jurisdictions are moving away from this requirement, but the "difficulty of proof of loss" is still considered in many situations in determining whether a liquidated damage clause should be enforced. (See U.C.C. section 2–718 which reflects this consideration in determining whether liquidated damages clauses are valid or void.)

Some cases involve liquidated damage clauses that underestimate damages. An example is found in contracts for burglar alarm services which typically provide for a rather small sum of damages (perhaps $50) for failure of the system to operate in its intended fashion. Such clauses are generally enforced. They do not raise the problem of being a penalty and are generally subject to attack only on such grounds as unconscionability.

Contract provisions may also limit the remedies available to one party. A seller of goods may insist on a contract term that provides for repair or replacement (usually at the seller's option) as the exclusive remedy in the event the goods do not perform as warranted. Contract terms may exclude some types of damages such as consequential damages. While such limitations may be subject to an unconscionability argument, they are generally found to be valid so long as they do not result in leaving the victim of a breach with no effective remedy. (See U.C.C. section 2–719(2) for a statutory handling of this issue.)

§ 133. Specific Performance

An order compelling a party to perform the contract can be issued only by a court exercising the powers of a court of equity. This remedy is stated to be available only where the "remedy at law" is inadequate. This means that specific performance can be obtained only where the money damage remedies discussed above (the remedies traditionally granted by a court of law as distinguished from a court of equity) will not suffice to provide a sufficient remedy for the victim of a contract breach.

The most common ground for finding that the damage remedy available at law is inadequate is that the subject of the contract is unique. If a contract involves the sale of unique property, then money damages will not place the plaintiff in as good a position as contract performance because the money cannot be used to buy the same property elsewhere.

For reasons that may be partly historical, real property is considered to be unique. In a particular case, goods may also be unique. Such contracts meet the first test for specific performance (that the remedy at law be inadequate). Under U.C.C. section 2–716, specific enforcement of contracts for the sale of goods may be had "where the goods are unique or in other proper circumstances." What constitutes "other proper circumstances" is left for development by case law. Cases which have granted specific performance under this section include long term supply contracts for goods that are in short supply. In these cases the goods themselves were not unique (petroleum products for example), but if a seller breaches during a time of shortage, the buyer may be able to prove that no market existed in which the buyer could enter into a comparable long term contract with another party.

Since specific enforcement decrees are granted by courts exercising the powers of equity, other rules of the law of equity must be considered to determine whether this remedy is available. For example, the plaintiff must establish that the contract when made was fair, just and equitable. The plaintiff must not be guilty of sharp practices in the transaction in question. Full analysis of the requirements imposed by courts of equity is beyond the coverage of the typical contracts course.

§ 134. Remedies Available in Actions Based Upon Detrimental Reliance (Promissory Estoppel)

Section 90 of the Restatement, First, provided that promises could be enforced when they foreseeably induced reliance of a definite and substantial character. (See § 69, *supra.*) It is clear that Professor Williston, at least, was of the opinion that a promise made enforceable by detrimental reliance would justify the same remedy as any other legally enforceable promise. Assume Uncle stated to Nephew: "I will give you $10,000 to buy a car." In reasonable and foreseeable reliance, Nephew purchased a car for $5,000. In Williston's view, Nephew could enforce Uncle's promise and recover $10,000. Under this view of the law, persons with actions based upon section 90 would have the full range of expectancy of the bargain or reliance damages discussed above.

The Restatement, Second, contains a revised version of section 90. Reliance under this Restatement need not be of a definite and substantial character and "the remedy granted for breach may be limited as justice requires." It is evident from this change that the authors contemplated circumstances in which the plaintiff may only recover reliance damages. One might anticipate that today, Nephew would recover only $5,000, the amount actually spent for the car.

B. REMEDIES IN SALES OF GOODS

§ 135. Buyer's Acceptance, Rejection and Revocation of Acceptance of Goods

A basic remedy of a buyer of goods under the U.C.C. is the right to reject non-conforming goods. Where there is any defect in tender in a single lot contract (section 2–601) or a defective tender in an installment contract which substantially impairs the value of that installment and cannot be cured (section 2–612(2)) the buyer has the right to reject the tendered goods. Rejection must occur within a reasonable time after the delivery of the goods and is ineffective unless the seller is seasonably notified (section 2–602).

Rejection is possible only where goods have not been accepted. Under section 2–606, acceptance can occur in any one of three ways: a) after a reasonable opportunity to inspect, the buyer signifies to the seller that he will take or retain the goods; or b) after a reasonable opportunity to inspect, the buyer fails to make an effective rejection; or c) the buyer does any act inconsistent with the seller's ownership of the goods.

When goods have been delivered and the buyer has had reasonable time and opportunity to inspect them, one of two things is going to happen very quickly. The buyer is either going to make an effective rejection of the goods or the buyer will be found to have accepted them. A rejection can be effective even if it is wrongful. If the buyer wrongfully rejects, the seller will have a remedy against the buyer, but it is a different remedy than would exist if the buyer had accepted the goods. If goods are wrongfully rejected, the seller still has the right to the goods and his ordinary action is for the difference between contract price and resale price under section 2–706 or contract price and market price under section 2–708(1). If the goods are accepted, the seller has an action for the contract price under section 2–709.

Even after the buyer has accepted the goods, there is still the possibility that this acceptance can be revoked under section 2–608. The legal requirements for revocation of acceptance are quite different from the requirements for rejection.

First, if the buyer had rejected, the seller would have the burden of proving that the tender conformed to the contract. If the buyer is attempting to revoke acceptance, section 2–607(4) places on the buyer the burden of proof as to all the requirements for revocation. Second, the buyer who is attempting to revoke acceptance must prove an "excuse" for the acceptance of the goods which can be either that he accepted the goods on the reasonable assumption that the non-conformity would be cured and it has not been or that his acceptance was reasonably induced by the difficulty of discovery of the defects or by seller's assurances (section 2–608(1)). Third, the buyer must prove that there was a non-conformity in the goods which substantially impairs their value to him (section 2–608(1)). And finally, the buyer must revoke acceptance within a reasonable time after the buyer discovers or should have discovered the grounds for revocation and before any substantial change in the condition of the goods which is not caused by their own defects (section 2–608(2)).

If an acceptance is properly revoked, the situation is the same as that which would have existed had the goods been rejected (section 2–608(3)). (See § 159, *infra*, for discussion of seller's performance and buyer's right to reject.)

§ 136. Seller's Remedies for Breach

When the buyer breaches a contract for the sale of goods, before the goods have been accepted, the seller may resell. If the resale is made in good faith in a commercially reasonable manner and in compliance with Code requirements, the seller may recover the difference between the resale price and the contract price plus incidental expenses, less expenses that could be avoided (U.C.C. sections 2–706 and 2–710). If there is no resale which is made in accordance with section 2–706, the seller may recover the difference between the contract price and the market price at the time and place of tender plus incidental expenses and less expenses which could be avoided (sections 2–708(1) and 2–710). Some authorities would permit the seller to elect to use a resale price or market price, whichever is lower, as the measure of damages.

Where the buyer has accepted the goods or where they were destroyed after the risk of loss had passed to the buyer, the seller may maintain an action for the price (section 2–709(1)(a) and (2)). The seller can also maintain an action for the contract price where the goods are identified to the contract and he is unable to resell them at a reasonable price (section 2–709(1)(b)).

The above mentioned remedies give no adequate relief for breach to the seller who is in a situation where his profits are partly dependent upon the volume of his sales. Consider the Ford dealer who contracts to sell a new car for $21,000. Assume that this price is the fair market value of the car and is $2,000 more than the dealer's cost of buying the car and preparing it for delivery. Before taking delivery, the buyer repudiates the contract.

If the buyer made a deposit before he breached, the dealer could retain $500 of the deposit. (Seller can retain $500 or 20% of the contract price, whichever is smaller, section 2–718(2)(b).) Assuming that no deposit was made or that the dealer is not satisfied with only $500, how should the dealer's damage be ascertained? The dealer cannot maintain an action for the price as the car was not accepted or destroyed nor is the seller unable to resell it for a reasonable price (section 2–709). The dealer can resell the car and sue for the difference between resale and contract, but assuming he sells it for $21,000, he will have nothing but the incidental damages allowed by section 2–710. He can sue for the difference between contract and market, but this too will be little or nothing. Yet the dealer has sustained damages in the amount of $2,000. At the end of the year he will have sold one less car because of this breach because the person who finally purchases this car for its market value of $21,000 would have purchased another car for that price. One sale was lost, and the dealer's profits for the period in question will be $2,000 less as a result. Even if the business was losing money, the dealer's losses would have been $2,000 less had he made this one additional sale.

The dealer may recover damages in the amount of $2,000 from the buyer under section 2–708(2). This section applies where the other remedies are inadequate. It permits the recovery of the profits, including reasonable overhead, which the seller would have made from full performance by the buyer. It will most frequently be applicable to retailers, wholesalers and manufacturers who are operating at less than full capacity, but may also assist any other seller whose profits are predicated in significant part upon the volume of his sales.

§ 137. Buyer's Remedies for Breach

If a contract for the sale of goods is breached by the seller, the buyer may "cover" by making any reasonable purchase of substitute goods in good faith and without unreasonable delay. The buyer may recover the difference between the cost of cover and the contract price together with incidental and consequential damages less expenses saved (U.C.C. sections 2–712(1) and (2) and 2–715). If the cover is made in good faith, it does not matter that the price was not in fact the lowest available. Where justified by the circumstances, the goods purchased in substitution need not be identical to those provided for in the contract.

If the buyer does not cover, then the measure of damages is the difference between the market price at the time when the buyer learned of the breach and the contract price, together with incidental and consequential damages less expenses saved (sections 2–713(1) and 2–715). Note that market price is determined at the time for performance in the case of seller's remedies (§ 136, *supra*). This was the common law rule for buyer's damages. The Code uses the time when the buyer learned of the breach which can be sometime after the seller was in fact obligated to ship or otherwise perform under the contract. In a rising market, the difference can be significant. In cases of repudiation, a buyer can learn of breach before the time fixed for performance. Section 2–713 would appear to provide that this earlier time (when the buyer learned of the breach by virtue of seller's anticipatory repudiation) is the time to be used to determine market price. If that is the interpretation which the authors intended, then the reference which is made to section 2–713 in the text of section 2–723 is inappropriate. That section provides that when actions founded on anticipatory repudiation come to trial before the time fixed for performance, market price shall be determined by the price prevailing when the aggrieved party learned of the repudiation. This provision is logically necessary when sellers sue for breach based upon anticipatory repudiation, but it expressly references the section relating to buyers' remedies.

Market price in the case of seller's breach is determined by the price at the place of tender except in cases where the goods were delivered. Where buyer rejected the goods after arrival or revoked his acceptance, market price is determined on the basis of prices at the place of arrival.

If the buyer has accepted defective goods, he may recover the difference at the time and place of acceptance between the value of the goods which he accepted and the value which the goods would have had if the goods had conformed to the contract warranties (section 2–714). Note that this computation does not utilize the contract price. The contract price is not relevant for determining the diminution in value due to the seller's breach.

If the buyer can establish special circumstances, he can recover further damages determined in any reasonable manner (section 2–714). A buyer may also recover incidental and consequential damages as described in section 2–715. The Code rejects the requirement that a party show that the breaching party "tacitly agreed" to assume liability for the particular damages in question (§ 127, *supra*, and comment 2 to U.C.C. section 2–715), but the common law limitation of damages to those arising from facts which the breaching party had reason to know at the time the contract was made is expressly preserved.

§ 138. Buyer's Right to the Goods

Common law decisions limited a buyer's right to specific performance to cases in which the goods were unique. The Code incorporates this rule in section 2–716 but adds "or in other proper circumstances." Some cases have granted specific performance in situations in which the buyer could not obtain a comparable contract on the open market. For example, some cases specifically enforced long term requirements contracts for petroleum products in a period of time in which the products in question were in fact readily available, but few if any sellers would commit themselves to future long term deliveries (§ 133, *supra*). It might be stated that the goods as such were not unique but the contract terms were. The "other proper circumstances" language is sufficiently broad that the Code will not impede the development of further case precedent specifically enforcing contracts for the sale of goods if in fact the courts are so disposed.

There are additional circumstances in which the buyer may obtain the goods themselves. This relief may be obtained where the goods have been identified to the contract and the buyer is unable to make a cover purchase (section 2–716(3)) or, under certain circumstances, where the buyer has made part payment and the seller becomes insolvent (sections 2–502 and 2–711(2)(a)).

IX. PERFORMANCE

A. PROMISES AND CONDITIONS

§ 139. Introduction

The subject of performance involves an analysis
of the legal duties that may become due under a
contract with special concern for when a given
duty to perform will arise and what the effect will
be if a duty of immediate performance is breached.
Contract duties are created by words of promise.
A promise is an undertaking or commitment that a
certain event will or will not occur in the future.
When there is a duty of immediate performance of
a promise, failure to perform in full is a breach.

In the most simple example, a contract may
contain one absolute promise. X says to Y: "If you
will climb that pole, I will pay you $10," whereup-
on Y climbs the pole. This unilateral contract has
but one promise, and the duty to perform that
promise arises immediately upon the making of
the contract.

Assume a slight change in the facts: Y states
that if X will climb the pole, Y will pay $10 to X
next Tuesday. There is again but one promise,
and the duty of performance is absolute. It is not
a duty that is immediately due and owing, but it is
an absolute promise because we know that Tuesday will come. The duty is not subject to any
conditions.

281

In addition to promises, contracts often contain conditions. A condition can be defined as an event, the occurrence or non-occurrence of which gives rise to or extinguishes a duty. Section 224 of the Restatement, Second, defines the term more narrowly as "an event, not certain to occur, which must occur, unless occurrence is excused, before performance under a contract becomes due."

Conditions can exist because they are expressly stated in the terms of the contract. Assume that a contract for fire insurance provides that Owner promises to pay a premium of $750 and Insurance Co. promises to pay for all losses to Owner's house up to some maximum dollar amount if it is damaged or destroyed by fire. This bilateral contract contains two promises. The promise by Owner to pay the premium is not subject to any conditions and is thus an absolute promise. The promise by Insurance Co. to pay for losses resulting from fire is subject to a condition. The condition is damage resulting from fire. Fire loss is an event, the occurrence of which will give rise to Insurance Co.'s duty to pay. If the event does not occur, the duty to pay will never arise. This condition is an "express" condition. It arises or is found as a term of the contract because it was set forth expressly in the terms of the contract.

In bilateral contracts, parties exchange promises and each is found to have bargained for the promise of the other. However, the ultimate thing that each party seeks is performance by the other.

Since promises are not always faithfully performed, a party to a bilateral contract may wish to protect himself by negotiating a contract term which makes performance by the other an express condition to his duty to perform.

Express conditions are created by the parties in the terms of their bargain. The courts simply recognize their presence and enforce them. If the parties chose to make something an express condition, the courts generally require that this condition be fully and literally fulfilled before the conditional duty will be found to have arisen. No particular language is required to create an express condition, however, terms such as "if," "provided that," "on the condition that," or "subject to" are commonly used to denote the parties intention that an event will function as a condition.

Assume that Jane plans to hire Dan to cut her lawn for $15. A mutual exchange of promises will produce a valid enforceable contract, but the practicalities of the situation are such that Jane does not really intend to sue Dan. Jane wants a promise because that will increase the likelihood of Dan's performance. However, she also wants to make certain that she will not have to pay $15 unless the job gets done. Jane's purposes will be served if she negotiates a contract in which Dan promises to cut the lawn and Jane promises to pay Dan $15 "provided that Jane will have no obligation to pay unless the lawn is completely cut."

The cutting of the lawn is a promised performance. It is also an express condition to Jane's duty to pay. Corbin referred to this as a promissory condition, but the important thing to realize is that the same event can be both a promise and a condition. Failure to cut the lawn has two very different legal effects. It is a breach of promise by Dan for which Jane could sue. It is also a failure of the condition to Jane's duty and thus prevents Jane's duty of performance from ever arising.

Implied conditions are found in contracts where the terms of the contract clearly indicate that one party must do something to permit or facilitate the performance by the other. X agrees to paint Y's house with the color of paint to correspond to a sample to be furnished by Y. Y's furnishing of the sample is an implied condition to X's duty of performance. While this condition was not expressed in the contract language, it is so clearly contemplated by the parties that it is implied in their agreement. As with an express condition, such implied duties of cooperation must be completely and literally fulfilled before the conditional duty will arise.

Where no condition is expressed or implied in the terms of a contract by the parties, a court may construe a condition to accomplish a just result. Conditions which are imposed by courts are generally referred to as constructive conditions.

Assume that Dan promises to cut Jane's lawn and Jane promises to pay Dan $15 for this work.

The contract contains no express or implied conditions. (In fact, there may be implied conditions such as the condition that Jane will not water the lawn on the day it is to be cut, but at least there are no express or implied conditions relating to Jane's duty to pay.) On their face, both promises appear to be absolute, however the law will impose a constructive condition that the lawn cutting must be substantially completed before Jane's duty to pay will arise.

This condition is imposed to do justice; to avoid imposing upon Jane a duty of immediate performance of her promise to pay until she has received the substantial benefit of her bargain. Since the parties themselves did not provide for such a condition, the court need not require full literal performance of the cutting job. Substantial compliance with the condition is sufficient to find that it is fulfilled and that Jane's duty to pay has arisen. Jane would thus be better off if she had bargained for an express condition because she could then insist on full performance before her duty to pay would arise. Of course, if the lawn is only substantially cut, Jane can deduct for the part of Dan's promise that was not performed. (See §§ 126 and 128, *supra.*)

It might be helpful to think of promises and conditions in the sense that promises are the basis of actions for breach of contract. They are asserted by plaintiffs to show the duty that the defendant breached. Conditions are defensive. They are asserted by defendants to demonstrate that their duty to perform never arose.

§ 140. Express Conditions

An express condition is one that is created by the terms of the contract. Express conditions will be found only where the contract states that an event must occur before a duty is to arise. While no specific or formal language is required to create an express condition, a condition will not be labeled "express" unless the parties' intent that it operate as a condition is expressed in clear language. This may be done by use of words of condition such as "provided that," "upon the condition that," or "if." Courts may also consider the entire contract as well as factors such as the subject matter and the relative situation of the parties.

It helps to keep in mind that an express condition must fully and literally occur before the duty that is subject to this condition will arise. This can cause one party to incur a forfeiture if the condition is substantially fulfilled but has failed in some minor detail. If the court refuses to find that something is an express condition, it can still find that it is a constructive condition in which case substantial fulfillment is sufficient and minor discrepancies will not result in a forfeiture or loss of contract benefits. For this reason, courts are not ordinarily motivated to find that a condition is expressed in the contract.

Assume that a fire insurance contract states: "The insured agrees to maintain an automatic water sprinkler system in good working condition." If the insured fails to maintain the sprinkler system in working condition and sustains a fire loss, the rights of the parties will depend upon the interpretation placed on the quoted language. If maintenance of the system is an express condition to the insurer's duty to pay, then failure of that condition will prevent the duty from arising. The insured will receive no payment. If maintenance of the system is a promised performance, then the insured is liable for any damages caused by breach of that promise. The burden of proof would be on the insurance company to show what part of the loss, if any, would have been avoided if the sprinkler system had been operating at the time of the fire. Whatever actual damages the insurance company could prove resulted from breach of the promise would be deducted from the insured's fire loss claim.

Maintenance of the sprinkler system would undoubtedly be held to be only a promised performance in this example. That may not be the result that the insurer desired, but no language of condition was used. Further, since the insurance company prepared the contract, any doubtful questions should be interpreted against the insurance company.

Assume a contract in which Joe is to harvest Al's hay and Al is to pay Joe $2,000. Absent unusual facts, all courts would find that the hay must be cut before the duty to pay will arise, but there is no language in the contract that expressly states that cutting is a condition to payment. Cutting the hay will likely be found to be a constructive condition to Al's duty to pay.

Assume the contract provides "Joe promises to complete the cutting of the hay by July 14, and Al will pay $2,000 for that work." The completion of the hay cutting by July 14 is not a condition that is expressed in the language of the contract. Finishing by the 14th is a promised performance, and if Joe does not finish until the 15th, he will be liable for any damages caused by this breach. Finishing by the 14th is a constructive condition to Al's duty to pay and if this condition is not substantially fulfilled, Al will have no duty to pay. If finishing by the 14th were treated as an express condition, then full literal compliance would be required and absent some basis for excusing the condition, Joe would not be paid if he did not finish until the 15th. The harshness of this result is reason for a court to avoid finding that the parties intended an express condition unless they used language in the contract that clearly mandates this result. If Al seeks this result, he might request additional language such as: "Al will have no duty to pay unless the entire job is fully completed no later than the 14th;" or "completion of the hay cutting by the 14th is hereby made an express condition to Al's duty to pay."

§ 141. Constructive Conditions; Precedent and Concurrent

Two centuries have passed since Lord Mansfield set forth the scheme for constructive conditions in Kingston v. Preston (1773), wherein it is stated:

> There are three kinds of covenants: 1. Such as are called mutual and independent, where either party may recover damages from the other, for the injury he may have received by a breach of the covenants in his favour, and where it is no excuse for the defendant to allege a breach of the covenants on the part of the plaintiff. 2. There are covenants which are conditions and dependent, in which the performance of one depends on the prior performance of another, and, therefore, till this prior condition is performed, the other party is not liable to an action on his covenant. 3. There is also a third sort of covenants, which are mutual conditions to be performed at the same time; and in these, if one party was ready, and offered, to perform his part, and the other neglected, or refused to perform his, he who was ready, and offered, has fulfilled his engagement, and may maintain an action for the default of the other; though it is not certain that either is obliged to do the first act. His Lordship then proceeded to say, that the dependence or independence of covenants was to be collected from the evident sense and meaning of the parties, and, that, however transposed they might be in the deed, their preceden-

cy must depend on the order of time in which the intent of the transaction requires their performance.

Promises which, by the terms of the contract, are to be performed prior in time are ordinarily construed to be conditions precedent to those promises which are to be performed later in time. A promised performance which requires a period of time, such as painting a house or cutting a lawn, is ordinarily construed as a condition precedent to the promised performance which consists of a single act such as payment of money.

Where both promises are capable of being performed simultaneously and the contract does not require that one occur first, the promises are treated as mutually dependent or concurrently conditioned upon each other. In this case neither party has a duty to perform until the other has performed or tendered performance. Both could theoretically wait for the other forever, neither would ever have a duty to perform, and there would never be a breach. As a practical matter, the party who wishes to conclude the transaction must take the step of performing or tendering his performance so as to give rise to a duty of performance in the other party. In these situations, the duty of each party to perform is conditional. It will not arise as an absolute duty until the other party has performed or tendered. The shorthand language for describing this situation is to say that the performances are concurrently conditioned upon each other. "Concurrent conditions" are not a different type of condition. This term simply describes the situation where neither party has an independent duty to perform because the duty of each is dependent upon the other acting first. This is the "third sort of covenants" to which Lord Mansfield referred.

Constructive conditions are imposed by the court to do justice to the parties. Justice is accomplished if the conditions substantially occur or are substantially fulfilled. Justice does not require that a court construed condition be literally and fully performed.

Where the constructive condition is an event which is also the promised performance, the condition is fulfilled if the promise is substantially performed. It can also be stated that the condition is fulfilled unless there was a material breach of the promise (§ 143, *infra*).

§ 142. Implied in Fact Conditions

An implied condition or implied in fact condition is an event which is not expressly made a condition by the language of the contract but which the parties necessarily contemplated as part of their agreement. The standard example of such a condition is the implied condition of cooperation which will arise where some participation or cooperation by one party is necessary to permit the other to perform or to enjoy the fruits of the contract.

If X contracts to fumigate a bank vault in exchange for which the bank agrees to pay $300, there is an implied condition that the bank will take the appropriate actions to open its vault and give X access thereto. The bank's duty of cooperation would also appear to be an implied promise.

The significance of the categories of conditions— express, implied, and constructive—is the difference in the approach which courts will use to determine whether the conditions have been fulfilled. Constructive conditions are created by judicial construction to produce just results and it is sufficient for this purpose that they substantially occur or are substantially fulfilled. Express conditions are created by the parties in the expressed language of the contract. The basic rule, therefore, is that they must be fully and literally fulfilled although courts will usually avoid this interpretation if the result would be a forfeiture. The very harshness of this rule causes courts to strain from time to time to avoid finding a condition to be "express."

It is frequently stated that implied conditions are to be treated the same as express conditions and that full and literal compliance with such conditions is necessary to give rise to a duty of performance. Some authors state that express conditions and implied conditions are "true" conditions in that they are both found to be terms of the contract because the parties so intended. Thus both should be accorded equal respect. In fact, however, because implied conditions are found from the sense of the transaction rather than from express words of the agreement, courts can interpret implied conditions in a reasonable fashion, if not a loose fashion. This permits courts to avoid technical problems with seemingly minor discrepancies which plague us in the express condition area.

It might be concluded that implied conditions must fully and literally occur, but because such conditions arise by implication, courts are rather free to articulate them in a reasonable fashion giving appropriate consideration to the events which have in fact occurred.

§ 143. Substantial Performance; Effect of Breach

Where one party's performance is a constructive condition to the other party's duty to perform, breach by the first party may prevent the other's duty of performance from arising. Since the duty is both a promise and a condition (a promissory condition), the first party's failure to perform is a breach of promise for which any resulting damages may be recovered. If there was a complete failure to perform, this would also be a failure of the condition to the other party's duty and the other party's duty to perform will not arise. However, since constructive conditions need only be substantially fulfilled, if the first party substantially performed, the condition has been fulfilled.

Assume that X contracts to build a house for Y for $150,000 payable on completion. X's obligation to build is a promissory condition. It is both a promised performance and a constructive condition to Y's duty to pay. Assume further that X stops performance when the house is completed except for the gutters and downspouts that were included in the plans. X has breached the promise to build in accordance with plans, and Y can recover damages for this breach (§ 128, *supra*). However, it can be assumed that X has substantially performed his obligation and thus the constructive condition to Y's duty to pay has been fulfilled. Y has a duty to pay the contract price minus his damages.

It can be stated that X has substantially performed thus giving rise to Y's duty to pay. It can also be stated that X's breach is a minor breach as distinguished from a material breach and thus Y has a duty to pay. If there has been substantial performance or substantial fulfillment of the constructive condition, then the breach by X is by definition a minor breach. If X has not substantially performed, then his breach is a material breach and Y's duty to pay will not arise unless the condition is excused for some reason.

Since express conditions must fully occur (§§ 139 and 140, *supra*), a "substantial performance" or "minor breach" analysis would not be appropriate if the construction contract between X and Y made full compliance with plans and specifications an express condition precedent to Y's duty to pay.

The term substantial performance is most frequently used in service contracts such as construction contracts. The term material breach is commonly used in contracts involving the sale of land and was used in common law cases dealing with the sale of goods. (The U.C.C. avoids use of these terms. For example, see sections 2–601 and 2–612.) However, substantial performance and minor breach are often used interchangeably, and the following analysis of substantial performance is also relevant for determining whether a breach is material or minor.

In determining whether a condition has been substantially performed, the majority of cases utilize some or all of the factors listed in Restatement, Second, section 241, which provides:

In determining whether a failure to render or to offer performance is material, the following circumstances are significant:

(a) The extent to which the injured party will be deprived of the benefit he reasonably expected;

(b) The extent to which the injured party can be adequately compensated for the part of that benefit of which he will be deprived;

(c) The extent to which the party failing to perform or to offer to perform will suffer forfeiture;

(d) The likelihood that the party failing to perform or to offer to perform will cure his failure, taking account of all the circumstances including any reasonable assurances;

(e) The extent to which the behavior of the party failing to perform or to offer to perform comports with standards of good faith and fair dealing.

Many cases also consider the willful, negligent, or innocent behavior of the party failing to perform which was the language used in Restatement, First, section 275 which addressed this subject. It should be noted that although the Restatement makes the behavior of the breaching party but one of five factors, most decisions indicate that if the plaintiff's departure is willful, there has not been substantial performance. Willfulness does not mean maliciousness, it merely means a knowing or bad faith departure.

As discussed above, a promised performance may also be a constructive condition to the other party's duty to perform. If the condition has been determined to have substantially occurred, any breach of the promise is properly termed a minor breach. Conversely, if the breach is found to be material, there has not been substantial performance of the condition.

Suppose that A, an accomplished attorney, has just obtained a large verdict in a personal injury case. The defendant appeals and A, with his client's consent, contracts with B, an appellate practice specialist. B agrees to write all necessary briefs for the appeal and A promises to pay B the sum of $5,000 "when the brief is in final form and ready to file with the court."

B reviews the transcripts and does the necessary research. B prepares drafts of the brief. B has a "final draft," but both B and A agree that there is one further point that B should research which may affect one portion of the brief. B is appointed to the position of Attorney General of the U.S., and he advises A that he cannot finish the brief. A refuses to pay B and B sues on the contract.

The first issue which must be resolved is whether A's duty to pay is dependent upon the occurrence of an express condition, the completion of the brief. It might be argued that the language used expressly provides that completion of the brief is an express condition to A's promise to pay. However, such an interpretation would lead to the result that B cannot sue on the contract unless he has fully and completely performed (§ 140, *supra*). Because of the harshness of this result, the courts would not be disposed to find an express condition, and since the language used in the contract does not appear to compel that result, the completion of B's performance would most likely be found to be a constructive condition to A's duty to pay (§ 141, *supra*).

The issue that must now be analyzed is whether B has substantially performed or, stated another way, whether the condition to A's duty has substantially occurred. Whichever way the question is stated or framed, the answer will be determined by application of the same factors. Thus, applying the factors set forth in Restatement, Second, section 241, *supra*, a court has five points to consider. (a) A did receive the substantial benefit of his bargain. The necessary organization and analysis has been accomplished. The missing work can presumably be performed by A or another attorney. (b) Since A has a cause of action against B for breach (B has breached at least part of his promise regardless whether he has "substantially performed"), A can set-off his damages against the contract price. A's damages are presumably measurable and ascertainable (§§ 126–128, *supra*) and A can therefore be adequately compensated for the benefit of which he was deprived. (c) B has rendered significant performance pursuant to the contract. This is important because it reflects the magnitude of forfeiture which B will incur if he is not permitted to sue on the contract. While there is some hardship upon A as a result of B's breach, it would appear that it would be a great hardship upon B to terminate the contract. (d) The contract does not provide for future performances, so the fact that B is not going to cure is not crucial. (e) B's breach was willful in the sense that he could have rejected the position of Attorney General and stayed home to finish the brief. He has knowingly departed from his duty, however, he is not acting in bad faith. Because of the nature and importance of the position which B accepted, his breach will not be found to be a violation of any standard of good faith and fair dealing.

As analyzed, the factors lead to the conclusion that the breach by B was not material and the condition to A's duty to pay did substantially occur. Therefore, B should be able to recover the contract price minus damages caused to A by B's breach.

It should be noted that in many cases the analysis of the Restatement factors will result in some points in favor of finding substantial performance and some against. The result is not predicated upon the numerical total of factors favoring and factors opposing a finding of substantial performance. The courts will base their decisions upon the factors which are most critical in the case before it.

The discussion in this section utilizes the terminology of substantial performance in analyzing the question whether a condition should be deemed to have occurred. This is the vocabulary commonly used in cases and in the Restatement. It might lead to less misunderstanding if the discussion focused upon fulfilling a condition by "substantial occurrence" of the condition. The effect of a partial failure of a promised performance is that there is a cause of action for breach. In determining whether the other party's duty of performance becomes absolute, the proper question is whether the condition to that duty has occurred by virtue of having been substantially performed. However, because the condition in question is also a promised performance, the "substantial performance of the promise" language is common-place.

§ 144. Guidelines to Identify Promises and Different Types of Conditions

No court ever interprets a term of a contract and labels it a promise or a condition without knowing what effect that label will produce. No law student or attorney should attempt to place labels on contract events without considering what results will best carry out the evident intention of the parties.

As an example, assume the court is interpreting an agricultural lease which contains language indicating that all noxious weeds are to be removed. If the language is interpreted to be an express condition to the tenant's right to remain in possession of the land, then any deviation from the full and literal requirement will create a basis for the landlord contending that the tenant should be removed. In the case of a long term lease, significant investments in long term crops could be forfeited due to the tenant's failure to remove weeds.

If the language in the lease is interpreted to be a promise, then the failure of the tenant to remove weeds would be a breach of promise for which the landlord could seek damages. Proving the dollar value of damages resulting from having a few weeds on the property would not be a task which the owner's counsel would approach with joy. If the promise to remove weeds is of sufficient importance to be also a constructive condition to the tenants' right to remain in possession, then possession could be terminated for a substantial failure of that condition or a substantial breach of the promise to keep the premises weed free. If removal of weeds is a condition to the tenant's right to continue in possession, finding this to be a constructive condition rather than an express condition would provide a distinct advantage to the tenant.

It would be a mistake to adopt a theory that courts interpret contracts however they please to produce whatever results they wish. But it is quite reasonable to expect that a judge will not wish to read an agricultural lease to provide that removal of weeds is an express condition to the tenant's right to continue in possession. Courts tend to interpret the contract term as language of a promise in such situations. This permits the owner to recover all of the damages which he can prove, and if the situation becomes bad enough, then the tenant can be terminated because of the substantial failure of a constructive condition.

In the drafting of documents, wise counsel pay particular attention to these issues. If they wish to be able to obtain damages if an event does not occur, then they must make that event a promised performance. If they wish to be able to take or avoid certain action if an event occurs or does not occur, then they must make that event a condition, preferably an express condition. Of course, the same event can be both a promised performance and an express condition. Experienced counsel know, however, that making a certain event a promised performance may provide a court with a ready-made reason not to interpret that same event to be an express condition.

There is an additional problem with the vocabulary used by courts when discussing conditions. In some jurisdictions such as California, courts commonly use the term "condition" to refer to what has been described above as an express condition.

Assume a simple contract in which Paul is to paint Mary's house for $10,000. Utilizing the vocabulary discussed in the preceding sections, one would state that there is no express condition but that the painting of the house is a constructive condition to Mary's duty to pay and her duty will not arise unless that performance is substantially rendered. If the promise to paint was not fully accomplished, one would then apply the factors set forth in Restatement, Second, section 241 to determine whether performance had been substantially rendered and the constructive condition thus substantially fulfilled.

In some jurisdictions, court opinions might state that there is no condition present, but that Mary need not pay if there has been a failure of consideration (meaning a failure by Paul to paint). These courts will then proceed to apply the section 241 factors to determine whether Paul's duty was substantially performed. If it was, Mary must pay the contract price less any damages for Paul's shortcomings. If Paul's duty to paint was not substantially performed, Mary's duty to pay will not arise because there was a "failure of consideration."

The difference between these two approaches is only in the semantics used. Using either vocabulary, Mary's duty does not arise until the duty to paint is substantially fulfilled. If Paul commits a material breach of the contract, Mary's duty will not arise.

§ 145. Conditions Subsequent

It is possible to fashion a condition so that it extinguishes an existing duty of performance rather than giving rise to a duty. Such a condition, by definition, occurs after the duty has already arisen, and can therefore be called a condition subsequent. In most situations where conditions are stated in the form of a condition subsequent, they are in substance simply conditions precedent. For example, father (F) contracts with his adult college student son (S) in which F makes a valid enforceable promise to pay S the sum of $500 per month for four years, provided that if S drops out of school, F's duty to make payments will cease. F's duty to make the monthly payments is stated to be an absolute undertaking creating an unconditional duty of performance. It is stated to be subject to being terminated by the occurrence of the event of S leaving college. S's leaving college appears to be a condition the occurrence of which will terminate a duty. It thus might be classified as a condition subsequent.

F's duty to make each monthly payment is actually subject to the condition precedent that S remain in college up to the time the payment is due. While the language of the agreement infers that F's duty is absolute but will be terminated upon the occurrence of the event of S dropping out, in fact there is no duty of immediate performance until the condition of staying in school has occurred. Because the language used is that of condition subsequent, many courts would designate it as such a condition.

Examples of conditions which are truly subsequent in substance rather than merely subsequent in form are not common in contract law. S sells B a tractor. The contract provides that S warrants certain features, that B must give notice of breach at least 120 days before filing suit, and that any action for breach of warranty must be brought within two years of the date of sale. Giving notice 120 days before filing suit is a condition precedent to liability. An action cannot be maintained without such notice. Filing an action within two years is a condition subsequent. After notice has been given, S has a present duty owing to B. The failure to file suit within two years time will terminate that duty and thus might be labeled a condition subsequent. True conditions subsequent are encountered with some frequency in the law relating to real property.

Before one gets too confused by the precedent and subsequent classifications, it might be helpful to know that in contract law there is really no difference between the two. For purposes of contract analysis, one can simply refer to the cutting of the lawn, the absence of rain on Saturday, or the staying in college as a condition without designating whether it is precedent or subsequent. The result will not be affected by the failure to designate the type of condition. However, in the area of pleading and procedure significance may be placed upon the difference between a condition precedent and subsequent in terms of who has the burden of pleading and proof, the party seeking to enforce the promise usually being required to plead and prove a condition precedent and the party seeking to avoid liability for breach of promise sometimes being required to plead and prove the occurrence of the condition subsequent which terminated his duty.

The definition of "condition" in section 224 of the Restatement, Second, (section 139, *supra*) does not encompass events that terminate a duty of performance. Thus all "conditions" are precedent in the vocabulary of the Restatement, Second. Events that terminate an obligor's duty of immediate performance are covered in Restatement, Second, section 230 and are treated as a discharge. (See § 185, *infra*.)

B. EXCUSE OF CONDITIONS

§ 146. Excuse of Conditions

A dependent or conditional promise does not ripen into a duty of immediate performance until the condition to which it is subject is fulfilled or excused. Thus, even though a condition has not occurred, the duty of the other party to perform may still arise if the condition is legally excused. Conditions may be legally excused in at least seven ways: (1) by the making of a proper tender which is rejected; (2) by the failure of a prior condition; (3) by an anticipatory repudiation of a promise by the other party; (4) by voluntary disablement or prospective inability of the other party to perform; (5) by waiver; (6) by estoppel; and (7) by impossibility of performance of the condition.

§ 147. Excuse of Condition by Tender

The improper rejection of a tender of performance is a legal excuse for non-occurrence of the condition precedent, and the other party's duty of performances becomes absolute.

This rule is typically useful when contract performances are concurrently conditioned upon each other. The party who wishes to see the transaction advance must tender his performance in order for the other party's duty to arise (§ 141, *supra*). When this is done, the other party may not avoid his obligations simply by rejecting the tender. A tender of money must be in cash or its equivalent (cf. U.C.C. section 2–511(2)). If a personal check is tendered or if a tender is defective for any similar technical reason and the other party does not object on that ground, he waives the objection (§ 152, *infra*). To illustrate, if A agrees to sell a specific automobile to B and B agrees to pay A $1,000, A's refusal to accept B's tender of the money excuses the condition to A's duty, and A's duty to transfer the automobile becomes absolute. Therefore, B could immediately file suit for breach of contract and prevail.

§ 148. Excuse of Condition by Failure of a Prior Condition

The non-occurrence of a condition may be excused if it is subject to a condition which has failed. To illustrate, suppose B contracts to build six $80,000 homes on O's land, with O to designate the sites. The contract is entered into in July with construction to begin in September. O fails to designate the sites for the houses before winter comes. The land freezes, making construction during winter months impossible. Normally, B could not recover from O without proving that he had performed the act of building the houses, thus fulfilling the condition precedent to O's duty to pay. But O's selection of the sites is either an express or an implied condition precedent to B's duty to build. Failure of the condition precedent of designating the sites is a legal excuse for the non-occurrence of B's condition. B may sue O, since O's promise to pay has become absolute because of the excuse of B's condition precedent. B may recover the profits he would have made on the job.

§ 149. Excuse of Condition by an Anticipatory Repudiation of a Promise, or by Voluntary Disablement or Prospective Inability to Perform

An anticipatory repudiation of a contract occurs when a party to the contract denies any intention to perform the contract prior to the time performance is due. A statement by a party to the effect that he is encountering difficulties in preparing to perform, that he is not pleased with the bargain, or that he is otherwise uncertain whether performance will be rendered when due is not sufficient to constitute a repudiation. The words must actually manifest an intent not to perform.

In bilateral contracts, an anticipatory repudiation has the legal effect of excusing the non-occurrence of conditions to the repudiating party's duty to perform. The practical effect is that the non-repudiating party may properly suspend his own performance or preparations. The non-repudiating party has a defense to going forward with the contract performance.

An anticipatory repudiation may also give rise to an immediate cause of action for breach. Some common law decisions deny an immediate right of action if the innocent party has already fully performed and is simply waiting for the date on which payment will be due. U.C.C. section 2–610 gives an immediate right of action in all cases.

Prospective inability to perform exists when circumstances indicate that it is highly unlikely that a party will be able to perform. If X contracts to sell Blackacre to Y, the fact that Blackacre now belongs to Z does not constitute prospective inability. X might be able to acquire title from Z thus making performance possible. If it is established that Z is a public utility which needs Blackacre to discharge its utility functions, then it is evident that X will not be able to acquire title and there is a prospective inability to perform.

A voluntary disablement occurs when a party to a contract engages in conduct which destroys or seriously impairs his ability to perform. Assume that S contracts to sell and B to buy Blackacre for $10,000 on July 1. On June 1, S conveys Blackacre outright to C. By his conduct, S placed his ability to perform beyond his own personal control.

Voluntary disablement and prospective inability give the other party a legal excuse for the non-occurrence of conditions to the performance which is apparently not going to be performed. If a party overcomes his inability to perform prior to the time for performance and attempts to reinstate the contract, the contract will be reinstated if the other party has not changed position in reasonable reliance in the interim. In the land sale contract illustration above, if S reacquired title prior to the time for performance and B had not in the meantime purchased another parcel of land or otherwise changed position in reliance, S could enforce the contract. If B had relied by suspending preparations for performance, B could be given a reasonable extension of time within which to perform.

§ 150. Prospective Inability to Perform and Repudiation Under the U.C.C.

U.C.C. section 2–609(1) provides:

(1) A contract for sale imposes an obligation on each party that the other's expectation of receiving due performance will not be impaired. When reasonable grounds for insecurity arise with respect to the performance of either party the other may in writing demand adequate assurance of due performance and until he receives such assurance may if commercially reasonable suspend any performance for which he has not already received the agreed return.

This subsection is applicable to a situation involving prospective inability to perform such as might arise when a seller who has agreed to deliver goods on credit acquires information giving rise to doubts as to the buyer's ability to pay. It can also be a very important tool for the innocent party who receives a somewhat ambiguous communication which might be a repudiation. The innocent party may demand assurances as to the other party's intention to perform as well as his ability to perform. The innocent party thus need not choose at this peril between the alternative routes of mitigating damages by contracting elsewhere or standing by waiting to see whether the other party intends to perform.

Failure to respond within a reasonable period of time to a justified demand for assurances is a repudiation. The Code states that this reasonable time is not to *exceed* 30 days. In appropriate circumstances, the reasonable time in which a response must be given to a demand for assurances could be a very short period of time, even thirty minutes or less.

Under U.C.C. section 2–610, a repudiation with respect to a performance the loss of which will substantially impair the value of the contract, gives the innocent party the right to suspend his own performance, and to declare an immediate breach or wait for a commercially reasonable time before treating the contract as breached. Thus the innocent party has a defense to going forward with his own performance. In addition, the innocent party may elect to treat the repudiation as an immediate breach. This is true without regard to whether there is any need to act immediately upon the repudiation.

U.C.C. section 2–611 permits retraction of a repudiation so long as the innocent party has not: (a) cancelled, (b) materially changed his position in reliance, or (c) otherwise indicated that he considers the repudiation final.

§ 151. Necessity to Demonstrate the Ability to Perform

Where a party is excused from tendering and acquires a cause of action because of an anticipatory breach, he is still ordinarily required to show that he could have performed but for the actions of the guilty party. Thus, if B anticipatorily repudiates his promise to hire J to sing in B's night club and J thereafter sues for breach of contract, the fact that J was disabled and could not have sung during the period in question would prevent J from recovering. The fact that J committed himself to sing for X after B repudiated is not a bar to J's action because this was a proper effort to mitigate damages which was necessary as a result of the repudiation. The repudiation excused the condition that J remain ready and able to perform (§ 149, *supra*).

§ 152. Excuse of Condition by Waiver

A party whose duty of performance is subject to a condition may communicate to the other party that he will not insist upon the occurrence of that condition. If the condition is not a material part of the bargain and its occurrence does not materially affect the benefit to be received by the promisor, its non-occurrence can be excused by waiver. One may not waive the right to receive a performance which is a significant or material part of the bargain (§ 98, *supra*). A material part of the bargain can only be deleted by a contract modification which must be supported by consideration at common law. Some statutes such as U.C.C. section 2–209 permit modification without consideration (§ 68, *supra*).

The doctrine of waiver can be used to excuse a condition when the waiving party has indicated a willingness to proceed with the contract without regard to whether the condition is fulfilled. Waivers may be withdrawn and the condition reinstated so long as this can be done and is done in a manner which is not unfair or unreasonable to the other party.

§ 153. Excuse of Condition by Estoppel

Waivers become irrevocable where the other party reasonably relies thereon to the point that the term waived cannot be reasonably reinstated. To illustrate, suppose S promises to convey Blackacre to B in exchange for B's promise to pay $10,000 on July 1. Time is made of the essence. B tells S on June 1 that he is having difficulty raising the money, and S states that he will not insist on performance before July 30. If B relies to his detriment on S's statement, by ceasing diligent efforts to raise the money by July 1, S will be estopped from reasserting the condition of performance on July 1. S may be permitted to establish a new date for performance earlier than July 30 if that is reasonable, giving recognition to B's reliance.

A party who has wrongfully prevented the occurrence of a condition can be estopped from asserting the failure of that condition. Where there is a duty to assist or not interfere with the occurrence of a condition, one who fails to cooperate and thereby prevents the fulfillment of the condition cannot rely upon its failure. A condition of party approval can be excused if the party withholds approval wrongfully. Some court opinions will explain these results by stating that the party is estopped from asserting the condition.

§ 154 Excuse of Condition by Impossibility

Impossibility of performance is often thought of merely as a method of discharge from a contractual duty (§ 176–177, *infra*). However, if it becomes objectively impossible to fulfill a condition which is not a material part of the agreed exchange, impossibility may excuse the condition. Where a forfeiture could result from requiring the fulfilling of a condition which is only incidental to the bargain, the condition will ordinarily be excused. Suppose B promises to build a house for O. O promises to pay $75,000, provided B obtains an architect's certificate. B builds the house according to specifications, but the architect dies before a certificate can be obtained. The certificate, although an express condition precedent to the right to payment, is only incidental to the major thing for which the parties bargained, and this condition will be excused by impossibility.

§ 155 Effect of Severability

A contract to paint a fence for $250 is an "entire" contract. Assuming that painting is a condition to the duty to pay (§ 141, *supra*), the painter must substantially perform the entire job before the duty to pay will arise (§ 143, *supra*).

If a painter contracts to paint two separate fences, one for $250 and one for $300, the contract might be severable. If this is the case, then completion of the first fence will be construed to be a condition to the payment of the $250, and painting the second fence a condition to the $300.

Finding contract performances to be severable has several important results. A painter who receives payment for each job as it is finished will have an easier time with his financial commitments than one who does not get paid until the entire job is completed. The painter who paints one fence and fails to paint the other will be able to enforce a right to payment for the first fence if the contract is severable. He will be liable for such damages as result from his failure to paint the second fence, but he will not find himself unable to assert any right as might be the case if the contract were entire (§ 143, *supra*).

The question of severability of contract performance is ultimately resolved by determining the parties' intentions. A contract can be severable if (a) performance by each party is divisible into two or more parts which are not inter-dependent upon each other for their value; (b) the number of parts due from each party is the same; and (c) performance of each part by one party is or appears to be the agreed exchange for a corresponding part by the other party. The question whether each part is the agreed exchange for the other part is a key to a finding of severability.

If a contract is found to be severable, the breaching party will be liable in an action for damages for the part which he breached. As to other parts of the contract, the failure of the breaching party to perform a severable portion will not bar his action on the remainder of the contract, or his right to perform thereunder.

C. CONSTRUCTION CONTRACTS

§ 156. Construction Contracts and Forfeitures

Construction contracts and many other service contracts present the prospect of forfeiture to the contractor in the event the owner is found not to be obligated to pay for improvements made on his property. Assume that C contracts to build a house for O for $65,000 and that the contract expressly provides that O's duty to pay is subject to the condition that C build in full and complete conformance to plans and specifications. The house is completed when it is discovered that the living room is a foot too narrow, or that the house is five feet too far back on the lot, or that the pipe in the walls is not the brand specified. Assume that the defects are not the product of a willful breach or bad faith.

There has been a partial failure of a condition which appears to have been made an express condition to O's duty to pay. Following the ordinary rules, the contractor must rebuild the house or not get paid (§ 140, *supra*). Some courts will agonize at length over the fact that express conditions must be completely fulfilled. Others will blithely ignore the fact that there is an express condition involved and treat the case in the same manner as one involving a constructive condition (§ 141, *supra*). But in the end, in most instances, there will be a statement that the law abhors a forfeiture, and the contractor will recover the contract price less provable dollar value of the discrepancies which may be nothing (§ 128, *supra*).

If the defects in the house are of a nature that can be corrected without undue economic waste, the proper result would appear to be to require the contractor to make the corrections before the owner's duty to pay will arise. Even this is not required in all cases. Where enforcing a requirement of full and literal compliance with a condition will cause one of the parties to suffer a forfeiture, the doctrine of substantial performance will frequently be applied to fulfill or excuse what appears to be an express condition.

If the defect is serious, such as one which involves the structural soundness of the building, or involves a willful departure by the contractor from plans and specifications, recovery will most likely be denied.

§ 157. The Condition of Approval by a Third Party or by a Principal Party to the Contract

A contract may provide that the duty of a party to accept and pay for the performance which he is to receive is subject to the condition that it be approved by a third party. Where there is no element of forfeiture involved, such as in the ordinary contract for the sale of goods, this express condition is literally enforced and will usually not be excused even by the death or incapacity of the third party. Fraud or collusion will excuse the condition, of course, but the fact that the third party acted arbitrarily, capriciously or unreasonably in refusing to approve the performance does not constitute grounds for excusing the condition.

When the element of forfeiture is introduced, the standard of conduct required of the third party changes. Consider these factors: (1) What is the magnitude of the forfeiture involved? (2) What is the nature of the approval being sought? Is the thing being approved something of utilitarian value with a measurable performance such as an air conditioning system, or is it a matter of aesthetics and taste such as the quality of a nightclub singer? In the latter instance, the third party will be permitted to exercise a greater degree of latitude and discretion. (3) How unreasonable is the third party's conduct? Has he refused to inspect at all or refused to inspect thoroughly? Does he give logical reasons for his disapproval or only reasons which are totally irrational or arbitrary and capricious? (4) Who is the third party and how was he selected? A renowned expert may be given wider latitude than a run-of-the-mill engineer or other professional.

While some courts reject such terminology as "unreasonable," "grossly unreasonable," "arbitrary" and "capricious," it would appear that some classification is helpful. It is worth considering that if the third party is to be held to the standard of acting "reasonably," then the court may be substituting the general standards of the community for the judgment of the person the parties selected. If other architects in town say that a paint job is acceptable, the architect who says it is not will likely be found to have acted unreasonably. Of course, the parties did not contract for the judgment of other architects in town.

Where it appears that the parties have selected a particular third party to give or withhold approval as to a matter which involves a measure of aesthetics, taste and fancy, the honest judgment of the third party is unlikely to be disturbed. This is the probable result even in the case where a forfeiture will result. Where the third party approver has apparently been selected simply because that party is one of those qualified to act or where the third party is passing judgment upon a question of utilitarian function and worth, then the presence of a threatened forfeiture will cause a court to examine the soundness of the decision of the third party.

In these situations a condition of third party approval may be excused if it is withheld for reasons which the court finds to be inappropriate.

Where the duty of a party to perform is subject to his own approval or satisfaction, some restrictions must be placed upon his discretion if one is to find a contract at all. If he is totally free to disapprove for any reason, his promise is illusory, and there is no consideration (§ 55, *supra*). Where the approval involves a matter of aesthetics and taste, some courts say that honesty is the standard, and honest dissatisfaction is enough to cause the condition to fail and permit rejection of the performance. Where the performance is one involving utilitarian standards of an objectively measurable nature, the courts usually imply a duty to act reasonably in exercising the discretion to reject.

D. GOOD FAITH AFFECTING PERFORMANCE

§ 158. Good Faith and Contract Performance

The U.C.C. provides in section 1–203: "Every contract or duty within this Act imposes an obligation of good faith in its performance or enforcement." Court opinions note that every contract imposes a duty of good faith or a duty of good faith and fair dealing upon the parties. Serious problems are encountered when one attempts to define or describe the type of conduct or obligations which the duty of good faith or of good faith and fair dealing imposes. There is also a wide range of opinions as to when such obligations are owing.

Section 1–201(19) of the U.C.C. provides: " 'Good faith' means honesty in fact in the conduct or transaction concerned." This definition, which some refer to as the "pure heart and empty head" test of good faith, is a rather narrow and minimal standard. It applies to all transactions within the Code. (See § 95, *supra*.)

Article Two of the U.C.C. has a number of sections which specifically require good faith in some phase of a transaction. Where the party involved is a merchant, these express mandates of good faith are interpreted to mean "honesty in fact and the observance of reasonable commercial standards of fair dealing in the trade." (See section 2–103(1) (b).) This expanded requirement of good faith will apply, for instance, if a contract for the sale of goods permits the merchant seller to fix the price (section 2–305(2)).

Contract law in the United States does not impose a general requirement of good faith in the negotiation stage. The contract is what gives rise to the obligation of good faith and that obligation is applicable to matters relating to the "performance or enforcement" of the contract. An existing contract may impose a requirement of good faith in the negotiation of renewals or the negotiation of contracts concerning related matters.

Some foreign legal systems impose an obligation of good faith in the negotiation process, and there have been significant writings on this subject in American journals. The German concept of *culpa in contrahendo* imposes significant duties in pre-contract negotiations. The common law, in contrast, imposes primarily negative duties upon parties in the negotiation stage, such as the duty not to misrepresent facts.

A few cases have found liability arising out of pre-contract activities where no contract resulted, but most have been based upon a reliance theory. (See Hoffman v. Red Owl Stores, Inc. (1965) and Wheeler v. White (1965).) However, it has also been held that a letter of intent imposes upon both parties an obligation to meet and negotiate in good faith in an effort to conclude an enforceable bargain. Refusal to negotiate is a breach of this duty that can produce liability, at least for reliance damages.

The obligation of good faith can become relevant in a number of areas. Contract terms which involve approval may be defined in terms of good faith. The implied obligation of cooperation or non-interference with the other party's performance may be reflected in terms of a good faith obligation. A party's right to reject goods because of a defect in tender or to withhold performance on the basis of a technical failure of a condition precedent may be circumscribed by an overriding obligation of good faith or good faith and fair dealing. It should be noted that the use of "reasonableness" as a standard might provide a higher obligation than a requirement of "good faith" if "good faith" is to be defined simply in terms of honesty in fact.

In the examples in the preceding paragraph, good faith does not assume the status of a promised performance for the breach of which a party has a right of action. Good faith becomes simply a standard, not unlike "reasonable," which is used to determine whether conditions are fulfilled or excused or whether promises were fully performed or breached. (See for example, Restatement, Second, section 241 relating to substantial performance in § 143, *supra*.) Good faith is used as a standard to define and describe rights rather than as a right in and of itself.

There are growing numbers of cases which award tort damages based upon violation of obligations of good faith and fair dealing in certain types of contract relationships. These cases are sometimes referred to by the plaintiff's bar as "tortious breach of contract." Prominent among them are cases in the insurance field but there are also a few in areas such as employment termination (§ 97, *supra*). The tort theory opens the potential for recovery for emotional distress and for punitive damages in aggravated circumstances. Use of a tort theory also permits the trier of fact to determine the propriety of a party's actions by applying community standards of conduct rather than those to which the parties agreed in their contract.

E. SALE OF GOODS

§ 159. Performance of Contracts for the Sale of Goods

The U.C.C makes a sharp distinction between single lot contracts and installment contracts in determining the rights of buyer and seller where a tender of performance is in some way inadequate. Therefore, the initial inquiry must be to determine whether section 2–601 (single lot) or 2–612 (installment contract) is controlling.

Section 2–307 sets the basic rule that unless otherwise agreed, contracts for sale require tender in a single delivery, but that section also recognizes that circumstances may give either party the right to make or demand delivery in lots. Section 2–612 defines "installment contract" as "one which requires or authorizes the delivery of goods in separate lots to be separately accepted."

If the contract does not require or authorize delivery in separate lots, then it is a single lot contract and section 2–601 defines the rights and duties of the parties concerning proper tender. The buyer may accept the whole tender, reject the whole or accept any commercial unit or units and reject the rest "if the goods or the tender of delivery fail in any respect to conform to the contract." Literally interpreted, this indicates that the buyer may reject all or part if the tender is one minute late or one widget short. It is difficult to formulate a more "pro-buyer" rule. The buyer's right to reject is subject to the duty of good faith (section 1–

203) which would require that the buyer act honestly (section 1–201(19)). Section 2–601 does not contain language expressly dictating the requirement of good faith, and thus even if the buyer were a merchant, there would apparently be no requirement that he observe reasonable commercial standards of fair dealing in the trade in accordance with section 2–103(1)(b). It is generally accepted that the higher standard of good faith contained in section 2–103(1)(b) is applicable only where Code language expressly requires good faith (§ 158, *supra*).

Section 2–508 gives a seller the right under certain circumstances to cure a defective tender. Section 2–508(1) simply restates the common law rule that where time for performance has not yet expired, the seller who failed on the first try may try again to make a tender which conforms to the contract. Section 2–508(2) is more significant in that it gives the seller additional time to make a conforming tender where the buyer's rejection caught the seller by surprise, that is, where the seller had reasonable grounds to believe the tender would be acceptable. It has been suggested by some that a tender of money damages may "cure" a late tender.

Under pre-Code law, the buyer had the right to reject a tender where the seller was guilty of a major breach but was forced to accept a tender and be content with his right to damages where the breach was minor. This rule forced the innocent buyer to determine at his peril whether the seller's breach was major or minor, a task from which buyers in single lot contracts have been relieved under section 2–601. Under the Code, the buyer has the right to reject for any defect in tender, but the innocent buyer must still determine at his peril whether the court would conclude that rejection was not in good faith. It has been suggested that if the buyer is honestly dissatisfied with the tender, then his rejection is in good faith. If the buyer is dissatisfied with his bargain rather than with the tender, then rejection would not be an act done in good faith.

If a contract for the sale of goods requires or authorizes delivery in installments then section 2–612 is applicable to determine whether the buyer may reject a non-conforming tender. As section 2–601 is pro-buyer, section 2–612 is pro-seller, and the classification of the contract as single lot or installment may determine the final result in many cases.

Except in the case of defects in the required documents, section 2–612(2) gives the buyer the right to reject an installment only if the non-conformity substantially impairs the value of that installment *and* cannot be cured. The question of the right to declare a breach of the total contract is covered by section 2–612(3) which provides:

(3) Whenever non-conformity or default with respect to one or more installments substantially impairs the value of the whole contract there is a

breach of the whole. But the aggrieved party reinstates the contract if he accepts a non-conforming installment without seasonably notifying of cancellation or if he brings an action with respect only to past installments or demands performance as to future installments.

The draftsmen of the Code rejected the terms major and minor breach. The Code does not define "substantially impairs the value," but comment 4 to section 2–612 provides in part:

Substantial impairment of the value of an installment can turn not only on the quality of the goods but also on such factors as time, quantity, assortment, and the like. It must be judged in terms of the normal or specifically known purposes of the contract.

The intent and purpose of section 2–612(2) is explained in comment 5 which provides:

Under subsection (2) an installment delivery must be accepted if the non-conformity is curable and the seller gives adequate assurance of cure. Cure of non-conformity of an installment in the first instance can usually be afforded by an allowance against the price, or in the case of reasonable discrepancies in quantity either by a further delivery or a partial rejection. This Article requires reasonable action by a buyer in regard to discrepant delivery and good faith requires that the buyer make any reasonable minor outlay of time or money necessary to cure an overshipment by severing out an acceptable percentage thereof. The seller must take over a cure which involves any material burden; the buyer's obligation reaches only to cooperation. Adequate assurance for purposes of subsection (2) is measured by the same standards as under the Section on right to adequate assurance of performance.

The U.C.C. does not specifically define breach by a buyer, but section 2–703 provides alternative remedies to the seller where the buyer "wrongfully rejects or revokes acceptance of goods or fails to make a payment . . . or repudiates with respect to part of a whole. . . ."

Matters related to a buyer's right to reject goods or to revoke acceptance of goods are covered in § 135, *supra.*

When you have completed your study of this chapter, you may wish to analyze questions 27–30 at the end of this book and compare your analysis with the one given there.

X. THIRD PARTY
BENEFICIARIES

A. WHAT PARTIES MAY ASSERT
CONTRACT RIGHTS

§ 160. Third Party Beneficiary Contracts

Contracts may be formed in which one party's performance is to be directly rendered to or indirectly confers a benefit upon a third party. Early common law courts had difficulties with the theoretical aspects of permitting a third party who had no privity with the promisor and from whom no consideration "flowed" to enforce the contract (§ 52, *supra*). Today all American jurisdictions have accepted principles of contract law which allow enforcement of such third party beneficiary contracts.

A third party only acquires the right to enforce a contract if the court finds that the principal parties to the contract intended to create legally enforceable rights in the third party. This test has been expressed using varying terminology in different jurisdictions. Some require a finding that the third party was a "direct" beneficiary, some require that the third party be the "primary" beneficiary, and others inquire whether the contract was made for the "express benefit" of the third party. The critical test is whether the third party was intended to have enforceable rights under the contract.

Courts have sometimes indicated lack of certainty as to whose intention actually controls. When a purported third party beneficiary seeks to enforce a promise, the better view is that the promisee's apparent intention should control in determining whether enforceable rights were created in the third party. The Restatement, First, reflected the common view that if the promisee's purpose was "to make a gift to the beneficiary or to confer upon him a right against the promisor to some performance" the third party had enforceable rights. In some jurisdictions such as Pennsylvania, court decisions indicate that both the promisee and the promisor must intend that the third party be a beneficiary.

§ 161. Identification of the Third Party

Historically, third party beneficiaries with enforceable rights have been classified as donee or creditor beneficiaries. A third party without enforceable rights has been identified as an incidental beneficiary to the contract. The distinction between donees and creditors is predicated upon whether the promisee was attempting to confer a gift upon the third party or attempting to discharge an obligation, real or assumed, which was owing to the third party. This classification can be significant because many jurisdictions apply different rules concerning the time the rights of a third party vest (§ 164, *infra*,) depending upon their status as a creditor or donee. In addition, a few jurisdictions, e.g., New York, will not permit a donee beneficiary to enforce a contract unless a family relationship exists between the donee and the promisee. The classification is not always clear since there are situations in which both a charitable motive and an attempt to discharge a real or assumed obligation are evident on the part of the promisee. There is also a category of cases, such as employer contracts with persons who are to provide benefits to the employer's employees, in which an attempt to define the motive as charitable or as intending to discharge an obligation is difficult and not really helpful.

The performance of a contract between A and B, in which A agrees to paint B's weatherbeaten house, will benefit C, B's neighbor. C is, however, nothing more than an incidental beneficiary since there is nothing to indicate that B's motive was to confer a benefit upon C. The performance of a contract between A and B in which A agrees to paint C's house is a direct benefit to C. C is an express beneficiary and the primary purpose of the promisee, B, in entering into such a contract appears to be to confer a benefit upon C. C will be found to be a third party beneficiary, donee or creditor depending upon the motivating force behind B's conduct, and C may acquire enforceable rights under the contract. If B's motives are partly charitable and partly to satisfy an obligation, C will ordinarily be classified as a donee beneficiary in jurisdictions when the rights of a donee are superior to those of a creditor.

The Restatement, Second, section 302, does not use the donee-creditor classification but retains the incidental beneficiary terminology. The term "intended beneficiary" is used in the Restatement to describe a third party with enforceable contract rights. To determine if a third party is an "intended beneficiary," an inquiry must first be made into whether "recognition of a right to performance in the beneficiary is appropriate to effectuate the intention of the parties" and then one must inquire whether:

(a) the performance of the promise will satisfy an obligation of the promisee to pay money to the beneficiary; or

(b) the circumstances indicate that the promisee intends to give the beneficiary the benefit of the promised performance. (Restatement, Second, section 302(1)(a) and (b).)

§ 162. Intended Beneficiaries in Special Situations: Government Contracts and Assumption of Secured Indebtedness

Third party beneficiaries can be found to have acquired enforceable rights in situations in which the presence of third party interests is not readily apparent. Anytime a contract will have the effect of producing a direct benefit for certain individuals or for a class of people, it is necessary to analyze the question whether the promisee intended that these persons have enforceable rights.

There are many types of contracts which are made between government agencies and private parties or other governmental units which have as their primary purpose provision of benefits to a class of citizens. An issue regarding third party rights can exist in contracts providing for such things as job retraining for persons whose employment in the lumber industry was terminated by the creation of a new redwood tree park or replacement housing for persons dislocated by a redevelopment project.

In contracts to which governmental entities are parties, one might assume that the government would prefer to do its own contract enforcing and reserve the right to rescind or modify a contract or determine the manner and extent of enforcement action. Thus one might assume that giving a right of action to a third party beneficiary might not be "appropriate to effectuate the intention of the parties." However, third parties have been found to have enforceable rights in similar situations and the Restatement, Second, section 302 gives the following illustration:

10. A, the operator of a chicken processing and fertilizer plant, contracts with B, a municipality, to use B's sewage system. With the purpose of preventing harm to landowners downstream from its system, B obtains from A a promise to remove specified types of waste from

its deposits into the system. C, a downstream landowner, is an intended beneficiary under Subsection (1)(b).

Third party rights may also "creep in unnoticed" in transactions in which some aspect of the agreement involves one party contracting to render a performance which will satisfy an obligation owing from the promisee to the beneficiary. One significant area which raises a third party beneficiary issue involves obligations secured by a mortgage or other security interest in real property. These obligations may be a personal obligation of the debtor or the debtor may have no personal liability thereon. This is a problem which involves issues outside the area of contracts, and it is complicated in most jurisdictions by anti-deficiency legislation which restricts or precludes the secured creditor from holding the debtor personally liable for portions of the debt not repaid by foreclosure.

When a debtor is personally liable for a secured loan on property which he is selling, he will ordinarily want the buyer of the property to assume the loan. "Assume" means promise to pay. If the buyer merely takes the property "subject to" the loan, the buyer will likely lose the property if the debt is not paid, but he has no personal liability for any deficiency if the property does not sell for enough to repay the entire debt. If the grantee (buyer) assumes the loan and the debt is not paid, the creditor may foreclose on the property and, subject to applicable anti-deficiency statutes, may hold the original debtor liable for the balance. Since the original debtor has the right to enforce the promise of the grantee to pay the balance, the creditor may also sue that assuming grantee on the theory of subrogation. (A creditor, under certain circumstances, has the right to bring a direct action against persons who owe money to his debtor.)

The law regarding third party beneficiaries may become involved when the following transaction occurs: A, the owner of Blackacre, borrows money from L and executes a note and a mortgage giving L a security interest in Blackacre as well as a personal promise to pay. A sells Blackacre to B who takes the property subject to the mortgage, thereby assuming no personal obligation to pay the loan. B later resells the property to C who assumes the loan, thus personally promising to pay it. The loan is in default. L forecloses and sells the property, but there is still $50,000 unpaid as the selling price did not cover the full amount of the loan. Assuming no anti-deficiency statute problems, A is liable to L for the $50,000. Assuming that A is gone or insolvent, may L hold C personally liable?

L cannot reach C on a theory of subrogation. B was not personally liable for the loan, so A has no right against B. This breaks the chain and prevents L or A from reaching C on a subrogation theory. L's alternative theory is that he is a third party beneficiary of the B–C contract. In the B–C contract, C promised to pay the outstanding loan to

L. B was not indebted to L, so at first glance, L does not appear to be a creditor beneficiary. Creditor beneficiaries are found, however, where the purpose of the promisee was to satisfy a creditor, actual or supposed, and it might be that B supposed or feared he might be personally obligated to L. L can assert the status of donee beneficiary, but it is not an easy task to convince a court that B's purpose was to confer a gift upon the mortgage holder. However in cases involving this issue, a number of jurisdictions have allowed L to recover against C on a third party beneficiary theory.

§ 163. Rights of the Promisee Against the Promisor

When the promisor fails to perform the promise made for the benefit of a creditor beneficiary, the creditor beneficiary may bring action against the promisor or may proceed against the promisee on the original obligation. If the creditor does proceed against the promisee, the promisee will be damaged as a result of the promisor's failure to perform. The promisee may sue the promisor for these damages.

In the case of a donee beneficiary, the promisee is not personally harmed by the promisor's failure to perform. If the donee beneficiary does not take action against the promisor, the promisee has no remedy at law. For this reason, the promisee is permitted to bring action against the promisor to specifically enforce the contract.

B. DEFENSES AGAINST THIRD PARTIES' CLAIMS

§ 164. Rights of Third Party Beneficiaries; Vesting of Rights

Because the third party's rights against the promisor are dependent upon the third party beneficiary contract, the third party's rights are subject to defenses which the promisor has in that contract. Thus if no valid contract was formed or if it is not enforceable against the promisor, the promisor may assert this defense against the third party beneficiary. If the beneficiary consents, the promisor and the promisee are generally free to modify the contract to the detriment of the third party or to rescind the contract. However, such modifications or rescissions without the consent of the third party beneficiary will not be effective if they occur after the beneficiary's rights have vested.

Different jurisdictions find rights to have vested upon the occurrence of one of three events. First, there are cases which hold that rights vest immediately at the time the contract is made. This is true even when the beneficiary does not learn of the contract until a later time. Second, a number of cases hold that rights vest at the time the third party acquires knowledge of the contract and agrees to accept the benefits thereof. Acceptance is ordinarily presumed in the absence of an express rejection. Third, probably the most commonly applied rule requires a change in position by the beneficiary in reliance upon the contract in order to vest his rights. Ordinarily, only a slight change in position is required, e.g., filing suit against the promisor.

Many states apply different rules to donee and to creditor beneficiaries with the donee beneficiaries' rights usually vesting immediately or when they have knowledge and assent and the creditor beneficiaries' rights vesting later in time, usually after some reliance. The reason for the distinction is that the creditor will ordinarily have a right of action against his principal debtor, the promisee. Some states vest the rights of third parties more quickly if the beneficiaries are minors. The inability of a minor to "learn" of his rights and "assent" has led some courts to provide for the immediate vesting of minors' rights upon the making of the contract. Other jurisdictions follow a single rule for vesting without regard to the nature of the beneficiary. The Restatement, Second, section 311(3) takes the position that rights vest when the beneficiary "materially changes his position in justifiable reliance on the promise or brings suit on it or manifests assent to it at the request of the promisor or promisee."

Where immediate vesting is applied, it can constitute a trap for the unwary. A and B enter into a contract in which B agrees to perform a promise for the benefit of C who is totally unaware of what is transpiring. Shortly thereafter, A and B rescind their agreement, possibly to enter a different agreement in which B's promise will be performed for A himself. In a jurisdiction which applies immediate vesting, C acquired an enforceable right against B when the A–B contract was made, and the subsequent A–B rescission does not affect C's right.

§ 165. Defenses Assertable Against the Third Party Beneficiary

Assume that Joe and Mary had a business transaction and that Mary claims that Joe owes her $10,000. Thereafter, Joe entered into a contract with Dan in which Joe promised to render a service and Dan promised to pay $10,000 to Mary. Now Mary has brought action against Dan for the $10,000.

The promisor can assert against the third party defenses arising under the third party beneficiary contract. Since the sole basis for Mary's action against Dan is the Dan-Joe contract, any defenses which Dan might properly assert under that contract are available against Mary. This would include defenses relating to formation such as misrepresentation or mistake or defenses relating to enforcement such as violation of public policy. It would also include a defense arising out of failure of a condition precedent to Dan's duty to perform such as Joe's failure to perform the service that he agreed to render for Dan.

The only defense that might arise under the Dan-Joe contract that cannot be asserted against Mary would be the defense of modification or rescission that occurred after Mary's rights had vested. (See § 164, *supra*.) For example, if Mary learned of the Dan-Joe contract and changed position in reliance upon her right to recover from Dan, her rights under that contract would be vested no matter which vesting rule the court applied. If Dan and Joe later modified their contract, such as by providing that Dan would pay the $10,000 to Joe instead of to Mary, this modification cannot defeat Mary's vested rights. This is the only significance of vesting. If there has been no attempt to rescind or modify the contract to reduce the third party's rights, then vesting is not an issue and no discussion of that point is required.

A promisor may not assert against a third party defenses that arise out of the transaction between the third party and the promisee. Thus, Dan may not assert against Mary defenses which Joe might have had if Mary had sued Joe. The nature and details of the underlying transaction between Joe and Mary is of no relevance to Dan. Whether Joe actually owed Mary any sum of money or whether Joe had a defense that he could have asserted against Mary is not important. For reasons satisfactory to himself, Joe entered a contract in which he obtained from Dan an agreement to pay $10,000 to Mary. If the Joe-Dan contract is legally enforceable, it is none of Dan's concern whether Joe was actually obligated to pay Mary.

Assume facts as set forth in the first paragraph of this section except that instead of promising to pay $10,000 to Mary in exchange for Joe's services, Dan promised to "pay the debt that Joe owes to Mary." In this situation, the measure of Dan's obligation is the amount that Joe owes to Mary. Thus the details of the Joe-Mary transaction would be relevant in an action by Mary against Dan, and Dan could properly raise and prove defenses that Joe might have had against Mary. Dan is not being permitted to assert defenses in the Joe-Mary transaction as a defense to his own obligation to perform. Dan is being permitted to prove defenses that Joe might have had against Mary because the amount legally owing from Joe to Mary is the measure of Dan's obligation.

When you have completed your study of this chapter, you may wish to analyze question 31 at the end of this book and compare your analysis with the one given there.

XI. ASSIGNMENT OF RIGHTS AND DELEGATION OF DUTIES

A. ASSIGNMENT OF RIGHTS

§ 166. Assignment of Rights; Delegation of Duties Distinguished

Most rights are capable of being transferred. Once a transfer has been accomplished, the transferor's interest in the right is extinguished and the right becomes the property of the transferee. A transfer of a contract right is called an assignment.

Duties are not transferable in the sense that rights are. Many duties are delegable, but the delegator remains responsible for the performance. If the party to whom the duty is owing agrees to the delegation and promises to release the delegator, a novation results and the delegator is released (§ 183, *infra*).

It is not uncommon to read or hear that one party "assigned the contract" to another. This is an ambiguous expression which must be interpreted by use of surrounding facts and circumstances. An "assignment of the contract" may mean that the assignor intends to perform the contract duties and manifests an intention only to transfer the contract rights. This is the typical situation in which the assignment is made to a lender as security for a loan. For example, a lender may advance money to a contractor and take an assignment of the right to payment on certain construction contracts. This is done to protect the lender in the event the contractor does not repay the loan. It would be most unlikely that a court would find that the lender has assumed the duty to build the structures.

The expression "assignment of the contract" may mean that the assignor intends to transfer the contract rights subject to performance of the contract duties with the result that the assignee is not bound to perform but will not receive contract benefits unless performance is rendered by the assignee. This result is reached in a number of cases in which the assignor "assigns" a bilateral executory contract for the purchase of real property in exchange for the payment of a nominal sum or other sum clearly less than the market value of the property. An example might be X assigning to Y for $500 cash X's rights in a contract for the purchase of Blackacre from S for $400,000. Courts have held that the assignee only acquires the right to the contract performance if he tenders the return performance. While the assignee may not have undertaken a duty to perform, he is not entitled to the return performance unless he does in fact perform.

"Assignment of the contract" may also mean that the assignor manifests an intention to transfer the contract rights and to delegate the contract duties. In this case, the assignee, by consenting to the transaction, impliedly promises to perform the delegated duties. The assignee/delegatee may thus be liable to the other party to the contract or to the assignor/delegator for breach in the event of nonperformance.

It is usually clear from the nature of the transaction between the assignor and assignee whether the parties contemplate that the assignor will be expected to perform the contract duties even though the assignee is to receive the performance. However, when the nature of the transaction is such that it is apparent the assignee must perform if he is to receive the contract benefits, it may be difficult to determine whether the parties intended that the assignee should be obligated to perform.

Assume that Henry has contracted to sell 1,000 widgets to Joe for $50,000. Henry then "assigns" this contract to Jane for $500. The U.C.C. (section 2–210) and the Restatement, Second, (section 328) take the position that the assignee who accepts the assignment under these circumstances becomes bound to perform. As noted in the Restatement, however, in the case of assignment of executory contracts for the purchase and sale of real property, courts generally hold that the assignee does not assume personal liability for the contract performance. In real property transactions, the sale of property which is subject to a mortgage or other encumbrance does not impose upon the buyer personal liability for the payment of the encumbrance unless the buyer expressly assumes that obligation. Some cases expressly consider that analogous situation in holding that an assignee of an executory contract for the purchase of real property does not assume personal liability for payment of the purchase price.

§ 167. What Rights Are Assignable; Effect of Prohibitions Against Assignment

Rights arising from a contract are generally assignable. The other party to the contract, the obligor, may properly object to an assignment of right to receive his performance only where his duty is somehow materially changed, where the risk of not receiving the return performance is materially increased, or the value of the contract performance is substantially reduced. Examples might include the attempted assignment by a buyer of his rights under a requirements contract, the rights of a borrower under a loan commitment, or the contract right of a famous person to have his portrait painted. In most of these cases, the problem at least partly involves an attempt to delegate duties which are not properly delegable.

Most obligors would prefer not to have to deal with assignees, and it is thus not unusual to encounter contract provisions which attempt to prohibit or restrict assignability. Since the assignment of contract rights is a common source of business financing and has other economically beneficial purposes, contract provisions which purport to limit the right to assign have been strictly construed by the courts. A contract provision which states that the "contract will not be assigned" has typically been interpreted to prohibit delegation of duties but not assignment of rights. A contract provision to the effect that "rights shall not be assigned" is typically interpreted to constitute a promise not to assign. In that case, an attempted assignment is fully effective and the obligor is left with an action against the assignor for breach of his promise not to assign. Even a contract provision which contains language to the effect that "any attempted assignment of rights is null and void" is usually interpreted as being only for the benefit of the obligor and only having the effect of permitting the obligor to refuse to deal with the assignee. Thus the assignment can still be valid as between the assignee and the assignor or the creditors or subsequent assignees of the assignor. Unless expressly covered, contract terms prohibiting assignments may also be found not to forbid assignment of all right to damages for breach of the entire contract or a right to payment arising out of the assignor's full performance of his contract obligation.

In addition to the restrictive rules of interpretation of contract provisions which attempt to prohibit assignment, there are various statutory restrictions which are designed to preserve freedom to assign rights. The U.C.C. (section 9–318) prohibits any restriction upon the assignability of the right to receive payment for goods sold or leased, or for services rendered. It also prohibits any restriction upon the assignment for security of any other right to receive money which comes within Article Nine of the Code. In contracts involving transactions in goods, the U.C.C. (section 2–210) prohibits any restrictions upon assignment of the right to damages for breach of the whole contract or a right arising out of the assignor's full performance of his contract duties.

Policy considerations have produced common law and statutory restrictions upon the assignment of certain rights. The assignment of tort claims for personal injuries is prohibited at common law because it violates public policy. It is sometimes stated that public policy considerations preclude the assignment of all tort claims, however, the logic of the policy considerations does not necessarily extend to property damage claims, and these can be assigned in some jurisdictions. Most states have statutes which either prohibit or restrict the assignment of contract rights to wages or salary for personal services. Some statutes permit the assignment of all or part of a contract right for wages if the wages have already been earned prior to the time of assignment. Some require the signature of a spouse.

The Federal Government and many state governments have restrictions on the assignment of claims against the government. These laws are ordinarily interpreted to relieve the government of the duty of dealing with the assignee but do not affect the validity of the assignment as between the assignor and the assignee.

§ 168. Requisites of an Assignment

Restatement, Second, section 324 provides:

It is essential to an assignment of a right that the obligee manifest an intention to transfer the right to another person without further action or manifestation of intention by the obligee. The manifestation may be made to the other or to a third person on his behalf, and, except as provided by statute or by contract, may be made either orally or by a writing.

Care must be taken to distinguish between a manifestation of intent to transfer a right to the assignee and a statement which identifies a source of payment or a promise to pay. Attorney X may state to Attorney Y: "Write the brief and you will get one-half the fee." This may be a promise of payment and may fix the amount and time when the payment is due, but it does not manifest an intent to transfer to Y the present right to collect the fee or any part of it.

The U.C.C. (section 1–206) imposes a writing requirement providing that the assignment is not enforceable beyond $5,000 in the absence of a sufficient writing. In addition, all assignments which are covered by Article Nine of the U.C.C. (see § 172, *infra*) must be effected by a signed security agreement (section 9–203(1)(a)).

At one time, the common law required that the contract which created the assigned right had to be in existence in order to have a valid present assignment. It was not necessary that the right have already been earned by performance, nor did it matter that the right was created by an option contract, but there had to be an existing contractual relationship from which the assigned right would arise. An attempted assignment of rights which might arise under contracts to be made in the future was treated as a promise to assign. The effect of this distinction is that the party seeking to obtain the right in question was required to contend with issues relating to the enforceability of the promise to assign and with third parties who claimed an interest in the right. The distinction could also affect the availability of defenses which the obligor could assert against the would-be assignee. (See § 173, *infra*.)

Recent developments have modified the common law rules in two ways. Where there is an existing business or employment relationship, a present attempt to assign a right which will arise out of a future contract anticipated in this existing relationship is now generally recognized as a valid present transfer of the right in question. The other change applies to assignments which come within the coverage of Article Nine of the U.C.C. This article authorizes an agreement between assignor and assignee by which the assignor's rights under future contracts will be effectively assigned the instant these future contracts are made. Technically this does not change the common law rule, but it results in instant assignment of all new contract rights without the necessity of further communication or paperwork between the assignor and the assignee. It also accomplishes the intended purpose of transferring the right in question to the assignee free of any intervening claims of third parties such as creditors of the assignor or parties claiming to be assignees of the same right.

§ 169. Assignment of Rights Embodied in a Tangible Object

If there is a tangible thing which represents a right, this thing ordinarily must be transferred from the assignor to the assignee before the latter can effectively enforce the right in question. The right to attend a football game and sit on the 40 yard line is represented by a thing or token which we call a ticket. An attempt to transfer that right to another person without giving that person the ticket will ordinarily not be sufficient to give the assignee the effective right to gain entrance to the game.

Rights are often evidenced by something such as a written contract. Such a writing does not represent the right. One need not surrender a written contract to enforce a right to payment thereon. There is no requirement that a thing which merely evidences the right be given to the assignee.

Where there exists a token or instrument which represents the right, the delivery of that thing is good evidence of the assignor's manifestation of intent to transfer. Such delivery is also a good basis for finding that a gratuitous assignment has been completed and is thus irrevocable. Failure to deliver the instrument or token which represents the rights may give the obligor a defense to rendering the performance to the assignee because of the assignee's inability to produce the token or instrument. However, the failure to deliver the instrument or token does not necessarily preclude a finding that there has been a valid assignment.

Numerous cases exist in which an assignor delivered a writing to the assignee which purported to constitute a present transfer of a right. Such deliveries have been found to constitute a valid present assignment and thus, where gratuitous, a completed gift, even where there was a token or instrument representing the right which was not transferred.

§ 170. Revocability of Assignments: Events That Revoke

An assignment becomes irrevocable if:

(a) it is made for consideration,

(b) it is represented by a token or document which has been delivered,

(c) the assignee has changed position in reasonable reliance upon the assignment, or

(d) the assignee has obtained payment from the obligor or judgment against the obligor or has entered into a contract with the obligor whereby the obligation has been modified.

Revocable assignments may be revoked at will by the assignor and are deemed to be revoked by the making of a subsequent assignment of the same right, by demand for performance or acceptance of performance by the assignor from the obligor, or by death or loss of capacity of the assignor or initiation of bankruptcy proceedings by or against the assignor.

§ 171. Partial Assignments

Before the law developed procedures permitting liberal joinder of parties, an obligor was free to ignore a partial assignment of a right. The partial assignment could have the effect of forcing the obligor to defend more than one suit arising out of the single transaction. Partial assignments are now permitted. The obligor is protected by permitting him to force the joinder in one action of all persons holding partial assignments of the same right, including the assignor if he reserves some portion of the right assigned.

§ 172. Multiple Assignments of Same Right; Coverage and Impact of U.C.C. Article Nine

Assignors with little cash and less morality may find themselves tempted to resell the same right two or more times by assigning it to successive assignees. An assignor who receives value warrants to his assignee that the right assigned actually exists and is subject to no defenses other than those stated. He also warrants that he has no knowledge of any fact which would defeat or impair the value of the assigned right and will do nothing to cause the right to be defeated. Successive assignments of the same right breach this warranty and subject the assignor to liability, but assignors who resell the same right to several people frequently have no visible assets from which to obtain satisfaction of a judgment. Since the obligor only intends to pay his debt once, the issue becomes one of determining which of the successive assignees has priority. Each assignee has parted with value and is innocent of any wrongdoing, yet only one will recover.

Article Nine of the U.C.C. covers all assignments which are made to secure the performance of obligations and all assignments of any sort which involve rights to payment arising from the sale or lease of goods or the rendition of services (sec. 9–102). There are some exceptions to the coverage of Article Nine (section 9–104 and particularly subsection (f)), but these tend to be confined to situations in which it is unlikely that there will be an opportunity for successive assignments of the same right. To be sure, there are some assignments which are not within Article Nine such as the assignment of the right to receive royalties for the sale or use of a patent or copyright, or the right to receive payment for the sale or rental of real property. Such assignments are within Article Nine if they are made to secure some obligation (section 9–102(1)(a)). If made as absolute assignments, they are not covered by Article Nine because they do not arise from the sale or lease of goods or rendition of services and are therefore not "accounts" (sections 9–102(1)(b) and 9–106).

Article Nine protects those who file financing statements and obtain signed security agreements from the assignor. The scheme is relatively simple. Filing a document (the financing statement) in a public office (often the Secretary of State) gives notice to all other potential assignees, lenders and other existing and potential creditors that the rights described therein have been assigned. With certain exceptions (e.g., section 9–312(4)), priority is given to the person who first filed the financing statement in the public office. There are some significant exceptions where filing is not required, e.g., section 9–302(1). The effect of Article Nine reduces the problem in most cases to determining whether anyone else has already filed a financing statement which covers assignments, and making certain that your client files before money or other valuable property is advanced to the assignor.

In those limited situations in which Article Nine is not controlling, priority among successive assignees is controlled by common law rules. The majority rule at common law, the so-called "American rule" provides that the first person who received an irrevocable assignment prevails over all subsequent assignees. An exception or qualification of this rule provides that the first assignee may be estopped from asserting priority where his failure to notify the obligor within a reasonable time resulted in a subsequent assignee being misled. This can occur where the assignor assigned to one assignee who did not give notice to the obligor. Assignor thereafter offers to assign for value to a second assignee who takes the precaution of first checking with the obligor to ascertain that there is a debt which is not yet paid and not yet assigned. If the first assignee's failure to give prompt notice results in the second assignee giving value for the assignment, then estoppel can be raised to preclude the first assignee from asserting his priority. Subsequent assignees have also prevailed when, acting in good faith and without reason to know of a prior assignment, they gave value and obtained payment or a judgment or a new contract in substitution for the assigned obligation or possession of the writing or thing (tokens) which represents the assigned right. (See § 169, *supra*.)

The apparent minority rule at common law, the so-called English rule, provides that the first assignee to give notice to the debtor prevails. This rule is based upon the theory that the giving of notice to the debtor is an act which the assignee should perform to perfect his rights as against other assignees or creditors.

§ 173. Defenses Available to the Obligor Against the Assignee

An assignment involves a transfer of rights. One basic proposition is that the assignee to whom those rights are transferred can have no better rights than the assignor possessed. This leads to the general proposition that the debtor or obligor can assert against the assignee all of the defenses that the debtor could have asserted against the assignor.

If the contract that created the assigned rights is subject to a defense arising out of its formation (§§ 99–124, *supra*), then this defense may be asserted against the assignee. These defenses are not waivable.

As a general rule, the obligor may also assert against the assignee any other defenses arising out of the contract without regard to whether the defense relates to matters that arose before or after the notice of assignment (U.C.C. section 9–318(1)(a)). However, there are two significant exceptions to this generalization.

The defense of payment is available to the debtor so long as payment was made before notice of the assignment and demand for payment by the assignee. After the assignee has demanded that performance be rendered to the assignee, the debtor may no longer make payments to the assignor and claim that the obligation was thereby discharged.

The debtor may expressly waive defenses against an assignee in the original contract. When one party to a contract plans to assign rights thereunder (typically a seller of goods or services contemplating assigning the right to payment), that party may seek a contract term in which the other party waives contract defenses against the assignee.

This simple contract term can have far-reaching implications because the debtor can end up paying money to the assignee for defective goods or for goods that were never delivered or services that were never rendered.

Common law decisions have avoided waiver of defense clauses in situations in which the assignor and assignee were closely related or both involved in the business transaction, however there is no general prohibition against such waivers. U.C.C. section 9–206 expressly permits waiver of defenses by "buyers or lessees" but by its terms it defers to consumer protection statutes and court decisions that provide otherwise. Most jurisdictions have such statutes protecting buyers in consumer transactions.

Some common law decisions provided that after notice of assignment, the principal parties to the contract could no longer modify that contract in such a way as to reduce the assignee's rights. U.C.C. section 9–318(2) expressly permits modifications that are made in good faith and in accordance with reasonable commercial standards so long as they relate to performances not yet rendered.

Another issue concerning defenses of a contract debtor against an assignee relates to matters arising outside of the contract that created the assigned right. Assume that Jim agrees to paint Donna's house for $7,000. While the work is progressing, Donna sells her used car to Jim for $4,000 on credit. Thereafter, Bank notifies Donna that Bank is the assignee of the Jim-Donna painting contract and demands that payment be made directly to Bank. The question is whether Donna can reduce her obligation by the $4,000 that is owing on the car.

U.C.C. section 9–318(1) provides: ". . . the rights of an assignee are subject to . . . (b) any other defense or claim of the account debtor against the assignor which accrues before the account debtor receives notification of the assignment." Thus the rights of Bank are subject to the $4,000 claim of Donna against Jim if that claim had accrued before she received notice of the assignment. The claim for $4,000 has accrued if it was already due and owing when Donna received the notice from Bank. For example, if Donna agreed to let Jim pay "in ten days," and she received notice of the assignment before the ten days had expired, then the $4,000 debt was not yet due and owing when she received notice, and she may not set off this claim against the Bank. Donna would be obligated to pay Bank the full $7,000 and would have to look to Jim for payment of the $4,000. Since lenders such as Bank ordinarily demand direct payment only when their debtor (Jim) is considered to be in bad financial condition, the right to set off the $4,000 against the total obligation is very important to the account debtor.

B. DELEGATION OF DUTIES

§ 174. Delegation of Duties: What Is Delegable

An obligor may properly delegate to another the performance of contract duties so long as the obligee will receive the substantial benefit of the bargain. If the performance to be rendered is one for personal services or otherwise calls for the exercise of skill and discretion, the performance will likely be found to be "too personal" to delegate.

Some performances are of such a nature that they are obviously too personal to delegate, e.g. contracts to teach, to sing or to paint a portrait. Even these duties would be delegable if one were to find an express or implied contract agreement permitting delegation.

The duty to pay money is delegable. The duty to deliver a fungible good, such as wheat, and similar impersonal activities would also be delegable in the absence of unusual facts or contract provisions which somehow cause the performance to be viewed as personal to the obligor.

Service contracts involving relatively mechanical activities such as painting a house, building a warehouse, or chopping wood would ordinarily be delegable. However, these garden-variety service contracts must be examined in their entirety to determine whether in the particular circumstance the parties contemplated personal performance. Even if one determines that the parties contemplated that the actual performance was to be accomplished by employees, the service may still be too personal to delegate if the duty of supervision is personal to the obligor.

Contracts for professional services such as those of an attorney or a physician are said to involve unique abilities and are thus stated to be non-delegable. However, the retention of the services of an attorney in a law firm would in ordinary circumstances constitute a contract for the services of the firm. Performance by another member of the firm thus does not involve a delegation of duties. A surgeon may properly obtain assistance of another during a lengthy operation and in fact may have an assistant or specialist perform a substantial part of a surgical procedure.

One might assume that contracts with corporations would be delegable in that the corporation would in any event have performance rendered by employees or agents. The parties were no doubt also aware that the ownership and control of the corporation might change during the course of performance of the contract. However, the obligee may have contracted with the corporation in reliance upon the ability and skill of its employees and its supervisors. Thus a delegation by a corporation must be subjected to the usual scrutiny.

The propriety of an attempted delegation of duties in a service contract also involves questions of the skill of the delegatee. A duty which might otherwise be delegable cannot be delegated to one who lacks the capacity or experience to complete the task in a satisfactory manner. For example, a contract to build a cannery to plans and specifications might be delegable to a qualified and experienced cannery builder, but a delegation to a delegatee who had no experience in construction of structures of this sort has been found improper, and the attempted performance by the delegatee need not be accepted by the obligee. Conversely, the qualifications of the delegatee may cause the court to find a proper delegation where the delegability of the duty is doubtful. For instance, a delegation by a corporation to its two sole shareholders may not result in any change in the personalities of the parties supervising the performance. A delegation by corporation number one to corporation number two which has purchased the facilities and retained all of the employees of corporation number one has been found not to affect substantially the performance of the contract. In such circumstances, the qualifications of the delegatee may cause the court to find the delegation proper. The ultimate question is whether the obligee can expect to receive substantially the same performance from the delegatee as the obligee had the right to expect from the delegator.

A contract provision which permits delegation will be enforced. Subsequent consent by the obligee to a delegation will be enforced if it is given for consideration or if the delegator has changed position in reliance upon the obligee's consent. A contract provision that prohibits delegation will most likely not be interpreted to prohibit the delegation of a duty that is totally impersonal such as the duty to pay money. However, such a provision expresses the parties' intention to treat the contractual duties as personal to the parties and can make non-delegable a duty which might otherwise have been delegated. For example, a contract duty to build a home might ordinarily be delegable, but a provision in that contract requiring performance by the promisor or otherwise expressly prohibiting delegation would be enforced. If a duty is delegable, an expression of objection by the obligee after the contract has been made will not prevent a valid delegation nor preclude performance by the delegatee.

§ 175. Liability of Delegator and Delegatee

A delegatee does not become liable for the performance of contract duties unless he assumes those duties by expressly or impliedly promising to perform. If the delegatee does assume, the promise to perform creates contract rights in the delegator who may bring an action for its breach. The delegatee's promise to perform also creates contract rights in the obligee who may bring an action as a third party beneficiary of the contract in which the delegatee assumed the duty of performance. Most third party creditor beneficiaries base their rights upon agreements in which a delegatee assumed contract duties. (See § 161, *supra*.)

A delegator remains liable for the performance of his contract duties despite the fact that the delegatee has assumed them. A denial by the delegator of further obligation under the contract constitutes a repudiation of contract even if the delegatee is competent to perform and expresses willingness to perform.

The obligee may consent to a novation whereby he agrees to accept performance from the delegatee. This agreement from an obligee releases the delegator from further obligation upon the contract. The consideration for the obligee's release of the delegator is the promise of the delegatee to perform (§ 183, *infra*).

If the delegator has repudiated his obligations under the contract, acceptance of performance from the delegatee without an express reservation of rights against the delegator may constitute implied consent by the obligee to a novation. If a duty is non-delegable because of its personal nature, acceptance of performance or part performance with knowledge that it was rendered by a delegatee will constitute a waiver by the obligee of the right to object to the delegation. Other than the above-stated situations, the acceptance by the obligee of performance from the delegatee does not release or waive any rights. If the duty is properly delegated, the obligee in fact has no choice but to accept performance by the delegatee. Thus, accepting part performance does not release the delegator from the duty to render the remaining performance. So also, acceptance of goods from a delegatee would not release the delegator from liability for breach of warranty arising from defects in the goods delivered.

When you have completed your study of this chapter, you may wish to analyze questions 32–34 at the end of this book and compare your analysis with the one given there.

XII. EVENTS THAT EXCUSE PERFORMANCE

A. IMPOSSIBILITY OR IMPRACTICABILITY

§ 176. Impracticability ("Impossibility") of Performance

Contract liability is strict liability. It is an accepted maxim that *pacta sunt servanda,* contracts are to be kept. The obligor is therefore liable in damages for breach of contract even if he is without fault and even if circumstances have made the contract more burdensome or less desirable than he had anticipated. (Restatement, Second, Introductory Note to Chapter 11.)

The common law first made exceptions and excused a party from contract duties where his performance had become impossible due to: (a) death or disability of one whose existence is necessary for the performance of the contract duty; (b) destruction without the fault of the promisor of a thing necessary for the performance of the contract; or (c) supervening governmental action which prohibits or purports to prohibit the performance of the contract. If a singer contracts to perform in a nightclub, the disability of the singer will excuse the duty to perform. In a contract for the sale of a specific cow, the death of the cow without fault on the part of the seller will excuse the duty to deliver. If a scrap dealer contracts to sell copper to a company in a foreign country, a government regulation which purports to prohibit the export of copper will excuse performance.

A supervening event that made performance more difficult or expensive or which made the contract as a whole less profitable or unprofitable did not excuse performance in early common law cases. Where parties sought to avoid contracts on such grounds, many court opinions labeled the situation one of "commercial impracticability" and stated a general rule that "commercial impracticability" is not sufficient to excuse performance since excuse of performance requires "impossibility."

As the law has developed over the years, courts have come to release parties from their contract obligations in various situations in which performance is not in fact impossible but is highly impracticable or is not possible of being rendered in the contemplated fashion. However, many courts have clung to the old vocabulary using the term impossibility to identify the basis upon which the contract duty is discharged even though the evidence indicated only that the performance was impracticable and not literally impossible. The Restatement, most writers and many cases use the term "impracticability" to describe this defense and this term is now generally accepted.

§ 177. Factors Necessary to Support Impracticability as a Defense

Four elements are required to establish the defense of impracticability. The first requirement is the occurrence of an event which has made performance, or performance in the contemplated fashion impracticable. Death, fire, illness, crop failures, canal closures, government regulations and similar events are the stuff from which these defenses commonly arise. These events are usually acts of God or of third persons or governments beyond the control of the parties to the contract. Some events make performance literally impossible which definitely satisfies this first element. The event may make performance in the contemplated fashion impossible but leave an alternative method of performance open. In this case, the degree of impracticability is the issue. Increased cost alone is not generally enough, but cost which involves economic waste through unreasonable allocation of labor and resources makes an alternative method of performance legally impracticable.

Where no event has occurred but the parties simply discover facts that existed at the time the contract was formed which make performance impracticable, the appropriate defense to analyze should be mistake. Some cases and the Restatement, Second, take the position that the party seeking excuse has a choice of defenses and may assert either mistake or impracticability.

A party seeking to utilize the defense of impracticability must establish that it is objectively impracticable (i.e., the thing cannot be done or at least cannot be done in the contemplated fashion) rather than subjectively impossible (i.e., I cannot do it). The promise to do the act carries with it the representation that the party has the usual skills and resources to accomplish the task, and thus he assumes the risk of his own shortcomings.

The second element which must be established is that the event must have occurred without the fault of the party who seeks relief in reliance thereon. Misconduct or negligence of the party may be sufficient to deny him the relief which he seeks.

The third factor is expressed in the U.C.C. and the Restatement, Second, in terms that the non-occurrence of the event must have been a basic assumption upon which the contract was made. Certain risks are allocated to one party by operation of law. The most common example is the risk that prices will change. The basic reason for entering a contract for future purchase and sale of goods, other than tying down a source which is necessary in some situations, is to protect oneself against price fluctuations. Thus a farmer may sell a crop before it is harvested because today's prices are adequate to assure a modest profit for the year. The milling company may buy that crop for future delivery because today's prices will permit it to compete in the market. Both parties are quite aware of the fact that prices will change. That is why they made the contract. Thus even a substantial change in prices does not excuse performance.

While the fact of change in market price does not excuse performance, market changes which result from events which the parties assumed would not occur may provide grounds for discharge. Comment 4 of U.C.C. section 2–615 states in part: ". . . a severe shortage of raw materials or of supplies due to a contingency such as war, embargo, local crop failure, unforeseen shutdown of major sources of supply or the like, which either causes a marked increase in cost or altogether prevents the seller from securing supplies necessary to his performance, is within the contemplation of this Section."

The fourth factor to be considered in determining whether relief should be granted on grounds of impracticability is whether the party seeking the relief has agreed to assume the risk of the event which is now asserted as a basis for discharge. The third factor may be characterized as an allocation of risk for certain events which is imposed on a party by operation of law. This fourth factor is one which is imposed upon the party because the party assumed a greater risk than what the law would otherwise have imposed. This might result from express language assuming such risk or by negative implication from such things as recital of events which will excuse and which omits the event in issue. The fact that the event which occurred was foreseeable does not automatically lead to the result that the party assumed the risk of its happening by failing to provide for it in the contract, nor in the application of the third factor does foreseeability "compel the conclusion that its non-occurrence was not such a basic assumption."

The language of the U.C.C. and the Restatement, Second, provides the basis for a substantial expansion of the types of cases for which relief will be granted. Certainly the law has progressed far beyond the old common law rules which purported to require actual impossibility before contracts would be discharged. However, oil embargoes by exporting nations, closures of canals and a worldwide shortage of yellowcake to supply atomic fuel for reactors produced litigation which provided an opportunity for courts to move into new areas in the subject of impracticability if they chose to do so. It seems fair to observe that recent court decisions have not been as liberal in excusing performance as some anticipated. In predicting results in this area it is wise to remember that there is still a significant judicial tendency to hold parties to their bargains, finding that they assumed the risk of events which now make their performance difficult.

B. FRUSTRATION OF PURPOSE

§ 178. Frustration of Purpose; "Economic Frustration"

After formation of a contract, events may occur that make the performance of the contract useless

to one of the parties. While the promised performance is not impossible or impracticable, it will be of
no value to the promisee.

Restatement, Second section 265 provides:

Where, after a contract is made, a party's principal purpose is substantially frustrated without
his fault by the occurrence of an event the non-
occurence of which was a basic assumption on
which the contract was made, his remaining
duties to render performance are discharged, unless the language or the circumstances indicate
the contrary.

This doctrine was apparently first recognized in
reported cases in the early twentieth century in
Krell v. Henry (1904). Plaintiff had contracted to
permit defendant to occupy plaintiff's flat on the
Pall Mall for two days during which the coronation
parades would be passing. The illness of King
Edward VII led to the cancellation of the pagentry.
The contract made no express reference to the
coronation. While there was nothing impossible
nor impracticable about the defendant using plaintiff's flat and paying money therefor, the contract
performance had become totally useless to the defendant, and the court found that defendant's duties were excused.

To excuse performance, it is essential that both
parties understand the purpose for which the contract is being made and that the failure of that
purpose makes the contract performance totally
valueless or almost totally valueless to the party

seeking relief. Many cases have been litigated in which a party attempted to apply this concept to a situation in which an event had occurred which frustrated his plans to make money from the contract performance. For example, parties have sought relief from long term leases of service stations when the highway is moved or gas and tire rationing is imposed. These efforts to obtain relief from unprofitable contracts almost invariably fail. The purpose of the contract is not frustrated; the only frustration is with the profitability of the performance. Courts sometimes refer to this type of situation as being one of "economic frustration," or "commercial frustration" and these are labels which a party wishes to avoid when seeking relief from a contract.

§ 179. Relief Afforded in Cases of Impracticability or Frustration

Despite the fact that a party seeks and obtains relief from performance of a contract on the grounds of impracticability or frustration of purpose, either party may be able to recover restitution damages, or reliance damages may be awarded in appropriate cases. The most obvious application of these remedies is to situations in which one party seeks relief from a contract after the other has conferred some benefit, thus being entitled to restitutionary relief, or has changed position in reliance upon the contract, in which case reliance damages can be awarded. A party who seeks relief of an equitable nature will be obliged to compensate for benefits which he has received and will likely also be obligated to pay for reliance damages reasonably incurred by the other party.

It is also possible for the party seeking to be relieved from the contract to obtain relief in the form of restitution. Where benefit has been conferred without compensation, the fact that a party seeks discharge should not necessarily preclude recovery for the benefits conferred. In the Coronation Cases (see discussion of Krell v. Henry, *supra*) the English courts denied recovery of rental already paid for flats despite the frustration of purpose. However, modern law would permit such recovery.

When you have completed your study of this chapter, you may wish to analyze questions 35–36 at the end of this book and compare your analysis with the one given there.

XIII. DISCHARGE

§ 180. Discharge by Performance and by Rescission, Release or Contract Not to Sue

The most common manner in which contract duties are discharged is by performance, but there are numerous other methods by which contract obligations can be terminated.

Two parties to a contract may discharge their respective duties by mutually agreeing to rescind their contract so long as a third party's vested rights are not affected. The relinquishment of each party's rights is supported by consideration in the bilateral situation since each is giving up his right to receive performance in exchange for avoiding his duty of performance. Where one party has already fully performed, release of the other by way of "mutual rescission" will raise a consideration issue at common law.

Under the general common law rule, a rescission need be in writing only if the agreement to rescind would work a transfer of title to land. The oral rescission is valid even if the statute of frauds requires the contract to be in writing. (See Restatement, Second, section 148.) State statutes which provide that a contract in writing can be modified only by another contract in writing, or by an executed oral agreement, have usually been

374

held to apply only to a "modification" and not to rescission. Under common law, a contract can be orally rescinded even though it expressly states it can be modified only by a written document.

The U.C.C. has adopted a different rule. Section 2–209(2) provides: "A signed agreement which excludes modification or rescission except by a signed writing cannot be otherwise modified or rescinded, but except as between merchants such a requirement on a form supplied by the merchant must be separately signed by the other party."

With respect to mutual rescissions of leases, real property law must be consulted to determine what is sufficient to constitute the surrender of a leasehold.

Where an innocent party responds to a material breach by stating that the contract is "rescinded," there is the risk that a court may interpret that term literally and thereby deny the innocent party any right to recover damages for the breach. If A has materially breached a contract with B, B has the right to rescind and thereby discharge all rights and duties under the contract. (If B has conferred benefits upon A, B may have an action against A in restitution. See § 131, *supra*.) B also has the right to declare a total breach, thereby relieving himself from the obligation to perform or to accept further performances from A but preserving his right to damages for breach of the entire contract. If B wishes to preserve the right to collect damages as distinguished from restitution, B should not be seeking to "rescind" the contract.

Mutual rescission can also contain a hidden trap. X agrees to harvest 1,000 acres of wheat for Y for a stated price per acre. After X has harvested 50 acres, the contract is "rescinded" by mutual agreement. Under the prevailing common law view, there is no presumption or inference that X has preserved his right to collect at the contract price for the work performed. However, X may still have a right to recover in restitution for the reasonable value of benefits conferred even if the parties did not preserve any rights under the rescinded contract.

The U.C.C. avoids these problems in transactions in goods by providing that when the parties mutually terminate a contract or when either party puts an end to a contract for breach by the other, remedies for breach of contract are preserved (sections 2–106(3) and (4) and 2–720).

The term "release" is used to describe a writing by which a duty owed to the person who signs the writing is discharged. The attempted release of all or part of an obligation without any bargained exchange has been a problem in the common law at least since the case of Foakes v. Beer was decided in 1884 (§ 51, *supra*). Some states have provided by statute for the release in writing of all or part of an obligation without consideration. U.C.C section 1–107 permits a written release without consideration, and this section applies to all matters within any article of the U.C.C. Some states have dispensed with the requirement of consideration for a release by case law.

Contracts not to sue are the invention of necessity. Common law decisions hold that a release, rescission or accord and satisfaction which discharges one co-obligor will release other co-obligors whose liability was founded upon a joint duty to perform the obligation in question. To avoid this result, the obligee may enter into a contract not to sue. As the name implies, this involves promising one co-obligor that no action will be maintained against him. This promise is given legal effect, but does not release other persons who might be obligated to perform the same duty. The liability of the other obligors is reduced by the amount paid for the contract not to sue. The Restatement, Second, section 295(2) takes the position that words which purport to release or discharge while reserving rights against another co-obligor should be interpreted as a contract not to sue. This would have the effect of preserving the liability of the other obligors in accordance with the stated intention of the person to whom the obligation is owing. Many states have reached the same result by statute. Even where rules have been adopted to protect a creditor in such situations, the law of suretyship will cause the release of a surety in certain circumstances in which the obligee discharges the principal obligor (§ 185, *infra*).

§ 181. Discharge by Substitute Contract

An obligee may accept a performance from the obligor which is different from that due under the contract, or the obligee may accept performance from one other than the obligor. If such performance is offered in satisfaction of the duty which is owing and if the obligee accepts the performance with knowledge of this fact, then the performance discharges the duty.

The same result can be obtained where the obligor promises to perform a different duty in substitution for that which is owing. If the obligee agrees to this substituted contract, an immediate discharge results.

If the obligee agrees to accept the substituted performance, but does not agree to an immediate discharge, then this is an accord agreement (§ 182, *infra*).

If a third party promises to perform the same or a different duty in exchange for an immediate discharge of the obligor and the obligee consents to this proposal, this is a novation which is discussed in § 183, *infra*.

§ 182. Discharge by Accord and Satisfaction

When an obligee agrees to accept and his obligor agrees to perform a different promise in lieu of that which is owing, such an agreement is called an accord. For example, A owes B $700. A offers to give B six tons of hay in lieu of the $700, and B accepts his offer. The parties have entered into an accord agreement. The making of this accord does not discharge the duty to pay the $700 unless the parties manifested that intention, and such an intent will not ordinarily be assumed. If one finds that the parties did intend an immediate discharge, then there is a substituted contract, and A is no longer obligated to pay B the $700 (§ 181, *supra*).

When A delivers the hay to B, thus performing the accord, this is termed the satisfaction. The satisfaction operates as a discharge of the original obligation to pay $700 as well as the discharge of the obligation to deliver the hay which was undertaken in the accord agreement.

The making of the accord agreement as distinguished from a substituted contract does not discharge the original obligation, but the better rule holds that the making of the accord suspends the original obligation until the obligor has had time to perform. Problems in this area usually arise when the debtor fails to perform the accord agreement. When the hay is not delivered to B, B has the election to sue on the accord agreement for breach of the promise to deliver the hay or to sue for the $700 which was originally owing since that obligation is not yet discharged.

An agreement to compromise a disputed claim is also commonly referred to as an accord agreement. This accord will be satisfied when the agreed upon settlement is paid. No consideration issue is presented so long as the parties are in fact compromising a validly disputed claim (§ 49, *supra*).

§ 183. Discharge by Novation

A novation is most frequently defined as a three party a transaction involving the original parties to the contract plus a newcomer. In the usual novation, one of the original parties to the contract is removed from the transaction and the newcomer is substituted in his place. This may not occur without the mutual assent of all three.

There are four elements of a valid novation: (1) There must be a previous obligation; (2) There must be a mutual agreement of all parties to the old and the new contract; (3) There must be an apparent intention immediately to extinguish the duties of the parties under the old contract, and (4) The new contract must be valid and enforceable.

To illustrate, suppose B, a builder, is under a contractual obligation to build a house for A for which A has agreed to pay $190,000 upon completion. If B approaches C, another builder, and offers the job to him and C assumes the job of building the house, there has not been a novation. All that has occurred is an assignment of the right to payment which will become due from A and the delegation to C of the duty to build the house for A. B remains liable on the contract, and A can still assert any appropriate objections to the delegation of the duty to build (§§ 174–175, *supra*). To constitute a novation, A must agree to release B from his duty to build in exchange for a promise from C to build, and A must promise to pay the $190,000 to C upon completion. B agrees to give up his right to receive $190,000 in exchange for being released, and C agrees to build in exchange for the right to receive $190,000.

X's creditor, Y, agrees to discharge X immediately if X will promise to pay money to Z or perform some other act for Z. The new obligation(s) need not be the same as those which existed in the original contract. X makes this promise to Z. This agreement is a novation.

Some states including California have statutes which define novation as the substitution of a new obligation for an existing one. As thus defined, novation is the term which would describe the substituted contract discussed in § 181, *supra*, and would thus apply to two party transactions (West's Ann.Cal. Civil Code Sections 1530, et seq.).

§ 184. Discharge by Account Stated

An account stated is an agreement by the creditor and debtor to the accuracy of a stated sum as the amount due. If a debtor has purchased items from a creditor or otherwise incurred obligations to a creditor and the creditor sends the debtor a statement of account, the act of keeping the statement for a period of time without objection by the debtor manifests his assent to be bound by its terms. The account can also be stated by the debtor or may be reached by mutual efforts of the parties. The creditor can sue upon this "account stated."

It is essential that the parties have had at least one previous transaction, i.e., a statement cannot create liability where none previously existed. An account stated cannot supersede a promissory note since such a note is viewed as better evidence of the debt than the account stated.

The statement of an account is not a compromise of a disputed claim. It is an agreement upon a computation of an obligation or obligations. It may be attacked as the product of a mistake, but the burden of establishing such a mistake is upon the attacking party. The party seeking to enforce the account has the benefit of not having to prove individual items of the obligation.

It has generally been held that an account stated operates as a discharge of the underlying obligation even though the account has not yet been paid. The Restatement, Second, section 282(2) states: "The account stated does not itself discharge any duty but is an admission by each party of the facts asserted and a promise by the debtor to pay according to its terms." In the Reporter's Note, the Restatement provides: "Whether an agreement has the effect of discharge, formerly attributed to an account stated, is now determined under the rules relating to substituted contracts . . . and accords . . .."

Inasmuch as the effect of an account stated is an admission by both parties of the amount due that is binding upon both in the absence of proof of mistake, it would ordinarily not be necessary to determine whether the underlying obligation is legally discharged prior to payment or at the time of payment.

§ 185. Miscellaneous Concepts That May Serve as Methods of Discharge

Duties under a voidable contract may be discharged by an exercise of the power of avoidance (§ 99, et seq., *supra*).

If a contract deals with an illegal subject matter or has some other aspect of illegality, the defendant can discharge or avoid his liability by asserting illegality as a defense or by the court raising illegality on its own (§ 120, *supra*). (In theory this may be a recognition that no legal duty ever existed rather than the discharge of an existing duty.)

The mere making of a contract for the benefit of a third party creditor beneficiary does not discharge the promisee's duty owed to the creditor, but such a duty is discharged when the promisor renders performance to the creditor beneficiary. Stated another way, the mere delegation of a delegable duty does not extinguish the delegator's duty, but performance by the delegatee will discharge the obligation (§ 175, *supra*). Performance to an assignee discharges the obligor's duty to the assignor.

If an obligor files a petition in bankruptcy and the trustee does not elect to continue performance, all contractual duties over and above what is paid in the proceedings are discharged.

Under the minority rule, the running of the time set for the bringing of an action for a breach of contract effectively discharges contractual duties, although it is the majority rule that the running of the statute bars only the remedy and does not discharge the debt (§ 63, *supra*).

In certain situations, contract obligations may be discharged by the rejection of a valid, unconditional tender (§ 147, *supra*). If the tender is accepted there is, of course, literal performance. The rejection of a proper tender discharges, at least temporarily, the duty of the party who made the tender to perform further, but if time is not of the essence, such a tender results in only a temporary suspension of the duty of performance, and performance may be demanded within a reasonable time. The tender of money for a consideration not yet received may also provide only a temporary discharge. To illustrate, suppose S contracts to sell a car to B for $12,000. Time for performance is not specified. A tender by B on July 1 only temporarily suspends his duty. B will still have to perform if S, within a reasonable time, tenders performance and gives B time in which to perform. But B's duty to perform would be permanently discharged if performance were due on July 1 and time had been of the essence.

If an obligor owes a duty to pay money for a consideration already received, a rejected tender does not discharge the debt, but it does stop the running of interest. Suppose R owes E $100. On July 1, R tenders E $100 in cash which E rejects. Although the debt is not discharged, E is not entitled to interest after July 1. (See § 125, *supra.*)

The release of a principal likewise releases the surety inasmuch as a release of the principal tends to militate against the interests of the surety. An actual release is not necessary; anything which "tends to militate against the interest of the surety" discharges the surety's duties. To illustrate, suppose R owes E $100. R delegates to D the duty to pay E and D assumes the debt. D thereby becomes primarily liable and R becomes a surety. If E were to release D, R would be discharged.

If a judgment is obtained for breach of a contractual duty, the duty to perform under the contract is "merged" into the judgment and is discharged. A second action on the contractual duty will not lie, and enforcement must proceed on the judgment.

The occurrence of a true condition subsequent (§ 145, *supra*) discharges the existing duty which was subject to that condition.

*

CONTRACTS QUESTIONS

The following materials are based upon portions of questions taken from bar examinations administered in the United States. The primary function of this material is to provide practice in issue identification. The commentary answers are neither models nor suggested as required modes of response. If these admonitions are kept in mind, the problems can be valuable in making a determining of your proficiency in the subject matter.

No. 1

P and D, who were acquainted with each other, resided in communities separated by 100 miles. On February 1, P wrote to D as follows: "Dear D. I have decided to give up my farm, Blackacre, and move to town. I thought you might consider buying it from me. I would like to get $175,000 out of it. I'll let you have ten days to think about it and talk it over with your wife. I know both of you would be very happy here. (signed) P." Does this communication consitute a valid offer, and if so, is it irrevocable for a period of 10 days?

An offer must manifest an intention to be presently bound and must create in the offeree the power to form a binding contract by an appropriate acceptance (§§ 5 and 27). P's letter indicates an intention to sell the farm, but the central question is whether he manifests an intent to be presently bound subject only to acceptance by D. There is no direct statement that P will sell to D, only that P wants to sell and thought D might like to buy. Conditional language ("would" and "thought you might") tends to negate an intention to be presently bound. The most compelling argument in favor of finding an offer is the statement that D will have 10 days to think it over. If P did not intend to give D the power to form a contract by accepting, then there would be no reason to give D a 10 day limit. The ultimate question is what D should reasonably understand to be P's intention.

Assuming that "I would like to get $175,000 out of it," can be interpreted to mean that P is proposing a price of $175,000, the terms are probably sufficient to find an offer. A rather high degree of certainty is usually required in real property transactions, but assuming that "Blackacre" is an identifiable parcel of land known to the parties, the terms are sufficient. The price is implied to be cash payable on delivery of the deed, and these performances are due in a reasonable time. While real property contracts usually cover a multitude of other details, local custom or usage will probably suffice to supply these terms. Failure to include these other matters might, however, have a bearing upon whether one finds that P manifested an intent to be presently bound.

Firm offers by merchants to sell goods can be irrevocable pursuant to U.C.C. section 2-205, but the U.C.C. does not apply to land transactions. Some jurisdictions have statutes which enforce promises not to revoke regardless of subject matter, but in the absence of such a statute, the promise not to revoke is not enforceable because there is no option supported by consideration (§ 23). Other bases for irrevocability are not applicable in this fact situation (§§ 24 and 26).

No. 2

S wrote P: "I have in mothballs six milling machines which I have not been able to use for three years. They are in good condition and may be inspected in my shop anytime this month. But I do plan to get rid of them one way or another during that time. Please let me know right away if you are interested at my price of $18,000 for the six." Has S made an offer to P?

Contracts for the sale of goods need not be definite as to all terms (§ 8), but there must still be a manifestation of intent to be bound to find an offer (§ 5). People tend to be less formal in transactions in goods, and intent to be bound is not dependent upon any formal words or phrases, but it still must appear to a reasonable person in the position of P that S has communicated a willingness to be presently bound to sell to P. In fact, S stated that he is going to "get rid of them one way or another" which tends to indicate that S may sell them to anyone at any time. This negates an intention to be presently bound to P because that would require that S refrain from selling the goods to another pending receipt of P's response. "Please let me know right away if you are interested" also connotes an inquiry. This communication can be characterized as a preliminary negotiation or solicitation for an offer.

No. 3

X made an offer in writing to B to sell his store for $130,000. B wrote X: "Accept your offer. This contract should be reduced to writing and signed by us." Is there an enforceable contract?

The question to be resolved is whether the parties have manifested an intention to be presently bound or whether one of them has simply manifested a desire to enter into a contract and an intention to be bound as soon as a written contract is prepared and signed. The common source of error in these problems results from failure to place proper emphasis on the need to find an intent to be *presently* bound. The U.C.C. provides for situations in which parties can be bound prior to completion of negotiations of terms, but the U.C.C. does not apply here and the usual approach is to deny enforcement of "agreements to agree" where further negotiation is contemplated. Likewise, there is no enforceable contract even where all terms are agreed upon if one of the parties has manifested a desire not to be bound until a formal document is signed.

In the instant fact situation, there may be further details which would ordinarily be resolved in the process of preparing a formal contract, and one could thus find that B has not manifested a present intent to be bound. However, B has chosen to use language ("accept your offer") which connotes present intent to be bound, and the anticipation of a formal writing should not preclude finding that the parties are already bound to a contract (§§ 5 and 40).

No. 4

A entered into an agreement with B, an artist, on January 2, whereby B agreed to paint A's portrait. The price was to be mutually arranged by A and B on January 9. On January 7, A repudiated. Is there a contract?

If the U.C.C. applied to this transaction, there could be sufficient certainty to enforce a contract, the price being a reasonable price at the time for delivery. This result would be reached if it was found that the parties intended to be bound before agreeing to the price (§ 8). However, since the dominant nature of this transaction appears to be services rather than goods, the U.C.C. would not apply, and the absence of agreement upon an essential term such as price would probably prevent finding a contract.

No. 5

On January 3, B wrote A that he would paint A's portrait for $3,000. On the same day A, without knowledge of B's letter, wrote B that he would pay $3,000 if B would paint his portrait. Is there a contract?

Identical offers which cross in transmission do not create contracts as neither party is exercising a power to accept (§ 11).

No. 6

S sent an offer to B which stated: "Will sell No. 2 winter wheat up to 10,000 tons at $180 a ton for delivery during January." B wrote S: "Would $175 per ton be agreeable for 5,000 tons?" Two days later B changed his mind and wrote: "Send 5,000 tons of wheat at your price." Both messages arrived in regular course of mail. Does B have enforceable rights against S?

Since S's communication is characterized as an offer in the question, this is given legal conclusion and need not be discussed. B's first response proposes a lower price and might be a counteroffer at common law unless it is viewed as simply an inquiry. The U.C.C. applies to this transaction, and section 2–207(1) requires an analysis of the question whether B's response is an "expression of acceptance." A response has been found to be an acceptance in some cases despite the fact that it indicated an intent to restructure substantially a proposed bargain in favor of the offeree. However, here there is no language which indicates that the offeree thinks he is concluding a bargain at this point. B's message is really an inquiry and not an expression of acceptance which could lead S reasonably to believe a contract was formed (§ 37).

Assuming B's letter were found to be a counteroffer, it would impliedly reject S's offer and would be legally effective when received. Even if it is not a counteroffer, it might be found to impliedly reject S's offer to sell for a higher price. In either case, S's offer could no longer be accepted after the rejection is received. The subsequent message appears to communicate an acceptance, and it would ordinarily be effective when sent because mail is a "medium reasonable in the circumstances." However, if the first of B's letters is found to be a rejection of S's offer, then the majority rule provides that a subsequent acceptance is effective only if it is received by S prior to receipt of the rejection (§ 42).

No. 7

P mailed to D an offer on the 1st and it arrived on the 2nd. On the 10th, P mailed a revocation, which would ordinarily be delivered on the 11th but which was in fact delivered at 2:00 on the 12th. D mailed an acceptance at 1:30 on the 12th. The letter of acceptance was never received. Was a contract formed?

In the absence of a stated time, an offer is effective for a reasonable time. This may or may not extend to 10 days after the receipt of the offer depending upon the nature of the subject matter, the identity and circumstances of the parties and other facts which might affect this determination. Since the offer was sent by mail, it is apparent that the subject matter cannot be something with an exceedingly volatile market and one might assume in the absence of other facts that a 10 day period for acceptance is not unreasonable. The fact that P thought it appropriate to mail a revocation on the 10th is some indication of an intent that the offer remain open at least to that time (§ 14).

With the possible exception of states which adopted the Field Code, revocations are not effective until received by the offeree. There is no basis for placing the risk of delay or loss in transmission upon the offeree; thus, the offer was not revoked before the acceptance was sent. Acceptances are effective when sent by an authorized means (older cases) or by any medium reasonable under the circumstances. Therefore, a contract was formed at 1:30 on the 12th. The fact that the acceptance was never received does not terminate the contract nor preclude its enforcement (§ 42).

No. 8

A sent to B an offer by letter. B wired acceptance. Is a contract formed when the wire is sent?

The common law rule required that an acceptance be sent by an authorized means, and the means which was used by the offeror would be impliedly authorized. From this it was reasoned by some courts that a method which was faster than that used by the offeror would also be impliedly authorized. Others took the opposite position holding that a mailed offer did not authorize acceptance by wire. The U.C.C. section 2–206 and the Restatement, Second, place the emphasis on the reasonableness of the medium used. Assuming that a court were to find that acceptance by wire was reasonable under the circumstances, the contract would be formed when the acceptance is sent. If wire is found to be an unauthorized medium for acceptance, then the acceptance will be effective when the wire is received. Under the Restatement, Second, if the wire is received within the time that a letter would have been received, then it becomes operative as of its time of dispatch (section 42).

No. 9

The Law Book Co. sent a letter to X, a young attorney: "We are sending you herewith a set of state reports. If you will compile a digest for us of all the worker's compensation decisions therein, you may keep the books free of charge." X began work. Later, after working six months, she received a letter from the Law Book Co. stating: "We have changed our minds about the digest, and so must withdraw our offer. Please return the reports to us at once, or start paying for them." X retained the books and finished the job two months later. The company refused the digest and instituted suit to recover the price of the books. What result?

X is performing a service for goods, and the U.C.C. can be applied to this transaction (U.C.C. section 2–304(1)). Since there was no communication of an acceptance by X, she will have a contract for research work only if the offer is interpreted as one which permits acceptance by performance rather than requiring a return promise. In case of doubt, the modern approach is to permit the offeree to accept by either method, thus X may well have chosen an effective means by which to accept (§ 31). U.C.C. section 2–206 supports this result.

Older common law cases imposed no requirement upon an offeree to notify the offeror that performance had been commenced. There were cases which indicated that the offeree must use reasonable effort to notify the offeror after performance was complete if the offeror had no convenient way of learning this fact (§ 33). U.C.C. section 2–206(2) would now control this situation. X's failure to notify the offeror within a reasonable period of time permits the offeror to treat the offer as having lapsed before acceptance.

Since X does not have an enforceable contract for services, retention of the books with knowledge that Law Book Co. is offering them for a price would manifest assent to pay that price. X would be liable.

No. 10

B signed and delivered the following to C on July 15: "Receipt of $100 is hereby acknowledged, and in consideration the undersigned agrees to convey Blackacre to C upon payment of $75,000 on or before September 15. (Signed) B." What are C's rights against B?

Assuming that this can be interpreted as an offer (e.g. that "Blackacre" can be identified and the terms are sufficiently certain as discussed in question #1, *supra*), this appears to be an irrevocable offer because there has been consideration given for it creating an option contract (§ 23). If the recital of consideration is in fact a sham, most jurisdictions would permit proof of this fact and deny enforcement of the promise not to revoke once the absence of consideration is established (§ 61). The language could be interpreted as an offer for a unilateral contract which contemplates acceptance by paying $75,000 rather than promising to pay. However, the offer may be manifesting indifference as to how the offer is to be accepted thus permitting acceptance either by promising to pay or by the act of paying (§ 31).

No. 11

A believed in good faith that he had a claim to certain property owned by B. In fact A did not have a valid claim. A sent a letter to B: "Will sell you my interest (in the property) for $1,000. You need not answer. Your silence will act as acceptance." Is a contract formed when B does not respond?

The release of an invalid claim can be consideration since A had a good faith belief in its validity.
Some jurisdictions would impose an additional requirement that A's belief be founded upon some
credible facts (§ 49). However, A does not acquire
enforceable rights against B under the stated facts
because in the absence of special circumstances,
silence will not constitute acceptance. B might be
able to enforce the contract if B subjectively intended to accept since A's communication expressly authorized this (§ 43).

No. 12

The Rex Co. was under a binding contract with
Jones to pay a monthly rent of $5,000 for a drug-
store, for three years, beginning January 1, 1983.
The Rex Co. paid $5,000 on January 1 and Febru-
ary 1. During the month of February, with permission of Jones, Rex Co. greatly improved the
rented premises at its own expense. On February
27, Jones told the Rex Co.: "I am happy about
these improvements. They have added to the
value of the building. I am going to reduce your
rent to $4,000 per month." That same day an
agreement was signed by both Jones and the Rex
Co. reducing the rent to $4,000. Could Jones later
insist on collecting the original $5,000 per month?

Consideration involves legal detriment incurred
as a bargained exchange for a return promise.
Thus what one did yesterday cannot serve as con-

sideration for a promise made today. "Past consideration is no consideration" (§§ 46 and 67).

On the facts given, Rex Co. has not made any change of position in reliance upon the promise to reduce the rent, thus there is no basis for enforcing the promise on detrimental reliance (§ 69). In the absence of a statute which permits modification of contracts without consideration, Rex probably remains liable for the full $5,000. Some cases enforce modifications by implying a rescission of the old contract and a making of a new one, however, in the case of a lease, it would be quite a fiction to find a surrender of the old lease under facts such as these.

No. 13

On June 1, O and C entered into a written contract in which C promised to build a road for O according to certain specifications, and O promised to pay C $100,000 upon completion of the job. The written contract included a promise by C to complete the road by January 1. C commenced work immediately, but soon discovered that the roadbed was rockier than he had expected, which fact, together with the fact of an unusual amount of rainfall, threatened C with considerable additional expense. In August, C called upon O and told O of these circumstances and informed O that he (C) would abandon performance unless a satisfactory adjustment of these difficulties could be made. After some discussion O and C drew up another written agreement, the terms of the new agreement being the same as those of the old except that O promised to pay $140,000. On December 28, C completed the job according to specifications. O has informed C that he will pay only $100,000. What are C's rights against O?

C had a preexisting duty to build the road pursuant to the original C–O contract. O will contend that C was incurring no new detriment and O was obtaining no new benefit in exchange for O's promise to pay the additional $40,000. However, the facts indicate that C encountered more rocks and bad weather than anticipated. If C had a good faith belief founded upon some facts that he had the right to terminate his performance under the contract, then his agreement to forbear from asserting this right could serve as consideration for O's promise to pay the additional $40,000. Many cases state that an owner's promise to pay extra money is enforceable where the contractor has encountered unforeseen difficulties. This is an appropriate analysis so long as it is understood that the difficulties must be of sufficient magnitude to provide a basis for excusing the contractor from performing or at least a good faith claim of excuse (§ 68).

No. 14

C was under an enforceable bilateral contractual obligation to build a road for O. After partly performing, C stopped. N, a neighbor of O who would be benefited by completion of the road, said to C: "If you will finish the job I'll pay you $1,000." C agreed and later finished the job. What are C's rights against N?

Assuming that N's communication was an offer, it matters not whether it calls for a promise or for performance as C did both. The central question is whether there was consideration for N's promise. Under the concept of preexisting duty, it can be reasoned that since C had a legally enforceable obligation to build the road, C incurred no legal detriment in doing so, and thus there is no consideration for N's promise to pay. This is the usual result even though the duty was owing to O rather than to N. On the other hand, if C had an opportunity to enter a mutual rescission with O or had some other opportunity to avoid further duties under the C–O contract, then it could be reasoned that N was making his offer to induce C to forego this opportunity. If one finds that C did forbear rescinding or avoiding the C–O contract as a bargained exchange for N's promise, then consideration can be found and the promise can be enforced (§ 48). N's promise would also be enforceable if the jurisdiction does not deny the existence of consideration based upon a preexisting duty owed to third persons (Restatement, Second, section 73, comment d).

No. 15

X, a wealthy lawyer friend of B, promised that if B would study a minimum of fifty hours a week throughout his law school career, X would pay B

$15,000 at the end of each school year. B did study at least fifty hours a week. Does B have rights against X?

The basic elements of a unilateral contract appear to be present, and the issue which will determine B's right to recover is whether there is consideration for X's promise. B stayed in law school and studied fifty hours per week, each of which involved doing an act which B was not legally obligated to do. Thus B did incur a legal detriment, and the question is whether this detriment was incurred as part of a bargain or as a bargained exchange for X's promise. X's position will be that X offered a gift to assist B in his desire to go to law school and study full-time and that remaining in school and studying diligently was simply a condition to the gift.

Anytime one notes a situation in which a person has promised to do or give something for or to another under circumstances which appear to involve donative intent, it is appropriate to explore the consideration issue very carefully paying particular attention to the question whether there is in fact a bargain. Detriment alone will not suffice because it may simply be a condition to a gift. One analysis which might prove helpful is to ask whether the promisor (X) is benefiting from the act of the promisee which is the asserted consideration. If so, this may be reason to conclude that there is a bargained exchange. A better inquiry might be to ask whether the thing which the promisee is asked to do is simply something which is necessary or appropriate to place the promisee in a position to receive the gift. If the promisee was requested to do more, then there would appear to be a bargain.

In the instant problem, a promise to make a gift of $15,000 per year to help a friend through law school would be a gratuitous promise, the attendance in law school being simply a condition of the gift. (One cannot help a friend through law school if the friend does not go to law school.) However, there is no reason why one need demand that the student study fifty hours per week. This is presumably not convenient or necessary to place B in a position to be able to receive the gift. While there is no indication that X will profit by B's performance, it is most likely more than a mere condition to a gift, and thus a bargain can be found (§ 53).

If no consideration is present, B could argue detrimental reliance. Whether attending law school and studying long hours was in fact induced by X's promise and is such action as would make nonenforcement of X's promise an injustice is a question which the authors had best leave to the reader to answer. X's recovery might be limited to the value of his reliance (§§ 69 and 134).

No. 16

T owned and operated a drugstore on premises owned by L. The lease was due to expire in six months. T signed an agreement in which T agreed to sell the business and the inventory to B for $200,000. B agreed to buy and pay the stated price "upon the condition that B can work out a satisfactory new lease with L." T promptly repudiated his promise to sell, and B sues.

T's promise to sell is not enforceable unless there is consideration to support it. B's promise to pay $200,000 is obviously sufficient legal detriment if B's promise is not illusory. The problem is whether B's power to prevent the occurrence of the condition to his duty to pay is so unfettered that B's promise is illusory. Since agreement by B to the terms of a lease with L does not appear to have any significance to B independent of his purchase of the drugstore, a court might find that B has made an illusory promise and thus given no consideration for T's promise to sell. However, agreements such as this have commercial utility. A duty of good faith and possibly even a duty of reasonableness could be imposed upon B to make the agreement enforceable (§§ 55 and 56).

No. 17

A owed B $150, a debt due on a valid contract. After B's right to enforce payment thereof was barred by the statute of limitations, A voluntarily delivered to B the following instrument: "Dear B: Enclosed is $50 of the money I owe you." B received payment on the enclosed check, but A made no further payments. Does B have an enforceable right to another $100?

A promise to pay an obligation which would be enforceable but for the statute of limitations is itself enforceable. An unqualified acknowledgment of the debt is usually held to be sufficient to imply a promise to pay. Mere part payment has been found to be sufficient to imply a promise to pay the otherwise unmentioned balance in some jurisdictions. The communication from A clearly acknowledged that there was an obligation owing in excess of the $50 which was being paid. Most cases would permit the creditor to prove the balance owing by extrinsic evidence and find that A's note impliedly promises to pay that amount. B should prevail (§ 63).

No. 18

A and B were partners in the shoe manufacturing business. A learned that B personally owed a large sum to X, a distributor of quality shoes. A feared that general knowledge of the financial condition of B would have a serious effect on their business. To prevent disclosure of this information as well as to secure an order for his factories from X, A orally agreed, for lawful consideration, to guarantee payment of his associate's debt to X. May X enforce A's oral promise?

A has made a promise to guarantee the debt of another, and this obligation would nominally come within the terms of the statute of frauds. However, A's primary purpose or main purpose in making the promise was to secure a benefit or advantage for himself. This is a recognized exception to the statute, and thus the absence of a writing signed by A will not prevent X from enforcing A's promise (§ 75).

No. 19

On February 26, A paid B $375 in consideration for B's oral promise that on the first day of each month for the next succeeding thirteen months, B would clean and oil certain machinery at A's mine. Is B's promise enforceable?

B's promise is by its terms not capable of full performance within one year and is thus within the statute of frauds. Part performance may affect the enforceability of contracts for the sale of goods or of interests in land, but this doctrine is not ordinarily used to enforce oral contracts which violate the one year provision. However, many cases permit contracts not capable of performance within one year to be enforced if one party has fully performed (Restatement, Second, section 130(2)). A has also relied upon the oral contract by making full payment, and A might contend that this reliance provides an alternate basis to make the promise of B enforceable. However, since A is entitled to recover the monies paid on a restitution theory, a court should not find that an injustice would result if the oral contract were not enforced.

No. 20

A owned a large tract of timberland in the northern part of the state. B desired to purchase some of the timber, so a portion of the property was marked off by stakes, and it was orally agreed that A would sell and B would buy all the trees standing on the plot for $3,000, with cutting and removal to be completed within two weeks at B's expense. Pursuant to this agreement, B entered upon the property the following day and cut and removed ten of the trees. Is the contract enforceable?

This is a transaction for the sale of goods under the 1972 amendments to U.C.C. section 2–107. Since the contract is for a price of $500 or more, it is within the writing requirements of U.C.C. section 2–201 which provides in subsection (3)(c) for enforcement "with respect to goods for which payment has been made and accepted or which have been received and accepted." THE contract can be enforced for the ten logs which were received and accepted, but this partial performance does not make the entire contract enforceable (§ 82). If the party against whom enforcement is sought were to admit the making of the contract "in his pleadings, testimony or otherwise in court," the subsection (3) (b) would permit enforcement to the extent of the quantity admitted.

No. 21

X orally contracts to buy a car from Y for $1,500. X pays Y $25 as a deposit. Is the contract enforceable?

At least some jurisdictions have held that a part-payment in a contract for an indivisible unit of goods makes the entire contract enforceable. A $25 payment on an oral contract for two cars at $1,500 each would presumably make the contract enforceable to the extent of one car (§ 82).

No. 22

A, a famous painter of biblical characters, invited offers for the purchase of a life-sized picture of Elijah he intended to paint. B's offer of $7,500 was the highest, and A agreed orally with B that he would paint the picture and sell it to B for that price. Is the contract enforceable?

Ordinary service contracts are not within the statute of frauds. One can enforce an oral contract to build a twin of the Sears Tower or the Grand Coulee Dam. If the A–B contract is for services to be performed by A, the statute of frauds does not apply. If this is viewed as a contract for future goods, then the statute of frauds would make the contract unenforceable unless further facts bring the case within one of the exceptions (§§ 73, 82, 87).

No. 23

S and B executed a written contract pursuant to which S agreed to sell 10,000 rabbits and B agreed to pay $15,000. The contract specified that the sale was f.o.b. S's ranch with performance to take place on April 1. A dispute arose and the contract was never performed. B sued S and sought to prove the following: (1) During negotiations, S stated that his hired man would deliver the rabbits, but S refused to deliver. (2) B told S that B would pay $5,000 down and $10,000 not later than April 15. S assented to this at the time the contract was signed, but thereafter S advised he would demand cash on delivery for the rabbits. (3) During the negotiations, S stated that he had excess vaccine for a certain rabbit disease and promised to give B enough to vaccinate all of the rabbits. S never tendered any vaccine. (4) In the industry, "1,000 rabbits" means 100 dozen rabbits. Thus B was entitled to an actual count of 12,000 rabbits under the contract. Which of these items may B prove?

The first question to be resolved by the court is whether the parties intended the writing to be a final expression of at least one or more terms of their agreement. Given the terms contained in the writing, there appears to be no logical reason why one would not conclude that it was a final expression. The final expression of the parties provided for tender at S's ranch (f.o.b. term), and this would operate as a discharge of any prior inconsistent agreements. Unless the evidence is being offered to prove mistake or some other defense, B cannot introduce evidence of the promise to deliver as this would contradict an express term of the written contract.

The writing provided for payment of $15,000 for the rabbits and this clearly means cash on delivery under both the common law and the U.C.C. (§ 141). Thus B's second item of evidence contradicts an implied term of the written agreement, and S will attempt to exclude it on that basis. While the language of court decisions would appear to support S's position, the results of many cases do not (e.g., Masterson v. Sine (1968)).

If this term is not found to be an express contradiction of the terms of the contract, then B can admit this evidence if the writing is found to be only a partial as distinguished from a complete integration. If the writing is a complete and exclusive statement of the terms of the agreement, then B cannot introduce evidence which will add the term which provides for credit. This issue will probably be resolved by inquiring whether parties situated in the position of S and B who were entering a contract of this nature would naturally have left this term out of the writing even though they meant it to be a binding part of their final agreement. Since this is a transaction in goods, the court could look to comment 3 of U.C.C. section 2–202 which phrases this question in terms of whether the terms " . . . would certainly have been included in the document in the view of the court . . ." in which case B would not be permitted to introduce them into evidence. It would not be illogical to conclude that S and B would certainly have included the payment terms in the writing had they intended it to be other than a cash sale, but this is a debatable point.

B's third matter relating to the vaccine is one which does not contradict the terms of the writing and thus can definitely be introduced unless it is found that the writing is a complete integration. This will involve questions similar to those discussed in the preceding paragraph with the answer turning on whether the court finds that this provision would have been included in the writing had the parties intended it to be part of their final agreement. If it would certainly have been included in the agreement, then B cannot present this evidence to the trier of fact.

B's fourth point involves evidence of usage of the trade which is offered to explain the meaning of contract language. Assuming that this method of counting rabbits is observed with such regularity in the rabbit trade in this geographical area that the parties are justified in expecting that it will be observed in the transaction in question, then B will be able to establish that this is a bona fide usage of the trade (U.C.C. section 1–205(2)). (If you think the example outlandish, see Smith v. Wilson, which is discussed in Hurst v. W.J. Lake & Co. (1933).)

While usage of the trade cannot contradict an express term of the contract (U.C.C. section 2–208(2)), it can be used to explain contract terms. If in fact "1,000 rabbits" means 100 dozen rabbits then proof of this trade usage does not contradict but merely explains. B should get this evidence admitted (§§ 91–92).

No. 24

Jones, a homeowner, wrote to the ABC Aircondi-tioning Co. asking the price, installed, of ABC's standard unit, the X–12. A salesman at ABC telephoned Jones on September 4, in reply to his letter and said that a special off-season price would be quoted, including installation. Later that day, the sales manager of ABC sent a telegram to Jones which, when received, read as follows: "We would furnish the X–12 delivered to your home for $898. Letter follows."

The letter which followed stated:

"You have been advised of the special price on the X–12, as per our telegram, for your immedi-ate acceptance. Enclosed is a catalog giving full particulars as to our established policies and warranties on our products."

The catalog contained a list price of $1,898 for the X–12 unit and a statement that "all prices quoted are exclusive of installation."

Jones signed and returned the letter by mail the same day with this endorsement: "Accepted. Sept. 6. J.B. Jones. P.S. Shipment must be imme-diate."

The next day, before the letter was actually received by ABC, the telegraph company advised ABC that, through the telegraph company's mis-take, the wire stated a price of $898 instead of $1,498. ABC immediately telephoned Jones and told him that the price quote should have been

$1,498; that is, $400 off the regular list price of $1,898 quoted in the catalog.

Discuss the rights of Jones.

This is a transaction in goods, and the communications from ABC appear to manifest the necessary intent and are sufficiently definite to constitute an offer. Jones can reasonably consider the initial phone call, the telegram, the letter and the catalog to find the manifestation of an intent to be presently bound. While mere price quotes are usually not offers, this was a specific response to an inquiry (§ 10). Acceptance by return promise is appropriate.

Jones' reply demands immediate shipment which might make it a counter-offer at common law, but under U.C.C. section 2–207(1) it would operate as an acceptance. It would be effective on dispatch assuming that mail is a reasonable medium under these circumstances.

While ABC is usually bound by the communication as delivered despite the error of the telegraph company, a court might reach the conclusion that Jones should have known that $898 was too low even for an off-season special. If Jones should have known a mistake was made, no contract will result (§ 109).

ABC promised free installation but the catalog stated that prices did not include that service. In cases of inconsistencies, later communications ordinarily control over earlier communications, but it is doubtful that a general statement in a catalog would supersede an express statement by the ABC salesman. Thus, if there is a contract, Jones is probably entitled to free installation.

No. 25

Prof is a new economics professor at state college. He is new to the area and wishes to pursue his passion for duck hunting. Having been advised to see Jack in Gridley, Prof went to that town and encountered Jake. Prof failed to note the difference in name, and Jake did not correct Prof when he called him Jack. Prof was most pleased at Jake's glowing reports concerning the number of ducks killed on Jake's pond last year. As Jake poured another drink, he assured Prof a warm bed, good food and fine hunting for $2,500. Prof read the standard contract form while Jake filled in blanks on another copy. Prof did not dream that the "other copy" was a different form, so he did not bother to "re-read" the actual copy he signed.

Prof actually signed an agreement to pay $4,000. Jake and Jack are two different people, and Jake's beds are cold as is his food. While Jake's figures concerning last year's kill are probably not too badly exaggerated, last year was the first really good year on Jake's pond in two decades. May Prof successfully disavow any contract obligations to Jake?

Misrepresentation of a material fact upon which Prof reasonably relies is a defense. There is authority for the proposition that intentional misrepresentation of a nonmaterial fact can also be a defense. If Jake has misrepresented his identity, that should be sufficient. The representations as to last year's kill were made to indicate likely prospects for the ensuing year and are thus "half-truths" which might provide a basis for relief if reliance thereon is reasonable. Representations as to bed and food are probably promises which have not yet been broken. However, if it can be shown that these statements related to how things have been, they could be found to be misstatements of fact (§§ 115–118).

Misrepresentation of the document and the price contained therein is clearly intentional and material, however Prof can anticipate problems showing reasonable reliance. In the alternative this problem can be cast as one of mutual mistake (§ 110).

Lack of capacity based upon voluntary intoxication is not ordinarily the best defense in the world, but it might have a bearing upon the outcome of a case in which the party pushing the liquor was obviously attempting to pluck a pigeon (§§ 103–104).

Unconscionability may be available as a defense if Prof can show procedural and substantive unconscionability. The misrepresentations and paper switching should establish procedural unconscionability. The facts do not indicate whether the $4,000 price is excessive. If it is clearly excessive, this would establish substantive unconscionability.

"Bad faith" is a term which might well be mentioned in discussion of this case and will probably appear in the court's opinion if Prof prevails. However, the parties did not owe each other a legally enforceable duty of good faith prior to the formation of the contract. Jake's "bad faith" in the dealings between the parties is not a source of substantive rights for Prof nor is it a defense which will relieve him from his contract duties if the other common law defenses discussed above fail. It is therefore in the role of a supporting argument, but should not be advanced as the legal basis for rescission of the contract (§ 95).

No. 26

B bought from S a considerable quantity of an industrial grease known as R-Lube, for 25 cents per pound. Thereafter, S developed a new lighter-weight grease suitable for some, but not all of the purposes for which R-Lube is suitable, taking great pains to keep the development work secret. By the end of the year, the new product was ready to market and was designated in S's records as "R-Lube Special." On January 2, S mailed to one thousand of his customers a card reading:

S is now offering for immediate order in any quantity not exceeding 2000 pounds, R-Lube Special at 20 cents per pound. This is an economy product of good quality. Detailed technical specifications will be provided on request.

S knew the new product was not heavy enough for B's operations and did not intend that a card go to B. However, one of the cards was sent to B due to a clerical error in S's office. B at once wrote S: "I am pleased to note the special price on R-Lube. Send me 2000 pounds."

When S received this letter he called B, explained the mistake and advised B that the current price of R-Lube was 28 cents per pound. B nevertheless insisted that he had a contract for 2000 pounds of R-Lube at 20 cents per pound. S consults you. What are his legal relations with B?

The U.C.C. applies to this transaction. The January 2 communication is probably sufficient to constitute an offer (§ 10). The contract price is only $400 and not within the statute of frauds. If it were, the requirement of a writing which specifies quantity should be found to be satisfied (§ 80) even though the quantity is not determined until there is an acceptance. Despite the clerical error, the communication to B is sufficient to give B the power to accept since it does not appear that B had reason to know of the error (§ 88).

If it can be found that the offer is ambiguous and that S should have known of this ambiguity and B did not have reason to know, then B might be able to enforce a contract on the terms which B understood; that is, a contract for "R-Lube" (§ 88). Even if the offer is not ambiguous, it might be found that the parties were mutually mistaken as to the subject matter of the contract and that no contract was found (§ 109). In the absence of a finding of ambiguity or mistake, B's response would be a counter-offer and rejection at common law (§§ 33–36). Under the U.C.C., it might be found that B has accepted S's offer forming a contract on S's terms for "R-Lube Special" (§§ 37–38, but see § 111). Whether knowledge of B's intended use could lead to liability for breach of warranty of fitness for a particular purpose when "R-Lube Special" failed to meet B's needs is a subject beyond the scope of this work.

No. 27

B agreed in a binding contract to lend C $3,000, C to execute a negotiable note for that amount with 6% interest, and C to provide for his obligation a surety acceptable to B. C brought D as surety and B refused to proceed saying that D was not acceptable. Actually B refused D as a surety because he (B) was short of money and did not want to make the loan. Is B liable for breach?

If B has the unfettered right to disapprove any surety for any reason, then B's promise is illusory (§ 55). A court would assume that the parties intended something more than an illusory obligation and would thus qualify B's right of approval and require that B act reasonably or in good faith in making his determination. If the standard which the court imposes is "reasonableness," then B's conduct will be compared to that of other people who lend money to determine whether others would have rejected D as a surety. If the standard imposed upon D is that of "good faith," then the court might make a more subjective inquiry to determine whether B's judgment was "honest" (§ 157). If B was honestly dissatisfied with D as a surety, then he has no obligation. However, the facts indicate that B was unhappy with the bargain and used his right of approval as a way of avoiding his promise, thus B acted in bad faith. The condition of approval should be excused, and B should be liable for damages (§ 153).

No. 28

Rich, a wealthy man, went to the Custom Shirt Company on September 1st to order a dozen shirts. He let Custom measure him for size, selected the silk to be used in the shirts, and signed a memorandum stating that he would pay $100 for each shirt that Custom would make for him, up to twelve shirts in all.

Custom ordered enough silk for twelve shirts at a total price of $240. Upon receipt of the silk, Custom cut it into twelve portions to make the cutting of the patterns easier. Custom then started making the first shirt and completed it on September 12th. It tendered the shirt to Rich on that day, but Rich refused it and stated he had decided to cancel the entire order.

Custom realized that it could not dispose of the silk which had been cut for the other eleven shirts because there is no market for cut silk. Custom also knew that if it went ahead and made the shirts and Rich refused to take them, the shirts could be sold to the trade for a price of only $48 per shirt. It would cost $40 for labor to make each shirt.

Custom decided to go ahead and make the eleven shirts after it received Rich's cancellation. When the shirts were completed, they were tendered to Rich, and he refused to accept them. Custom then sold the shirts, but the resale price of the shirts had suddenly dropped, and Custom received only $30 per shirt.

Custom now sues Rich. Is Custom entitled to collect from Rich? If so, how much?

This is a transaction in goods. If the memorandum Rich signed is an offer for a unilateral contract or one that invites acceptance either by promising to perform or performing, the offer becomes irrevocable once performance is begun. Performance had clearly begun prior to revocation. However, if the offer is one for severable performances, the offer could be revoked as to severable portions if performance had not begun on each. Cutting the silk, in light of the other facts given regarding the lack of a market therefore, is probably an act referable to the contract, and thus performance has begun with respect to all twelve shirts. The offer was therefore irrevocable, and Rich is liable for breach of the entire contract on September 12th, assuming that Custom is found to have given notice of the fact of acceptance within a reasonable time (§§ 33 and 39 and U.C.C. sections 2–206(2) and 2–610).

At the time of Rich's breach one shirt was finished. As to that shirt, Custom would be entitled to recover the difference between the contract price of $100 and the resale price of that shirt, assuming it was resold in compliance with the requirements of U.C.C. section 2–706. If the resale did not comply with the code, Custom may recover the difference between contract and market price at the time and place of tender (U.C.C. section 2–708(1)). In the view of some experts, a seller can choose between these two remedies taking that which produces the higher damages (§ 136).

As to the other 11 shirts, Custom had a duty to use reasonable commercial judgment with respect to the question whether to complete the shirts or salvage the material (U.C.C. section 2–704(2)). Hind sight discloses that the decision to proceed was unfortunate since $40 labor expense per shirt was incurred and the shirts sold for only $30. However, if it was reasonable to anticipate a sale price of $48 and if the cut material had no market, then a court should find the decision to invest $40 to complete was commercially reasonable, and Custom should recover the difference between the contract price ($100) and the resale price ($30) plus incidental costs (such as the cost of resale) less incidental savings, if any. If it were established that $30 was not a reasonable price for the shirts, Custom could have refrained from selling and brought an action under U.C.C. section 2–709 for the contract price holding the shirts as security for the payment of the judgment.

No. 29

Manor, the owner of a certain house and lot, engaged Broker to sell such property under the terms of a written agreement which provided, in part:

"I, Manor, agree to pay Broker a commission of 6% of the gross sale price of any sale of said property which is arranged by Broker for a consideration of not less than $275,000, such commission to be payable upon consummation of the sale."

Broker procured a buyer, Valley, who offered to purchase the property for $275,000, agreeing to pay $75,000 down and give a note secured by a deed of trust for the balance on certain stated terms. Manor grumbled at these terms, but accepted Valley's offer.

Prior to the time fixed for closing, Manor conveyed the property to Junior, Manor's 22 year old son who was seeking a performance bond for his new construction business. Valley learned of this conveyance, notified Manor that he was in breach, and purchased a similar parcel of property from Smith. Junior reconveyed title to Manor who tendered title to Valley on the specified day. Valley refused to perform, and Manor thereupon conveyed the property to Junior as a birthday present. What are the rights of Broker against Manor?

Broker might advance three distinct theories for recovery against Manor. Broker may assert that the language of his contract with Manor provides for payment of a commission when a sale is consummated and that this was accomplished when M and V entered into a valid enforceable contract. There is no obvious answer on this issue although one might reason that the parties logically intended that Manor would pay Broker when Manor got paid and thus "consummation" referred to completion of the transaction. If Broker provided the contract form, the inclination to interpret ambiguous terms of a contract against the draftsman might tip the scales against Broker (§ 89).

Broker's second theory for recovery is the contention that Manor's initial conveyance to Junior constituted a form of repudiation which excused Valley from its duty to perform. A party who voluntarily incapacitates himself by committing an act which seriously jeopardizes his ability to perform can be found to have repudiated (§ 149). Broker's position will be that there is an implied duty of cooperation and certainly an implied duty not to prevent consummation of the sale by breaching (§§ 56, 142, 148). Breach of this duty excused the condition precedent (consummation of the sale) to Manor's duty to pay (§§ 149 and 153). In the alternative, Broker can advance the argument that if Manor has not breached and thus excused Valley from performing, then Valley's duty to perform is not excused and Manor can still enforce the contract against Valley. Recovery on this theory would depend upon whether the court were to find that Manor has an implied duty to take legal action to "consummate" the sale with a buyer who will not voluntarily perform.

No. 30

M, the publisher of a newspaper, contracted with T, the operator of a supermarket. M agreed to publish for T in M's newspaper an advertisement each day for four weeks. T agreed to pay a certain sum, in four equal weekly installments. The contract document further recited: "A complete layout of each ad will be delivered to M not later than 10:00 on the day prior to the day on which the ad is to be published."

The first week of performance under the contract has passed, and T promptly paid the first installment. Each day during the week T had been from one to three hours late in submitting his layout to M. M complained to T each day about the delay. On the first day of the second week, T submitted the layout for T's eighth advertisement to M four hours late.

Assume that M consulted you immediately upon receiving this layout, and stated that T's advertising was more of a nuisance than it was worth unless layouts reached M promptly. Indicate, with reasons, your advice to M concerning his legal liability to T if: (1) he refuses to run the eighth advertisement, and (2) he informs T that he will render no further performance under the contract.

In the question above a contract is stipulated as existing between two parties. M has promised to run T's ads each day for four weeks. Failure to perform that promise would be a breach of contract unless the promise were shielded by a condition which neither occurred nor was excused. If M's promise to print is dependent upon the occurrence of some condition precedent, then the duty will not arise unless the condition was fulfilled or excused.

Under the terms of the contract, T was obligated to deliver ad layouts to M by 10:00 on the day prior to each publication. There was no contract language which explicitly stated that failure to deliver on time would prevent M's duty of performance from arising, thus there is no express condition. However, the delivery was a duty to be performed prior to the time fixed for the duty to print and this is one basis for finding that the delivery is a constructive condition precedent to the duty to print. More specifically, however, the delivery of the copy is clearly an event which T must cause to occur before the printing of the ads can be done. Therefore, timely delivery of the copy could be viewed as an implied condition of cooperation (§ 142).

M has accepted and run late copy each day thus far. Despite the fact that M has complained, his counsel must be wary of the possibility that a court could find that by accepting five late performances and proceeding with the publication, M has waived prompt performance as a condition precedent to his own duty. In the present situation, however, the layouts are being delivered at least one hour later than ever before. Thus even if some waiver might be found, the present failure goes beyond that to which M has acquiesced in the past.

There is at least a partial failure of a condition precedent to M's duty to perform. This is not an express condition, and even if it were labeled an implied condition, it is likely that a court would not enforce a rule requiring full and literal fulfillment or would define the implied condition to require delivery within a reasonable time rather than at 10:00 (§ 142). The test which M's counsel should anticipate being applied is one of substantial performance. (In jurisdictions such as California, the vocabulary to be anticipated is not whether a condition has been substantially fulfilled. California opinions might discuss whether T's breach constitutes a "failure of consideration," but the factors considered will be the same (§ 144).)

Restatement, First, section 275 and Restatement, Second, section 241 state factors to which courts commonly look to determine the presence or absence of substantial performance or substantial occurrence of a condition. Applying these factors to M's case, one finds that M has not given his counsel sufficient facts. We need to know more about M's printing operation and the problems which will result from receiving advertising layouts four hours late. This information is necessary to determine the extent of the harm to M or the extent to which he is being denied the benefits which he could reasonably have anticipated under the bargain. M's harm probably cannot be adequately compensated in damages, because having to hurry and rush an item does not usually produce damages which are measurable or quantifiable in dollars. There is no indication that T is going to suffer any loss in the nature of a forfeiture if one or more ads are not printed. It is too late for T to cure the defect in his performance on this occasion, and the prospects for timely performance in the future are not bright given the record to date. There are insufficient facts from which it can be determined whether T's failure is willful or a violation of standards of good faith and fair dealing, and it seems unlikely that M could prove this on the facts given.

On balance, one might conclude that if the four hour delay does create sufficient havoc with M's printing routine, M may be justified in his refusal to print this one advertisement on this occasion. Even if the four hour delay is such that the duty to print this ad does not arise, M's counsel should not advise him to declare a breach of the entire contract. Particularly in light of the fact that seven prior late performances have been accepted, it would be most unlikely that M could establish that this one longer delay was a sufficient breach to justify cancelling the entire contract. Such action would probably be a repudiation by M which would subject him to liability for such damages as T might be able to establish (§§ 143 and 149).

No. 31

A Federal agency contracted with a local agency wherein the Federal agency agreed to provide funds for redevelopment and the local agency promised to do certain enumerated things. Included was a promise by local agency to provide "suitable replacement housing" for all persons who would become obliged to move from their existing residences because of the redevelopment activities. After approximately one-half of the area to be redeveloped had been vacated and leveled, the Federal agency and local agency entered into modification of their agreement pursuant to which local agency's obligations with respect to persons uprooted by the project were rescinded. What are the contract rights of the affected persons against Federal agency or local agency?

The first question to be resolved is whether any persons other than the principal parties to the contract have legally enforceable rights therein. Restatement, Second, section 302 indicates that in order for these third parties to have enforceable rights one must find that "recognition of a right to performance in the beneficiary is appropriate to effectuate the intention of the parties and either

. . . (b) the circumstances indicate that the promisee intends to give the beneficiary the benefit of the promised performance." The promise in which the residents are most interested was made by the local agency to the Federal agency. Thus the Federal agency is the promisee. Did it intend to give these people the benefit of the promised performance? Is the recognition of a right to performance in the beneficiary appropriate to effectuate the intention of the parties? It may be more appropriate to ask whether the Federal agency intended to give the third parties the right to enforce this part of its contract or whether it should reasonably be found to have intended to keep all enforcement powers in its own hands (§ 162).

If one finds that the residents are intended rather than incidental beneficiaries, the next question is whether their rights had vested prior to the time the principal parties to the contract modified it so as to defeat their rights (§ 164). This probably requires that the specific persons who are intended beneficiaries be identified which in itself is not an easy task (§ 162). There is case law authority for vesting beneficiaries' rights when they rely, or, when they learn of the contract and agree to accept the benefits, or when the contract is made. The Restatement, Second, section 311(3) would terminate the principal parties' rights to modify the contract so as to deny benefits to third parties when those third parties have changed position in justifiable reliance or brought suit or manifested assent to it at the request of the promisor or promisee.

The affected people would have no contract right against Federal agency. That agency made no promise for their benefit and there is no right of action on any theory such as wrongful rescission.

No. 32

The construction contract between HO and C provided: "C shall not assign any right to payment hereunder." In violation of this term, C assigned to Bank his right to receive one progress payment under the contract. May Bank assert valid rights against HO?

Bank may recover from HO under the U.C.C. without regard to common law issues concerning prohibitions against assignment or against partial assignments. Article Nine of the U.C.C. provides in section 9–102(1):

. . . this Article applies

(a) to any transaction (regardless of its form) which is intended to create a security interest in personal property or fixtures including goods, documents, instruments, general intangibles, chattel paper or accounts; and also
(b) to any sale of accounts or chattel paper.

The right to receive payment for services rendered in this fact situation is an "account." (U.C.C. section 9–106.) HO is the party obligated to pay the account and is thus an "account debtor."

Having these definitions in mind, one turns to section 9–318(4) which controls this problem:

(4) A term in any contract between an account debtor and an assignor is ineffective if it prohibits assignment of an account or prohibits creation of a security interest in a general intangible for money due or to become due or requires the account debtor's consent to such assignment or security interest.

The assignment should be found to be valid (§ 167).

No. 33

C entered into a valid contract to build a home for X on X's lot in exchange for $140,000. X sold the lot to Y and assigned and delegated to Y X's rights and duties under the contract. Does C have any immediate rights against X? May C refuse to perform? What will X or Y's rights and duties be if C assigns his contract rights and delegates his contract duties to S, another local contractor?

Contract rights are freely assignable except in unusual situations in which the duties of the promisor would be somehow changed if they were to be rendered to another party. No such problem is presented here, and X may assign to Y the right to receive the services of the contractor.

Contract duties are delegable where the delegation will not deprive the other party to the contract of some significant part of his bargain. X's duty in this case is the duty to pay money which is most impersonal. C will not be denied any expected benefits if he is paid by Y rather than by X. Thus the X–Y delegation is proper.

While X remains liable to C on the contract and while C now enjoys the additional right to collect from Y, the practical effect of delegation of duties is that in some cases neither party chooses to pay but rather points to the other party as the appropriate debtor from whom C should collect. Whether C can demand that X reaffirm his obligations under the contract or that Y acknowledge his new obligation to C probably depends upon the extent to which the court will turn to the U.C.C. for a rule to apply by analogy in this situation (see U.C.C. sections 2–210(5) and 2–609).

For reasons noted above, C can assign to S his right to payment for the construction work. The delegation to S of the duty to perform cannot be accomplished without the owner's consent, however, unless it can be established that the owner will receive the substantial benefit of his bargain. If X or Y will not receive performance substantially equivalent to that which they had the right to expect from C, then this attempted delegation is improper. If C were simply the low bidder in an open bidding process, the delegation would probably be proper assuming that the delegatee, S, is a competent contractor. If X inspected the work of C and other contractors and then selected C to construct his home because of C's acknowledged quality as a homebuilder, the delegation by C to S of the duty to perform would be difficult to sustain (§ 174).

No. 34

A was lawfully indebted to B for $10,000. C and A entered into an agreement whereby C promised to perform A's obligation to B. C failed to pay B, and B sues C and A.

B has a right to recover against A. The facts stipulate that A is lawfully indebted to B in the amount of $10,000. A debtor cannot relieve himself of liability without the creditor's consent simply by finding someone else who is willing to promise to perform for him. Had C performed, this would have discharged A's obligation to B (§ 185).

B also has the right to recover against C as a third party beneficiary of the A–C contract. C can assert against B any defenses which C has on the A–C contract; thus, if the agreement between C and A is not legally enforceable, B has no rights against C (§ 165). C could not ordinarily raise against B any defenses which A might have had against B. However, in this case, C promised "to perform A's obligation to B." Thus the measure of C's obligation to B is the amount which A owed B and defenses available to A could therefore reduce C's obligation.

No. 35

On February 1, M brought her daughter to S's dress shop for fittings for a custom made wedding dress. No agreement was reached as M was examining both the $400 and the $600 models. All parties understood that the daughter was to be married on March 5.

On February 2, M wrote to S ordering the $600 wedding dress for delivery by March 2. S received this note and bought the necessary cloth on her next trip to the City. S returned to her shop and cut the cloth and began to stitch.

On February 9, the daughter's fiance was killed in an accident. On March 1, S tendered a completed wedding dress and demanded $600. M consults you. What are her obligations to S?

M's note of February 2 is apparently sufficient to constitute an offer to buy goods. Assuming it is signed, it satisfies the minimal requirements of the statute of frauds for a sale of goods. U.C.C. section 2–206 permits acceptance in any manner reasonable under the circumstances. This might be interpreted with reference to Restatement, Second, section 30(2) to give S the right to accept either by promising to perform or by simply rendering performance. However section 2–206(2) expressly permits an offeror to treat an offer as lapsed where he has not been notified of acceptance within a reasonable time, so even if beginning performance was an appropriate means of acceptance, the failure to give notice to M should provide M with a defense. It might also be effectively argued that the impending wedding created a situation in which M sought and needed an express promise to perform, and thus beginning performance without any communication might not be found to be a reasonable manner of acceptance under the circumstances.

If M did have contractual obligations to S, the death of the groom-to-be does not create a basis for asserting impossibility or impracticability of performance. M can still accept and pay for the dress. Daughter can still wear it. However, the cancellation of the wedding completely frustrates the promisor's purpose in entering into this contract and makes the other party's performance valueless (§ 178). The groom's death was an event the nonoccurrence of which was a basic assumption on which the contract was made. There is no reason to assume that M would be found to have assumed this risk, and the frustration occurred without fault on the part of M. Thus M can establish the elements of the defense of frustration of purpose and should be excused from her contract promise. Had the wedding been cancelled because of a disagreement between the parties, frustration of purpose would probably not be an available defense because this would be an assumed risk.

Assuming this was a valid contract, S should have the right to recover reliance damages for time and materials expended (§ 179). Had M notified S before substantial work was performed, M could avoid significant liability. Since S fully performed before notice was given, S will recover the cost of the materials and the value of S's services rendered. S will likely be denied any "profit" on the contract, but if the dress was made with S's labor, S will probably recover something close to the full contract price.

No. 36

Morel is a large-scale distributor of yogurt. For some years M maintained his own dairy herd to supply part of his milk requirements. In 1981, M decided to slow down and devote his time to the yogurt business. He sold his dairy herd and equipment to Toron, an experienced dairyman who then owned no other dairy stock. Toron agreed to pay $375,000 for the cattle and equipment, and M agreed to buy T's output of milk for the next 10 years at the market price at the time of delivery, provided that M would not purchase any quantity in excess of that which M actually required for the production of yogurt.

In 1983, two years after this transaction was completed, M was involved in a serious automobile accident which left him unable to continue business activities. Since his only child had gone to law school, M sold his plant and equipment to Borden and retired to Sun City. T has no acceptable alternative market for his milk and sues M for breach of contract. What result?

M agreed to purchase all of T's output of milk up to M's requirements. This is both an output and requirement contract. The quantity would presumably be the same if the parties had provided that M would buy all of his requirements from T provided that M would not purchase any quantity greater than that actually produced by T.

At common law, ordinary output contracts and requirements contracts were not found to create an obligation to remain in business and continue to have output or requirements. In the absence of some subterfuge, such as terminating requirements by selling the yogurt business to a child who then hired the father as general manager, the common law did not imply from the making of the contract any duty to continue to have requirements or output. However, common law courts recognized that such a term might properly be implied from the other terms or circumstances of a contract. Thus, in a case where X paid valuable consideration for Y's promise to purchase his requirements from X or sell his output to X, the fact that consideration was paid for the executory promise permitted the court to find an implied promise by Y to remain in business. Assuming that the court took evidence from which it could find that the $375,000 paid by T was more than the market price for the cattle and equipment without a milk contract, then T has paid consideration to M in exchange for M's promise to buy M's requirements of milk from T. From this a court can imply a promise by M to continue in the yogurt business.

U.C.C. section 2–306(1) addresses this general problem and indicates that the measure of the parties obligation is such as will occur in good faith. Comment 2 states that a shutdown for lack of orders might be permissible but a shutdown to curtail losses would not. But this section does not appear to provide any guidance for the resolution of the problem presented. It might be anticipated that a court would fulfill its obligation to analyze section 2–306 and then proceed to find, in accordance with common law cases, that the extra value which M received from T gave rise to a duty upon M to remain in the yogurt business for 10 years.

The conclusion that M was obligated to remain in business does not resolve the case. M's injury prevents M from continuing personally to manage the yogurt business. If the contract is interpreted as limiting the quantity to be purchased to that which M needs in a yogurt business to be managed by M personally, then M's injuries will make performance ". . . impracticable by the occurrence of a contingency the non-occurrence of which was a basic assumption on which the contract was made . . ." (§ 177 and U.C.C. section 2–615(a)). In this case, M would be excused from his implied promise to remain in the yogurt business.

Assuming that even a yogurt connoisseur would not claim that the operation of a yogurt business is a duty too personal to delegate, the probable conclusion is that M will not be excused from his implied promise to remain in the yogurt business simply because he is not personally able to manage it.

INDEX

References are to Sections

ACCEPTANCE OF OFFER

Auctions, 45

Bilateral/unilateral distinction, 26–32, 29–34, 35, 40, 42

By words,

    If variance in terms, can be a counter offer, 35–36

    Liberalization of exact conformity rule by the UCC, 37–38

    Must be an unequivocal promise, 32, 36, 43–44

Communication of,

    In bilateral contracts, 27, 41, 42

    In unilateral contracts, 33, 39

    Loss in mails, 27, 42

    Offer by mail, telegraph, 42

    Offer may dispense with communication, 42, 43

    Time when effective, 27, 41, 42

Conditional acceptance,

    Acceptance on condition, new terms, 35–38

    Future acceptance distinguished from, 40

    Ordinarily a rejection, 19, 35, 36

    Requests or suggestions as, 36

Effect of misrepresentation, 115

Effect of mistake or misunderstanding, 6, 109

    Misstatement of terms, 109

    Mistake as to parties, 109

Equivocal acceptance, 35–37

Essential elements,

    Intention to accept, 4

    Knowledge of offer, 11, 42, 44

    Part performance before knowledge, 11

Express words of acceptance may not be enough, 29–32

Future writing contemplated, 40

Schaber & Rohwer–Contracts, 3rd NS—16

ILLEGALITY
Exculpatory clauses, 121
Legal acts violating public policy, 120
Licensing statutes, 122
Nexus to contract, 120
Pari delicto, 120
Persons law designed to protect, 120
Remedies, 123–124

ILLUSORY PROMISES, 54, 55, 61

IMPLIED CONDITION
See Conditions; Performance

IMPLIED–IN–LAW CONTRACTS
See Quasi-Contract

IMPOSSIBILITY
See Impracticability

IMPRACTICABILITY
     See also Frustration of Purpose
    Generally, 154, 176–177, 179
Assumption of the risk, 177
Basic assumption, 177
Commercial impracticability, 176–177
Condition, excuse, 154
Death or illness, 177
Destruction of subject matter, 177
Economic impracticability, 176–177
Governmental action, 177
Mistake distinguished, 110
Relief afforded, 179
Severable units, 123, 155
Subjective, 149, 150, 176

INCAPACITY
See Capacity

INFANTS, 101
See also Capacity

OUTPUT CONTRACTS, 57

†